RADICAL
CONFIDENCE

RADICAL CONFIDENCE

"Unfiltered and unafraid, *Radical Confidence* is the perfect book for anyone who wants to finally reach the success they've always dreamed about."

—Marie Forleo, author of the #1 *New York Times* bestseller *Everything Is Figureoutable*

"Lisa Bilyeu is a phenomenal storyteller. Her ability to reflect on her own past experiences and translate them into empowering, transformative, and practical insights will provide readers the tool kit they need to build the lives they want."

—Jay Shetty, #1 *New York Times* bestselling author of *Think Like a Monk*

"In her book, *Radical Confidence*, Lisa challenges the deep-rooted beliefs that prevent so many of us from knowing or reaching for our dreams. Lisa shares her raw and honest journey, with a healthy dose of humor, to inspire us all to find our own inner purpose and power. She provides the practical tools to help anyone feel empowered to create a life they truly desire. If you want a road map for how to get started creating Radical Confidence in your life, this book is for you!"

—Dr. Nicole LePera, the Holistic Psychologist and author of the *New York Times* bestselling *How to Do the Work*

"*Radical Confidence* is just the book to cheer and galvanize you when life feels hard and your dreams unattainable. Lisa Bilyeu's sparkle and drive shine through every paragraph. She can spur you on, fire you up, and help you regain the conviction that anything is possible."

—Martha Beck, *New York Times* bestselling author

"This powerful book gives you the tools you can apply to your life right now to gain real, radical confidence. Through Lisa's sharing of her raw, candid, and inspiring journey, she not only empowers you to believe in the possibility of your own dreams but teaches you how to become the hero of your own life, too!"

—Jamie Kern Lima, *New York Times* bestselling author of
Believe It and founder of IT Cosmetics

"Lisa Bilyeu inspires so much confidence in others, and this book is a blueprint for a stronger, happier, more authentic life. No matter how you currently feel about yourself, about life, or about your future, get ready for change and a whole new understanding of what's possible for you. A must-read for a more confident life!"

—Brendon Burchard, #1 *New York Times* bestselling author

"People unconsciously judge you on the level of confidence they detect in you. Your success depends on this quality, and Lisa has distilled the art of having and projecting this aura into ten highly practical lessons. A must-read for anyone hungry for power in this world."

—Robert Greene, *New York Times* bestselling author of
The 48 Laws of Power

"If radical confidence scares you, good. You need this book. Lisa will push you through the fears that hold you back and show you that you are the only hero you need. The life of your dreams is within your reach. Lisa gives you a step-by-step guide to being the hero you need right now. Must-read. Smart. Fun. Actionable. There's a superhero inside you; Lisa will help you learn to fly."

—Mel Robbins, *New York Times* bestselling author and
award-winning podcast host

"From the life of a housewife feeling stuck to the $1 billion sale of her company, Lisa Bilyeu is the definition of a success story."

—Jenna Kutcher, author of *How Are You, Really?*

"Lisa reminds you to embrace the beauty of you, be compassionate, and be sensitive, but never to the point of losing yourself."

—Trent Shelton, host of the *Straight Up with Trent Shelton* podcast

"Lisa's mission is to empower all women to become the heroes of their own lives."

—Ellen Pompeo, actress and host of
the *Tell Me with Ellen Pompeo* podcast

"The book is amazing!"

—Jason Wachob, host of *The mindbodygreen Podcast*

"Whip-smart lessons in how you can conquer the negative voice in your head and be the hero of your own life."

—Dave Asprey, host of *The Human Upgrade with Dave Asprey* podcast

"Lisa will inspire you."

—Danica Patrick, host of the *Pretty Intense* podcast

RADICAL CONFIDENCE

11 LESSONS ON HOW TO GET THE RELATIONSHIP, CAREER, AND LIFE YOU WANT

LISA BILYEU

Simon Element

New York   London   Toronto   Sydney   New Delhi

SIMON
ELEMENT

An Imprint of Simon & Schuster, LLC
1230 Avenue of the Americas
New York, NY 10020

Copyright © 2022 by Lisa Bilyeu

First Simon Element trade paperback edition April 2024

SIMON ELEMENT is a trademark of Simon & Schuster, LLC

Simon & Schuster: Celebrating 100 Years of Publishing in 2024

For information about special discounts for bulk purchases, please
contact Simon & Schuster Special Sales at 1-866-506-1949 or
business@simonandschuster.com.

The Simon & Schuster Speakers Bureau can bring authors to your
live event. For more information or to book an event, contact the
Simon & Schuster Speakers Bureau at 1-866-248-3049 or visit our
website at www.simonspeakers.com.

Manufactured in the United States of America

10 9 8 7 6 5 4 3 2 1

Library of Congress Cataloging-in-Publication Data
has been applied for.

ISBN 978-1-9821-8141-3
ISBN 978-1-9821-8142-0 (pbk)
ISBN 978-1-9821-8143-7 (ebook)

To anyone brave enough
to pick up this book and consider change.

Contents

CONTENTS

CONTENTS

RADICAL
CONFIDENCE

WHAT THE HELL IS
RADICAL CONFIDENCE?

Radical (adj):   Turning something on its head by not giving an eff!

Confidence (n):   1.   The ability to believe in yourself even when you have insecurities, are vulnerable, or feel like total shit.

                        2.   A tool that can be strengthened, developed, or—when necessary—faked.

*H*i, I'm Lisa, and I want you to know that you don't have to hit rock bottom to change your life.

If anyone had ever sat me down and told me, "You'll spend eight years of your life as a housewife. It won't be that bad; you'll just lose your confidence, lose yourself, and squash all your hopes and dreams," I would have run screaming from the room, leaving a Lisa-shaped hole in the wall. Maybe even going all *Real Housewives* and flipping a few tables on my way out. But guess what? That's exactly what happened. I spent almost a

1

decade living each day totally detached from my hopes and my dreams. I lost my confidence, and I lost myself. So, how the hell did that happen?

Let me tell you, it wasn't overnight. It never is, despite the cliché of "I blinked and all of a sudden . . ." That's such BS. You never just blink. Ever. Major changes, good or bad, always come about slowly. The foundation gets laid little by little, bit by bit. A wrong turn here, a pit stop there, all may seem like harmless detours. All those little diversions come before the BOOM! It can be the smallest fender bender or a massive pileup. Either way, that airbag to the face makes you stop and realize that you're totally lost. "How the heck did I end up here?" you ask yourself. But while a big dramatic moment might be what it takes to get you to look around, the reality is that your dreams have been in your rearview for a while and you just didn't notice they were getting smaller and smaller and slowly disappearing out of sight.

My wrong turns were small choices and situations that didn't seem like a big deal at the time. Usually, I wasn't even aware that I was making choices. When someone asked how I was, I answered, "Oh, you know, fine," and I thought I was telling the truth. I certainly wasn't doing bad. I had a roof over my head, food to eat, was married to the man of my dreams, and had puppies to scrum on. Who was I to complain? Sure, most days I felt a kind of numbing sadness that I couldn't quite pinpoint, but so many people suffer from so much worse than anything I was going through. How bloody ungrateful was I?

The truth was that I was thoroughly and totally stuck. A place I now look back and call—dun dun dun—the Purgatory of the Mundane.

The Purgatory of the Mundane might be even more dangerous than hitting rock bottom. Rock bottom can jolt you into action, but the Purgatory of the Mundane just lulls you to sleep with a sweet lullaby and then keeps you right on snoozin'. You're comfortable, but you're not actually engaged. Your basic needs are met, but your hopes, dreams, and wildest desires are withering away faster than the Wicked Witch of the West at a water park. Poof! Gone.

The Purgatory of the Mundane is like an inner-tube pool floaty—easy to get into, even relaxing at first, but then it's really frikin' hard to get out (especially when you're trying desperately not to spill your drink or get your braids wet). The Purgatory of the Mundane motto is "It's not *that* bad." And it *isn't* that bad, but believe me, it's a sinister trick to fall for. The Purgatory of the Mundane doesn't want you to leave, and knows how to get you to stay right where you are, how to convince you that you don't deserve to go after your dreams, that you're guilty for wanting more, and that you're just being selfish and entitled to think that your life could be any better than it already is. But, guys, the truth is that unhappiness is unhappiness, no matter how you shake or bake it. Sprinkle on as many reminders as you want ("At least I'm not still single," "At least I have a paycheck"): That cupcake is still going to taste like boredom frosted with despair and baked through with paralysis.

Since you picked up this book and chose to spend a few of your precious minutes reading this introduction, I'm going to bet that the Purgatory of the Mundane sounds familiar to you. Maybe you already have the stamp in your passport and have even spent some time there yourself. Maybe you have frequent-flyer miles and you're there right now, up to your ankles in all that sticky, routine, boring-as-shit stuff that you've come to believe is your lot in life. If that's you, then you've come to the right book, and it's time to plot your escape. It's time to grow.

I know, I know! Growth is hard. It's scary. It's painful, and sometimes it downright sucks. But, homies, it's also absolutely necessary if you want to change your life. You cannot—I repeat, you *cannot*—reach your goals without growth. And even then, the truth is, there isn't a finish line. Life changes, you will change, and your goals will change. But that's what Radical Confidence is all about. It's a series of tools you can use time and time again, on every journey you damn well choose to go on. So, dog-ear pages! Underline sentences! Break out the highlighter! Fill it with sticky notes! This book is your game plan. Because whether you're starting a new business, developing a new habit, ending a phase of your life that no longer serves you, or making any change in your life, really, you'll need a game plan.

A few years ago, when I finally started to settle into the fulfilling, challenging, exciting life that I had created for myself, I started to notice something. People, usually other women, were always saying things like "But of course you can do that, you're so confident" or "I wish I had your confidence." My gut reaction to this was always, "Oh, hellllll to the no, not me! I'm not confident. I feel like shit about myself half the time, too."

We've been taught to see a confident person as someone who's genetically gifted. She's unstoppable and can do anything because her confidence can withstand a million slings and arrows without even a ding. She stands out there, hands on her hips, cape billowing in the wind, bothered by absolutely nothing. She never fails, she's never experienced negative self-talk, and she doesn't give a crap what people think about her. This confident woman might as well be Wonder Woman, and though I loooooove a good ol' superhero movie, this sure as hell is definitely not me.

I'm just Ordinary Woman. I fail all the time. In fact, I screw up on a daily basis. I know I really, truly suck at a lot of stuff. And I do care what people think about me. Sometimes I take criticism to heart because I know it's right. It's still very important to me to be a loving, supportive wife. I don't have a suit of armor, and my negative voice plays on repeat like a skipped record, in Dolby surround sound, and half the time, that dial is stuck on the *What Did I Do Wrong Today?* show on WTF FM, where the DJ has a British accent.

The more I thought about it, the more I realized why people saw me as confident: because I don't wait to feel confident to do something. I pack all my insecurities, doubts, fears, and negative self-talk into my Louis Vuitton bag, sling it over my shoulder, and off I trot. And that, my friends, is radical confidence.

Radical confidence is being honest with yourself and ditching the old excuses, like "I don't feel confident enough to do that." Radical confidence is knowing what you're good at and knowing when you suck, and acknowledging both without feeling bad about yourself. It's about being grateful for what you have and wanting more. It's about using your insecurities to drive you. It's about learning to control your emotions so they don't get in your way. It's knowing when to listen to the negative voice playing on repeat and when to pull the plug and throw the speaker out the damn window. Radical confidence is accepting yourself the way you are and, at the same time, being brave enough to believe you can change. It's about plugging your nose and diving headfirst into a challenge without worrying about whether you'll fail and drown. It's knowing that if you do fail (and let's face it, you probably will at first; failure isn't a dirty word), you can Get. Back. Up. It's about vulnerability and being willing to take long, hard looks at the raw answers to tough questions. It's about facing your ego and telling that bitch to calm down. Radical confidence is the life-changing magic of figuring shit out!

As women, we're bombarded from day one with ideas and beliefs that hold us back. Some of those are thrust on us by our families, some by our culture and society at large, and some are things that we put upon ourselves. They become so ingrained in us that we lose our ability to differentiate what we want from what we've been told to want. From the time we're little girls, we're taught that there is a certain way we should look, a certain way we should act, and a certain lifestyle we should lead. We learn to believe, like believe to our core, that we should put other people's wants and needs first, and anything else is just downright selfish. We're told what our future should be, and what path we should take to get there, as if our lives are like the British Parliament and everyone gets to scream and yell their opinion. So when it comes time for us to go after what we really, truly want for ourselves, we're bloody exhausted, right? We've wasted all our time and energy second-guessing ourselves. Our desires. Justifying our ambitions and explaining our choices in a pathetic attempt to make sure that everyone—from our parents and friends to our teachers, and even that great aunt we haven't seen since 2002—approves of our lives. Because I mean Goooood forbid they disapprove. This, right here, guys, is a dream killer, and we have to stop. Your life is exactly that. YOUR life. Your life isn't run by a committee, and everyone doesn't get an equal vote.

I was a dreamer and an artist from as far back as I can remember. I would sit in front of the TV for hours, drawing cartoon characters, dreaming I would one day be the next Walt Disney. Art AND movies? Come on! Well, that was until my mum told me it was now all made on computers. Do you hear that sound? That's the sound of little Lisa's heart breaking. Still, my enthusiasm for art, movies, and America remained strong. As a teenager, I spent my weekends sneaking into movie premiere after-parties with my best mate, where we'd stay one step ahead of security while I'd imagine that someday, such a party would be thrown in honor of MY movie.

INTRODUCTION

I was raised in a very traditional Greek family and brought up to believe that being a good Greek wife meant that taking care of your man was priority number one. My family, from my dad to my *yiayia* (grandmother in Greek), often reminded me that I must learn to cook and clean so that when I got married I could take care of my husband. But I was a bull when it came to holding on to my dreams. I fought like hell to study film and media at university and then to continue my studies in Los Angeles. Where happenstance totally changed the course of my life and I met my husband, someone who was just as passionate about film as I was, and it felt like I was thiiiiiiis close to making my dreams a reality.

Shortly after we were married, my hubby and I agreed that I would stay home for a year, maybe a year and a half, to handle the personal side of our lives while he focused on going out and making enough money for us to live out our dream of making movies together. This wasn't my ideal situation, but I jumped in with enthusiasm. The inner tube looked pretty good just floating there and seemed like something I could get down with for a little while before our next big move. If this was what it took to make movies, then of course I could do it.

One year stretched into two, two into three, and all the while, I tried to smile through it. Sure, I'd once had dreams as a kid that were so big they were colossal (and the Oscar for Best Director goes to . . . Lisa Charalambous!), but it took work and sacrifice to make big things happen. That's what I told myself, even as I was bored out of my skull every day, cooking, cleaning, and laying out clothes for my husband. But I just kept telling myself it was for the greater good. The greater good. The greater good. The greater . . . good?

Maybe you've been in a situation like this before. Where you sacrifice and sacrifice, and then you get to a point where you realize your sacrifices are good for everyone BUT you. Maybe it's with your family, with your job, or a relationship that has you tossing your own dreams in the trunk, back there with all the junk and spare tires, so that someone else's dreams can drive. You might even be able to convince yourself it's not such a bad idea: "I mean, it's not forever," you remind yourself. But it's hella stifling in that trunk, so while you're just trying to enjoy the scenery, your dreams are slowly suffocating. But here's the thing—no matter what you might think, no matter what someone else might try to tell you—it's never too late to let your dreams breathe. When you cut through the shoulds and start aiming for a life that's honestly fulfilling—that, my homies, is the greatest good.

But this can be scary. If you're like me, and you've spent much of your life being a people pleaser, putting your own needs first can feel like stepping out on a ledge and uh-oh! Here comes the vertigo! What if I fall . . . and fall on my face? Sure, that's a legit fear. But, also, what if you just went ahead and took that leap and landed on your feet?

I host my own show, *Women of Impact*; have spoken on the TEDx stage; and am a frequent guest on podcasts and shows. I count inspirational, world-rocking women like Nicole LePera and Mel Robbins as my homies. My goals and dreams are bigger, more audacious, and more badass than they've ever been before. I wake up every morning and ask myself how I want to spend every second. Then I go out and do just that. I'm out here, sweating my ass off to see how many lives I can change, how many people I can inspire, and how much fun I can have in the process.

And you know what? If I did it, you can do it, too! Because there's nothing extraordinary about me. I'm totally average, and I'm not saying that to diminish myself in any way. I'm saying it because I've accomplished all of this *without* being born with an extraordinary spark. I don't have some wild intellect or unparalleled talent. I don't have insane confidence. I wish I did—it would've saved me yeeeears of beating myself up and feeling shitty about myself. But alas, no. Just ask any of my former teachers.

I never had a rock-bottom, lightning-strike moment that lit a fire under my ass and jolted me into action. Nope, instead I got myself out of the Purgatory of the Mundane the same way I got myself into it. Little by little, bit by bit. Then, before I knew it, this mildly dyslexic gosling in a blah T-shirt and unmatching sweats, doing calf lifts to burn extra calories in the checkout line at Costco, had morphed into a braided, bad-bitch, boots-wearing swan who frikin' loves her life. Even on the hard days. Maybe even more so on the hard days, because those are the days that make me realize how strong I am and how much I can accomplish. It's always the hard days that shine a light on how truly far we've come, and how much farther we can go.

You don't need to wait for things to get better or for them to get worse to spark radical confidence. Radical confidence is a decision that you make every single day, to be totally frikin' honest and real with yourself about where you are and where you want to go. You start your journey, right here, right now, wherever, however, whoever you are.

Radical confidence isn't the goal. It's the tool you need to get to that goal. It's like a muscle. It takes work to build, and it takes more work to keep it. You wouldn't expect to get glutes of steel after doing one round of squats at the gym, would you? No! So why do we always expect that looking in the mirror and saying a few affirmations is all it takes to be confident? With confidence—as with butts—it takes reps to get results.

That's why all the lessons in this book are the tried-and-tested ones, ones that I've constantly used, refined, and reused on my own radical confidence ride. I don't want this book to just spark change; I want it to keep the fire burning. In fact, scratch that, I want it to fan the frikin' flames into a roaring bonfire! I'm all about tactics and techniques (no woo-woo shit here, homie). Because when those tough times come and emotions and negative thoughts start flooding in faster than Usain Bolt (oh, and they will come), I can't just will myself to do something—I need a damn game plan. And that's what this book is.

It's a blueprint—an action plan with personal stories as examples of how I'm not just talking the talk. I've been there, done that. I've walked the walk, tripped, stumbled, and fallen on my face time and time again, and I'm still out here, putting one foot in front of the other. Some of these stories I've truly never told anybody before—about times when I failed epically, felt completely ashamed, and thought I'd never recover. I'm going to tell you about times when I literally picked myself up off the cold floor, unpacked my emotions, and went on to kick some ass. I'll share tips and lessons I've learned from some of the brilliant women I've interviewed on *Women of Impact*, because I want you to see that you're not alone in this. As women, we've been buried in bullshit our whole lives, but that stops right here, right now, with this book!

No more hiding behind excuses, no more diminishing your dreams, and no more waiting for someone else to rescue you. Fuck fairy tales! It's time to storm the castle, because in this story, you are the hero of your own life.

YOUR DREAMS ARE A GAMBLE...
BET ON YOURSELF

Dream (n):   1.   A concrete, actionable goal that re-
quires having your feet planted
firmly on the ground.

2.   Something you have every right to
achieve.

I was always the dreamer in my family. There were rumors of a great-
grandfather who was an artist, but I had to go pretty far back in the
bloodline to find anyone who was like me. Everyone else was practical and
grounded. And so whenever I started to daydream about the big things I
wanted in my life, I'd get as far as "And I would like to thank the Academy"
before my acceptance speech was interrupted by a voice, yelling in Greek,
"*Lizou mou!* Get your head out of the clouds!" That voice sounded a lot like
my dad.

I know I'm not alone here, because so many of us are taught that
dreams are just like the tooth fairy and Father Christmas—things we outgrow because they aren't real. Dreamers are seen as people who aren't

anchored in reality, who spend a lot of time wishing and hoping, and very little time doing. The message that we get is that it's okay to have dreams, at least when you're young, but going after them as an adult is silly. So when I put my dreams aside in favor of a looooong ride on the Housewife Scalextric—a road that loops, going nowhere—I didn't protest initially; a big part of me felt like this was where I was always going to end up anyway. Who was I to think I actually deserved to go after my dreams?

In sharing my story of how this happened, I'm begging you, I'm actually pleeeeeading with you, homies, do not—I repeat, do not—do what I did! I was wrong, I was wrong! I was so wrong that I want to run up and down my street, waving my hands in the air and screaming my head off about how wrong I was. I was wrong not to reevaluate my goals. I was wrong to try to distract myself from my deep unhappiness. I was wrong for not questioning my initial choices, and I was wrong for choosing to let my dreams die.

And yes, I said *choose*. Because buying a Housewife Scalextric ticket and climbing aboard? That was a CHOICE I made. Riding that goddamn thing for eight frikin' years? Another CHOICE. Every time I thought about getting off but used a word like "can't" or "should," I was actually just making an excuse and prolonging my ride. I was choosing to make an excuse rather than find a way around the obstacles that stood between me and the sense of purpose that I so desperately craved. So, yep, this is a little tale about what *not* to do.

I Can Dream Big.

Once upon a time in London, there lived a teenage girl with frizzy hair, a flat chest, and a long last name that rhymed with "shag-a-lamppost." Her name was Lisa, and the world of adolescence wasn't all that kind to Lisa, due to the fact that, in addition to all the unfortunate things previously mentioned, Lisa also had a big nose, a unibrow, and an orthodontic head-brace, and was just an average—okay, maybe even less than average—student. But before you go feeling too sorry for Lisa, know that Lisa didn't feel sorry for herself. Because Lisa had movies.

Okay, I'm just going to go ahead and drop this third-person shit right now, because it will get annoying, and as you've probably guessed . . . I'm Lisa! While my female classmates were out drinking and snogging boys in the back seats of cars, I was chasing after a different kind of crush: Hollywood. Movies were my jam. Eighties flicks were my favorite, and I was drawn to anything that was an underdog story. I watched *The Goonies*, *The Karate Kid*, and *Adventures in Babysitting* until the tapes wore out (yes, that actually used to happen before everything was streaming). On the weekends, my best friend Nicole (a freckled ginger who was teased just as much as I was and had about the same amount of luck with the boys) would run around London, trying to find celebrities and sneaking into movie premiere after-parties. On Monday mornings, while all the popular girls were gossiping, Nicole and I were off in the corner, recounting our own adventure of sneaking into the *Eraser* premiere after-party. "Can you believe how big Arnold Schwarzenegger's hand was when we shook it?" I'd ask Nicole, and she'd shake her bright red locks in agreeing disbelief. "It was the size of a plate!" she'd whisper back.

Celebrity hunting was an escape for me, because school had always been a struggle. At one point, I was moved into "special" classes because my teachers thought I held my pencil wrong. I barely passed English—not because I couldn't speak it but because trying to interpret a poem left me totally confused. "What do you mean, she's about to commit suicide?" I'd think as my teacher went on and on about Sylvia Plath. "She was just talking about flowers."

Art was the only subject in which I excelled. I had always loved drawing, and while I might have been holding my pencil "wrong," I got it to bend to my will and do some pretty awesome things. However, all I wanted to do was draw—I was insecure, and drawing was one of the few things for which I was praised, so I white-knuckled it and held tight with all my might. I wasn't about to let go of the one thing that made me like myself. My teacher wasn't having it, though, and he insisted that, if I wanted to pass his class, I had to explore other mediums. I went home furious, and as I started to vent to my mum, she just matter-of-factly said, "Well, darling, do you want to be right, or . . . do you want to pass?" I hated the choices, but there they were, plain as day, coming out of my mother's mouth. This was a groundbreaking moment for me in my younger years, because I realized that, either way, it was my choice (a lesson I later forgot for eight years)—and I wanted to frikin' PASS.

Even so, I figured I might as well do what I could to make it interesting, so I became a bit of a renegade when it came to completing my assignments. My teacher said I needed to sculpt. Okkkkaaayyyy, so what could I sculpt with that would actually be fun and not the same old, same old clay that everyone else was using? I know. Wax! Where do I get wax? Candles! How do I melt them? In my mum's microwave! I practically burned off my fingertips because I touched it long before it had cooled down enough to mold, but, despite the blisters, I passed, and with good enough grades to get into university.

When I told my dad that what I wanted to do with my life was make movies, let's just say he was . . . not thrilled. He valued traditional skills and a stable career, as both had served him well in his life. My dad could teach Drake a thing or two, because he had truly started from the bottom. Growing up in a tiny village in the mountains of Cyprus, he had a hole in the floor for a toilet, left home at the age of twelve just to go to school, and as a teenager worked digging ditches in the mountains. When he moved to London and got a job in the mailroom of a shipping company, he saw it as a great opportunity. He worked hard, learned on the job, studied and took classes at night, and ended up running the entire company. He tried to instill this practical mindset in his children by giving us spontaneous math quizzes at the dining table and repeating "Time is money!" like it was his own personal theme song. I'll never forget the sound of him yelling this in his thick Greek accent as seven-year-old me took my time getting out of the car, having no bloody clue what this was supposed to mean, considering I wasn't getting paid to get out of the car.

When it was time for me to go to university, my mum encouraged me to study art, but I had decided on a film and media degree. But my dad was more horrified than Joey being asked to share food. He might as well have shouted, "A Charalambous doesn't major in media!" In Greek culture, parents face a lot of judgment over what their children are doing, so it was like the Greek version of keeping up with the Joneses. Keeping up with Jonesanopouloses! My dad wanted me to study something useful, like math, or English, but I didn't back down. We fought for two weeks until, finally, he relented. In an utterly nonjudgmental tone, he turned to me and matter-of-factly said, "Well, you'll end up at home with kids anyway, so it doesn't really matter."

Now, before you gasp at the horror, the truth is that he really didn't mean or see this as an insult, or as a way of diminishing my dream, because his mother and sister didn't even go to high school—so in his mind, my staying home and not necessarily needing an education were just unemotional facts.

But nothing was going to pop my bubble, and I went to university and killed it. With the opportunity to study something I was interested in, I learned that I actually liked school (and parties), and I started to come into my own academically and socially. On those first days of university, no one knows who is who. Who are the mean girls and if there is a Regina George lurking around the corner, ready to jump out at you at the first sign of weakness. Because let me tell you . . . oh, she smells the fear! And this was actually beyond frikin' exciting to me. The "Plastics" of the world didn't know I was insecure, and no one knew I had been bullied and teased. I got to start over, and that was exactly what I needed. I mean, who knew how easy it was to excel in an environment where people aren't making fun of you behind your back? Not me! It was a whole new feeling. It took me a few years to get there, but by my senior year, I had buckled down and become a serious student. I sat in the front of the class and raised my hand so much I practically tore my rotator cuff.

University did wonders for my personal confidence, too. Up until then, almost everyone I knew was Greek, Turkish, or Jewish and had a very similar upbringing to my own. Now I was surrounded by people of all races and cultural backgrounds. They thought it was cool that I was Greek. A total first! And boys paid attention to me. Yes, me! Little old Lisa Shagalamppost—who once relied on truth or dare to get a kiss—was now hot shit. I was being asked on dates! That's right. Plural. With an s. And that gave me the confidence to finally embrace all the things that made me different, like my obsession with hip-hop and the fact that I had dreams other than becoming a mum right after graduation. The more people accepted me for who I was, the more confident I became. Turns out, confidence wasn't the Loch Ness monster. It actually did exist. But the best part of this was that all the new people I was meeting had dreams as big as mine.

When I was growing up, my *yiayia* was fond of telling me that my story had already been written by the almighty bestselling author himself—God—and, as she saw it at least, that story ended with my being a wife and mother just like all the other women in my family. *Yiayia* meant this as a comfort, but I absolutely hated the idea that I didn't get to write my own story. I mean, what if I wanted something else for myself? This had never seemed like an option before, but now I had to look no further than my fellow classmates for dream-chasing inspiration. They were building all kinds of careers and creating their own futures, and if they could do it, why couldn't I? Making movies was my dream, and I was determined to see it come true.

So when my flatmate (roommate, for you Americans) gave me a pamphlet in my final semester of university for an eight-week course at the New York Film Academy in Los Angeles, I practically lost my mind with excitement. This was hands-on moviemaking in Hollywood, on the Universal Studios backlot. Uni-frikin'-versal! We would get access to their wardrobe and props department and get to shoot on their sets, like *The Wild West*. It was like someone climbed into my brain, transcribed my dreams, and now here I was reading it in Times New Roman on a piece of trifold paper. There was no way I wasn't going.

The only problem was . . . it cost money. And though I now had a college degree, what was the one thing I didn't have? You guessed it. Money! So off I headed to convince my dad to not only let me go but also foot the bill. Cue "Eye of the Tiger," because I was ready for a fight. Ding . . . Pups (as I call him) and I circled each other in the ring and went toe-to-toe. After ten rounds, I was left wounded, hurt, bleeding, and exhausted, but my determination was left standing. Like Rocky Balboa, I stood victorious, and I was headed to Los Angeles, baby! Almost.

Pups gave me one condition: As soon as I got back, I had to get serious about my future. And when my dad said future, what he meant was: Get a stable job. Stay at said job until I find a "good" Greek man. Marry said good Greek man so I could leave my job and stay at home to take care of my husband and the four kids we were surely going to have.

Now, this kind of future was about as far away as you could get from the one I actually envisioned for myself—which involved cameras, film sets, and emotional storytelling—but I wasn't going to tell my dad this now. Hollywood was on the line here, people! So we made an agreement, kissed on both cheeks (as the Greeks do), and the next thing I knew, I was boarding the plane, taking my seat in 48F, and London was disappearing into the fog below.

My best mate and partner in crime Nicole came with me, of course, and before heading to Los Angeles, we stopped in Las Vegas so that I could put my other major—partying, obvi—to use. At the end of the week, Nicole was burnt to a crisp, I'd acquired a great tan, and we both had hangovers that were grander than MGM. Now we were truly ready for LA.

I had rented a fully furnished studio at the Oakwood Apartments in Burbank, which was known for being the first stop in town for dreamers like me. When I walked into the convenience store and saw all the signed headshots of celebrities who had stayed in these very same apartments, I felt like I was staying in a five-star resort. Then, as if things couldn't possibly get any better, the very first person I see when I get to the NYFA, on my very first day, is a hot guy working in the office. Like, we're talking about chiseled-jaw, head-spinning, double-and-triple-take hotness here. Are you kidding me, Los Angeles? I was truly living the American dream.

The first four weeks of my course were spent in the classroom, before we were going to be released out into the world to make our own movies for the last four. From day one, my newfound swagger and I strutted into that classroom like we owned the joint—something that was made a bit easier by the fact that there was only one other girl in the class, a German girl named Vera who quickly became my new bestie. I was a sponge, soaking up everything I could, and having an absolute blast in the process. Then one day, a few weeks in, I walked into class and Hot Office Guy was standing at the front of the room. As soon as class starts, he introduces himself as . . . our new teacher! I almost laughed out loud. Teacher? Thiiiings just got more interesting.

But for some reason, Hot Office Guy seemed less than impressed with me. In fact, he flat-out ignored me. Bloody cheek. But also . . . I must say . . . intriguing. On the outside, I was cool as school, but on the inside, I couldn't for the life of me figure out what his deal was. I could break the ice with anyone, but Hot Office Guy was stone cold.

Then, on the last day of our last class, before we would begin our four-week practical making of our final film, we shot short films on the Universal Studios backlot on Wisteria Lane. Specifically, on the set of *Desperate Housewives* (trust me, the foreshadowing isn't lost on me here). As students, we were required to be escorted on and off the lot by a teacher, to keep celebrity-crazy kids from trying to sneak into Eva Longoria's trailer, which didn't really make sense to me. I mean, can you believe that there are people out there who look for celebrities by sneaking into places? Who does that? (But also, did I tell you how big the Terminator's hands are IRL?)

Vera and I had finished early, and I strolled over to ask Hot Office Guy if he could give us a ride off the lot. I expected what I always got from him, which was a straightforward answer, but to my surprise, he turned to me and smiled. "Sit your ass down," he joked. "You're not going anywhere." Before my confident self could even think of a cocky comeback, I blurted out "Okay." And, I sat. Okay? *Okay?* Lisa, you aren't a puppy at obedience school. You don't sit on command. Hot Office Guy and I ended up talking for some time outside on the grass of Gabrielle Solis's house while another group of students filmed. Finally, as they were finishing up, he told us he could leave and give us a ride, so we headed out to the truck. Vera—knowing how much I was crushing on him and being one of those homies where you don't have to say a word, she just has your back—let me take shotgun and then pretended to be distracted with what she saw out the window. Now that it was just the three of us, and we weren't in a classroom, Hot Office Guy seemed to warm up even more, and he even asked us what we were up to for the weekend. Girl, this was my in.

"A bunch of us are going to see a movie tonight," I said, totally casual. I was soooo casual, right? Very casual. Absolutely casual. "You should come!" Thank God the words came out casually, because inside I was freaking out. Should I have said, "You can come." Oh, no, that sounds sexual! Maybe I should have asked him, "Do you want to come?" How about, "Come with us." Or was that too casual? I'm secretly *Home Alone* screaming in my head. Hands on my cheeks and all.

Fortunately, he didn't seem to notice. "Sounds great," he said. "If I get off work in time, I'll come join you." I wrote down my number on a scrap of paper, and he drove off. Then I sprinted into my apartment to wait for him to call.

He didn't call.

I tried to shake it off, but I had to admit that this really bummed me out. Even if he didn't fancy me back, I thought this was at least a chance for us to be friends (ah, who am I kidding? He was hot as hell, and I definitely wanted him to fancy me back), but there was no way I was going to let this show. I walked into class on Monday determined to act like I'd completely forgotten that there was even a chance that he was going to call. So I devised a very intricate game plan. Step one, don't react. Step two, repeat step one.

At the end of class, as I'm getting ready to leave, he pulls me aside. "Hey, Lisa," he said, "I'm sorry I didn't call on Friday. I was going to, but then I fell asleep."

A beat. And another beat. Inside Lisa is screaming. You fell asleeeeeeep? I was more appalled than Rachel was when Ross fell asleep in the middle of her eighteen-page letter (front and back). It sounded like the lamest excuse that I've ever heard, but I reminded myself of my genius game plan, so I just laugh it off. I turn and walk right out the door, all the while thinking, "Be cool, Lisa, be cool." There was no way I would let him see I was bothered. No. Way. I was still playing it cool when my phone rang that night.

"Hey, Lisa," he says when I answer, "I'm sorry we didn't get to hang out this weekend, but one of my friends is having a movie premiere, and I wanted to see if you would want to go with me."

This is the part where I wish I could say I played it cool. That I made him work for it. But, alas, all the coolness I had earned went right in the trash, along with my Tetley tea bag. I answer before he's even finished asking. "Sure, Tom," I said, "that sounds great."

What I know now, which I didn't know then, was that Tom Bilyeu always has a plan, and seeming to ignore me was part of it. First, he had to wait until the end of our classes, because what if we went out, had a really awkward time, and then had to stare at each other for the next four weeks? Second, we had to hang out one-on-one. If he'd come along to the movie with me and all of my friends, there would have been zero chance for us to connect and have a real conversation. Third, he had to have an excuse.

Even though we were both adults and there was only a four-year age difference between us, a teacher taking a student on a date was a little bit of a gray area (and when I say gray, I mean totally forbidden). So a film premiere was perfect. If anyone asked, he could always say that he thought it would be a great opportunity for me to learn about the movie industry.

And last but definitely not least, Tom wasn't looking for a relationship, and I had to leave the country in a few weeks. Where was the downside?

The movie premiere was being held at the Directors Guild of America on Sunset Boulevard, and I went HAM getting ready. Not only is this a date but it's also a big deal. I spend two hours shaving, blow-drying my hair while rapping along to Eminem, and primping and prepping and trying on like seven different outfits before going back to the very first one I tried on. And then the doorbell rings. I can barely contain my excitement as I rush to answer it. I fling the door open, and Tom's standing there in . . . his work clothes. Yeah, he definitely didn't go home and change, because he's still wearing a shirt with the NYFA logo on it. The same one he wears Every. Single. Day!

We walked outside, and I was equally impressed with his car. His ride was a big, beefy "old man" Buick with a back seat that was so chock-full of stuff he could put Public Storage out of business. I wouldn't say that I was superficial, but in my conservative Greek culture, men's and women's roles were as defined as they were back in the caveman days. Man provide for woman, woman take care of man, that sort of thing. A nice car and nice clothes were a guy's way of signaling that he could provide. But then he did something that no one had ever done for me before—he opened the car door for me. The caaaaar doooor!

"CHIVALRY IS ALLLLIVE," I screamed to myself as I climbed into the Buick. Maybe I could get used to American boys. Or, at least, this one. So when he asked if I wanted to get a bite to eat, I nodded harder than a bobblehead. Then he pulled into a strip mall and took me to a Chinese restaurant with a B rating. "What the hell is this hole?" I'm thinking as I pick up the laminated menu. But ten minutes in, I couldn't have cared less about the rating, or the fact that my ass was going numb from the rip in the chair that was digging into my butt cheeks. Tom was unlike anyone I'd ever gone out with before.

The shocking, nonchalant bombs that came out of that man's mouth before we'd even ordered our entrées . . . He didn't know if he wanted to get married and had never really thought about kids (what? That's even a question in your mind?). He told me with such endearment that he talked to his mum every day. He didn't believe in God (huh?), and he just outright said, with no shame or hesitation, that he liked porn. Did I mention he just said it to me? Out loud? Like, in public?

This couldn't be any more different than the people I'd grown up with in North London. Everyone there got married and had kids. Everyone believed in God, because that was what our parents, grandparents, great-grandparents (you see where I'm going) did, and so it was a given, like the sky being blue. And no one—I repeat, no one—talked openly about anything to do with sex. I occasionally heard my dad and his friends tell rude jokes, but that was it, and I would have eaten soap before I let *Yiayia* know that *I* knew that the stork did not, in fact, deliver babies.

Tom was Marvin the Martian to me—totally bloody alien. He wasn't putting on airs, or graces, or cologne. And, maaaaan, I felt like I could breathe. Everything Tom said got me thinking and made me start examining my own beliefs about who I was, what I thought, and why I thought it. Then he stun gunned me with the paralyzing question, why do I believe in God? And the embarrassing truth was the only answer I could actually think of was "Because my dad told me to." Yep, I was twenty-one years old, and THAT was my reasoning. I'd never even considered that God was something I could choose to believe in. And I *had* seen porn before. Maybe, with Tom, I could admit that and not be judged. Tom wasn't trying to be perfect, and it started to dawn on me that might mean he didn't expect me to be perfect either (though I still left dinner starving because I thought a first date was too soon to stuff my face with egg rolls).

Tom was kind; he was attentive and a total gentleman. Plus, he wasn't the least bit pretentious or materialistic. I soon realized that his messy car, his work clothes, and the strip-mall restaurant weren't just signs that Tom didn't care about impressing me but signs that he didn't care about impressing *anybody*. He knew what he liked. For example, the food at this particular Chinese restaurant and the dozen free NYFA T-shirts he got so he didn't have to do laundry that often. He was totally confident in who he was, and that was very frikin' attractive.

His confidence in being himself put me in the same headspace, and it gave me total permission to be myself. So I didn't try to impress him (aside from not eating all the egg rolls). I hadn't had many expectations for this date—other than someday telling my grandchildren that their grandma once had a hot fling with a hot American dude—and since Tom wasn't looking for a relationship either, we were both just being our weird selves and talking about things that people rarely talk about on first dates—like God and porn.

And then, after that, we hung out almost every day. We never talked about having a relationship or if we were seeing anyone else, or where we thought this was going. It was always just, "What are you doing tomorrow? Cool, let's hang out." On my last week in the country, we went on a double date to have a s'more-out at Dockweiler Beach with some of his friends, and toward the end of the evening, his best friend asked us, "So, Lisa's leaving soon. What are you guys gonna do?"

Up to this point, we hadn't really discussed it. Mostly out of fear of admitting we had both really fallen for each other and it was finally coming to an end (cue "Summer Lovin'"). Then Tom said matter-of-factly, "I'm going to use all the money and vacation time I was saving to go to New York and visit her in London instead." He looked at me and smiled. That was the first I'd heard of this plan, but it got a big hell yeah from me! Even though he worked for the New York Film Academy, Tom had never been to New York, and I knew how badly he wanted to go, especially since he was thinking of moving there. The fact that he was willing to postpone this to come see me almost made me drop my marshmallow into the sand.

Within three weeks of my leaving Los Angeles, Tom got his first-ever passport. Within a week of that, he'd booked a flight, and just a couple of weeks later, I was watching him come down the jetway at Heathrow towing a bright pink suitcase that he'd borrowed from his mum.

We were staying with my mum, who made us sleep in separate rooms until my older brother Beeve (aka Steve) called her out on it. "Mum," he said, "Tom came all this way to see Lisa, and you're making him sleep in another room?" Tom had gone out of his way to make a good impression on my family and had brought everyone personalized gifts, so my brother wasn't just sticking up for me. He really liked this guy. Tom was also the first guy I'd dated whom I introduced to my dad. I was absolutely petrified. But since Tom was a "xeno" (a person who isn't Greek; an outsider), my dad didn't take the relationship all that seriously.

Two whole weeks seemed like a lot when he booked the trip, but they went by in a blink; before we knew it, it was almost time for Tom and his mum's suitcase to go home. Then when he got back, he wrote me an email and said the words I had been feeling: "I've fallen in love with you." Suddenly, the stakes were higher.

We were no longer hoping to see each other again. Now we were planning our lives around it, and doing whatever it took to make it work. We learned the fine print of visa laws, frequent-flyer miles, and all the other ins and outs of having roughly 5,437 miles between you and the person you love. Seven months later, on a warm summer night at Alexandra Palace, overlooking all of London, Tom got down on one knee and asked me to marry him. And, homie, I said yes!

We had a big, fat Greek wedding. And I don't mean that as a joke. I mean the movie is like watching our wedding video. It was exactly like it. Tom stood in a paddling pool and got christened. We had two hundred guests at the wedding—190 of them were from my side, and 10 were from his. The Americans got lit on a shot of ouzo, not knowing they weren't supposed to chug but rather sip it.

After our wedding, we honeymooned in Italy, but we definitely did not "when in Rome" it. Every night, I'd ask Tom where he wanted to eat, and God bless his cotton socks, he would answer, "The Hard Rock Cafe, of course." Finally, on the last night, I was salivating for some good ol' authentic Italian food, and I knew that if I asked Tom where he wanted to eat again, he was going to say the bloody Hard Rock Cafe! So I finally, for the first time, spoke up: "Please, I can't eat at the Hard Rock again," I said. "Can we pllleeeeeease go somewhere Italian?" Tom, without missing a beat, replied, "Babe, if you wanted to go somewhere else, why didn't you just say so? You kept asking me where I wanted to go, so I kept telling you. But if you want to go to a different restaurant, then of course. Anything for my baby!" By speaking up, I actually got what I wanted. And in this case it was to devour a bowl of pasta. Tom, not surprisingly, got a pizza.

Though I didn't realize it at the time, this was such a huge, important lesson: In life, as in dinner, you've got to ask for what you want, instead of hoping that someone else will give it to you. Even with all the Hard Rock burgers, it was literally a perfect honeymoon, and we were madly in love when we headed, for the first time ever, to our new shared home: America.

Our first stop in the US was Tacoma, Washington, where Tom had put all of his stuff in storage at his mum's house. There, we celebrated with his family who hadn't been able to come to England for the wedding, then packed up a U-Haul, hitched it to the beefy Buick, and started our drive south to Los Angeles. I felt like I was in a rom-com. Married to the man of my dreams and road-tripping to California? The romance! Tom swerving across the freeway when I got attacked by a giant vampire bat and screamed and flailed like I'd just seen Ted Bundy in the back seat? The comedy! Tom insisting that said "giant vampire bat" was actually just a grasshopper? More comedy!

Since we were trying to save as much money as possible, we didn't want to stop at motels, so we'd pull into parking lots to try to catch a few hours of sleep here or there before driving on. I'd get as comfortable as I could in the passenger seat and fall asleep with a gear shift digging into my thigh, and then wake up an hour later in a panic, thinking the car was about to roll out into the highway because the engine was running (which actually turned out to be just Tom switching the heater on to keep us from turning into frozen corpses).

We'd worked so hard to finally be living in the same place, to be able to be together without a gray cloud shadowing us with a return ticket. We felt like we'd already accomplished so much. We had big dreams for what our future would look like—making movies, living in a beautiful home, taking the world by storm. After all, we were heading to LA, baby. Our first stop when we arrived was Tom's friend's apartment in the Valley, where we stayed until we could find a place of our own.

I set about learning the American way, and walked half a mile with a garbage bag full of dirty laundry slung over my shoulder and officially visited my first laundromat, trying to convince myself that it was a cool and "American" thing to do. Just like in the movies! Except it was nothing like the movies: There was no spontaneous singing. There was no wise old

22

lady who read my future. There was no shirtless, six-pack-ab dude washing his only tank. It was just . . . laundry. For like, five hours.

I couldn't wait for us to have our very own place, and after a long four weeks, we found a seven-hundred-square-foot apartment in West Hollywood. Ahhh—a place that I could finally call home. We had come to the end of the rom-com, the credits rolled, and our life as husband and wife had officially begun.

From the time Tom and I met to the time we moved into that apartment, everything we had done had been in service of something bigger. Most of our goals and milestones were built around figuring out how we were going to be together, and we were always jumping through hoops and figuring out logistics to reach them. But that was finished. We were no longer scheming about how we could work around immigration restrictions, lessen family resistance, and save pennies for plane tickets to be with each other. We were together—and for good, at that. It was go-time—except I had nowhere to go.

Tom headed back to work at the New York Film Academy, and on his first day, I gave him a kiss and sent him off. I closed the door behind him and realized I had no idea what to do with myself. I had spent so much time and effort to get to this moment that I hadn't really thought about the logistics of what would happen next. I slowly walked over and took a seat on my mother-in-law's generously donated sofa. I looked around.

Now what?

I Can Change My Life.

Tom and I were partners, equals in our relationship, and one of the things he liked about me was that my dreams and ambitions were just as big as his. Now that we were married, we were going to hit the ground running to chase after our dream of making movies. Except . . . I didn't have a visa yet. So I couldn't work, nor could I get a driver's license. I fell into a routine of taking care of our apartment, cooking, and helping Tom out when I could, like walking Santa Monica Boulevard and passing out NY Film Academy flyers at Subway and the Coffee Bean for an extra buck. We were constantly looking for business opportunities that we thought would help us make some extra money and get us more involved in the industry. For a while, we had Bilyeu Photography; we'd shoot headshots for up-and-coming actors in the apartment's parking garage. With Kinkos-printed business cards, custom-made Bilyeu Photography T-shirts, and two employees (Tom and I count as employees, right?), I thought we had officially made it.

If this was a television show, a voice-over would now say, "Lisa and Tom had not made it. They had just hung a sheet in front of their car and were taking pictures that would help someone get rejected at a dog-food commercial audition."

I managed to get a few little industry jobs here and there. I worked as an on-set photographer for a film where the lead actress demanded that I and my camera stay far away from her. I obeyed, of course, until a producer bit my head off. "I hired you to take pictures of our star!" he yelled. "So where the hell are they?" I ended up guerrilla-styling it, hiding behind a couch and randomly clicking my camera in her direction, hoping that I got something usable. On another, small-budget project, I filled in for the props department, only to have an actor throw an empty matchbox at me when he ran out of matches to set on fire for the scene. Yes, you read that right. He threw a matchbox at me. Not quite the glamour and excitement of the film industry I had once dreamed of. The heart of the thirteen-year-old Lisa, who would stay up till 3:00 a.m. in her Edwardian house in London to watch the Oscars, was breaking. Tom's experiences were equally disheartening, and it became obvious that neither of us were down for being stepped on. That just wasn't how the Bilyeus rolled, so we were going to have to find another way.

Then, one day, Tom came home with an offer that seemed like our movie dreams really were about to come true. Through his teaching job, he had met some young, wealthy entrepreneurs who were looking to get into the movie business, and they wanted to hire Tom to write a script for them. The job would pay more than he was making teaching, so it seemed like a no-brainer. He'd take a year to write the script, and then we'd start making the movie. Academy Awards, here we come! I just had to keep doing what I was doing for another year, and, of course, I could do that.

Tom wrote and wrote, a year came and went, and reality started to sink in for his partners. It took a lot of money to finance a movie—a looootttt of money. So these guys had another idea. They already had experience building software companies, so they were going to do that again; the idea was that they would then sell that company and use the money to finance the production of their film. To keep Tom involved until they had the finances, they suggested he come on full-time as a copywriter. They figured it would take anywhere from twelve to eighteen months to get the company to the point where they could build it and then sell it for an amount that would finance their film.

Now, being a copywriter was never something that Tom had dreamed about, but they made this proposition veeeeeery interesting: They told all their employees to act and think of themselves as having any position in the company they wanted. If they wanted to be a partner in the company, then they should act in accordance. Tom, being Tom, took them very seriously, even though he was so low on the company totem pole that his desk was in the server room. Sure, everyone else at the company was older and had more experience, but if they told Tom to act like a partner, then, by golly, he was going to act like a partner. He saw it as the path to big things. "Babe, THIS is our chance," he said. "Our chance to make movies on our terms."

I never wanted another matchbox thrown in my face, so this sounded pretty damn good to me. I was determined to help Tom make the most of this opportunity. From our very first date, when he took me to that Chinese restaurant, I knew that Tom was ambitious. It was one of the things that I was incredibly attracted to and the thing I committed to supporting the day we took our vows. I knew the man I married and swore I would always support that. So if he truly believed that this was a life-changing venture, then I'd dive in, too. "Sink or swim, baby," I said to him. "Either way, we go together."

I Can Stop Making Excuses.

When Tom and I decided that I would stay home so that he could really focus on his job, we played a game—one you won't find in Vegas, unless we decide to someday open up the Bilyeugio—that we eventually began to call No Bullshit, What Would It Take? (NBSWWIT?). This game is all about dissecting what you think you want and analyzing what it would take to make it possible.

Instead of saying, "Tom can't become a partner in this company because he has no prior experience," we looked at, "What would it take for Tom to become a partner in the company with no prior experience?" At this point, we still thought the goal was to build a technology company, then sell it to fund films, so Tom becoming a partner was still in service of our bigger goal. We decided that what it would take was arranging our lives so that Tom could focus his attention and energy 1,000 percent on building the tech company. What would it take for him to do that? No bullshit—he didn't want to waste a minute of time or an iota of energy on anything that didn't move him to his goal. We even got into arguments about making the bed. He didn't want me to make it, because then he had to waste his time to unmake it. Making or unmaking the bed wasn't going to get him to his dreams.

Tom wanted to be all in with his new job, so we sat down and started stripping away all of our assumptions about how we would live our lives so that we could look at what it would really take for him to give 110 percent. First, Tom wanted to move. His new bosses lived in Marina del Rey, and he thought that we should live in Marina del Rey, too, so that if there was a business emergency at 2:00 a.m. on a Saturday, he could be there in seven minutes. Like a new expectant parent timing the ride from home to the hospital, whenever we looked at an apartment, we would do the same thing: "All right, baby, aaaaaaand start the timer!" If an apartment clocked in at eight minutes and twenty-three seconds, even if it was otherwise perfect, it was out of the running.

We also started to study the behaviors of the most successful people of our time, across industries, to see what we could learn about how they lived their lives. Tom had read that Steve Jobs maximized his day by eliminating making decisions that didn't matter or that took up valuable brainpower, like deciding what to wear. Ever wondered why you always saw him in black? Now you know. We talked it over, and since our eyes were still on the prize—the money and freedom to make movies—we decided that we would take a bite of the apple and go all in on the Steve Jobs Effect.

He would focus 100 percent on work, and I would handle 100 percent of the household responsibilities. Not only would I be president of Bilyeu Enterprises but I would also be the chief accountant, head chef, human and puppy resources (HPR) manager, and director of housekeeping. Was I particularly excited about this arrangement? No. But did I believe at the time that it would help get us to our goal? Hell yes. I laid out his gym clothes so that he could put them on first thing in the morning. While he was at the gym, I laid out his work clothes so he could get dressed right out of the shower, and I sent him to work with a lunch box so he wouldn't have to spend any time debating between El Pollo Loco and Fatburger.

I was never excited about the idea of staying home and focusing all my energy on housekeeping, but I knew that it was something I could do, and quite honestly, it was very important to me to support Tom. After all, it was in service of something bigger—our shared dream—and there was no way we were going to let that die. Besides, it was only for twelve to eighteen months.

So no problem. I could do this. I was only twenty-four, after all, so Tom and I had our whole lives ahead of us. There was no rush on having kids, or anything else, really. But after a year of Tom working overtime at the tech company, it was clear that they were nowhere near ready to sell it. "Babe, we just need another twelve to eighteen months," he told me. "Then we'll really be ready to sell." "Okay," I thought, "we've come this far. If a little more time is what the hubby needs, then a little more time is what I'll give him."

I had always wanted to live in America, and now I was in California, married to a man I loved like crazy, and that man was out every day, busting his butt, so that we could make our dreams come true. I could see the marina from my balcony, and when I talked to my friends back home, they oohed and aahed about my life in Los Angeles ("Tell me again about how you saw Jodie Foster at the Coffee Bean"). But the truth was, the novelty had worn off. Even if I'd seen Jodie Foster every morning (or at least MWF), that still wouldn't have made up for the fact that I was starting to feel like I had no idea what to do next. It was like my life had paused on the frame that said "To be continued . . . ," but the sequel still didn't have a script. I hated staying home, and I was bored out of my nut. Rather than face this fact, and just start writing the script myself, I did everything I could to distract myself from it.

I didn't want to look at the big picture of my life, so I got hyper-focused on the details. As soon as I got up, I'd launch into my day with a strict schedule that I had carefully constructed to distract myself from the fact that I didn't really have all that much to do. 7:30 a.m.: Feed the furbabies, Batman and Banzai. 7:38 a.m.: Strip down, close my eyes, and step on the scale. This is really where my day started during this time. Like you check the weather forecast to see if you should take a jacket or wear shorts, the number on the scale would almost always determine how I felt about myself that day. If I ever got introspective and started to think about why my weight was such a focal point, my defense mechanisms would toss out a distraction as if I was a dog in need of a really interesting squirrel to chase. Hindsight being twenty-twenty and all, it's clear to me now that I was also fixating on my weight because I felt like that was the one thing I could control, unlike all the other things in my life that I felt were slipping out of my control. Losing a pound or two made me feel proud, like I'd accomplished something. I'd even take point five of a pound down as a win. If I was up a pound, or if I'd gotten lax the day before and eaten two sugar-free popsicles instead of just one, that would impact whether I skipped cardio or ran on a treadmill for forty-five minutes.

But even a girl who's obsessed with her weight can only spend so much time at the gym, and I still had long, empty afternoons to fill. I learned to break up my week by tackling one big household task a day, which at least made me feel like I had a plan and a purpose. Then, to keep myself minimally entertained, I gamified them all. Look! Another squirrel!

I grocery shopped, I clipped coupons, counted pennies, and scouted sales like I was competing on *The Price Is Right*. Sometimes, I played little tricks on Tom: I'd buy the cheaper version of something we normally had, and then waited to see if he noticed a difference. When he didn't, I would feel like I'd scored. "Those paper towels were forty-seven cents cheaper, and Tom didn't even comment on the texture," I'd say to myself, stepping away to secretly pump my fist in the kitchen. Nailed it! If I wanted to go an extra round, I'd see how far I could stretch one paper towel, painstakingly tearing each one into halves to make sure I never used more than I needed. Doubling our money. One more squirrel!

One of my favorite competitive sports became carrying the groceries from the parking garage to the apartment. How many bags can I hold, and how far can I get, before I have to stop and readjust? Last week, I had five bags and made it to the elevator, but this week I made it all the way to our floor with six bags. Someone call the folks at *Guinness World Records*.

Tom's business partners were bodybuilders, so when Tom got into lifting and decided he wanted to bulk up, I was thrilled. Not just because it meant I was going to have a walking cheese grater for a husband but because it was a new challenge for me. At the time, the predominant thinking in bodybuilding was that, in order to build muscle, you needed to eat six meals a day. Yep, that's forty-two meals a week for one person. I was so starved for something different, anything different, that I saw bulk cooking as an exciting new task to fill me up (regardless of the fact that it was LITERALLY just more of the same. Another squirrel).

I started shopping at Costco so I could buy all of our food in bulk, and went hard on the meal prep. Have you ever seen a Greek girl grill thirty burgers and thirty chicken breasts, all at once, all by herself? Let me tell you, it's pretty damn impressive. I had a whole system and was a one-woman assembly line, marinating the chicken while the burgers cooked, trying to time and flip everything perfectly, and then portioning it all up so that we'd have lunches and dinners ready to go for the rest of the week. I challenged myself to cook more at once this week than I did the week before, and if I succeeded, I got the same sense of satisfaction I did when the number on the scale dropped. Bulk squirrel!

Some days, I groomed the dogs. Or organized the closet, or washed the car. It was thrilling. All of it. Absolutely thrilling. Occasionally, when Tom got home from work, he would notice all the chicken breasts ziplocked in the freezer and that the dogs were tangle free, but more often, he didn't. His days were long and stressful, and his own entrepreneurial enthusiasm was wearing off. Eventually, he got to the point where he would walk in from work, and the first thing out of his mouth was, "Don't ask me about my day." It became my own full-blown personal Fight Club. First rule of the Bilyeu household: Don't talk about his day. Second rule of the Bilyeu household . . . DON'T TALK ABOUT HIS DAY. But I can't talk about my day, either. What am I going to tell him? That this afternoon, the woman at the checkout counter liked my accent? Or that I finally got that stain out of the carpet? We didn't talk about our big dreams or making movies anymore. We didn't talk about what was next. Instead, we just headed to bed.

One day, I was traveling back to the UK with my sister, Lully, and we were going through customs when the immigration attendant, while checking my passport and visa, asked for my occupation. I hesitated for a moment, so my sister answered for me. "Housewife," she said nonchalantly. I stopped and froze in shock. "I'm not a housewife," I thought. "I'm president of Bilyeu Enterprises." That was how Tom and I had always referred to me and my role of taking care of the cooking and the cleaning and the . . . oh God. I was a housewife.

Now, let me just stop right here for a minute to drive home a point. There is nothing—I repeat, nothiiiiiing—wrong with staying home to care for the family. Not a frikin' thing. It's a bloody hard and valuable role, and I have enormous respect for women who hold down their household. But it wasn't the life I had dreamed of. It wasn't what I wanted, and it didn't make me happy or feel at all fulfilled, and to cope, I was developing some pretty unhealthy habits and patterns. Somewhere I had ended up without intention. And you want to know the worst thing about it? The thing that still pains me? I thought that I didn't have a choice in the matter, and that it was all out of my control. Oh, my, my—how wrong I was.

The mistake that we made was that we stopped playing NBSWWIT? after we got our first set of answers. In retrospect, we should have played every twelve to eighteen months, every time we needed to make a new decision or just assess whether our initial plan was still valid. We didn't realize that our odds of winning would have increased had we just played a few more hands, and, damn, I swear to you, girl, I will never make this same mistake again.

Now, when it comes to NBSWWIT? (Stop by the Bilyeugio gift shop to pick up your souvenir slogan T-shirt), I've become a bona fide high roller. I play the game constantly to make all the major decisions in my life. I make sure I know exactly what I want, and then I ask myself a series of questions to suss out exactly what I'm willing to do and what it will take to get it. But it took me some time to get to this point. And when I say some time, I mean *eight years*!

We don't let our dreams die by chance. They aren't taken away from us. We're not unlucky. It's a choice—only I didn't see it like that at the time. The first dream-killing choice I made was dismissing my own unhappiness. I had so much, had come so far, that I believed it was selfish to be unsatisfied with what I had. Rather than listening to that annoying voice that was quietly whispering that something was wrong, I put my fingers in my ears and "la la'ed" my way to trying to block it out, because I felt like holding on to my dreams meant that I was ungrateful for what I had. Was I unhappy? No doubt. But did I think unhappiness alone was a good enough reason to make a whole bunch of changes, changes that might make other people uncomfortable? I wasn't there yet. So rather than having the radical confidence to take the initiative myself, I just kept waiting for things to change on their own. After all, many people would have killed for my life. But you can be over-the-top frikin' grateful for what you have, and you can be maaaaaadly in love with parts of your life and be utterly miserable in others.

The truth is that all of us deserve to go after our dreams. We all deserve to do everything we can to live the life we want. If that sounds big, bold, scary, and incredibly audacious to you, then hell yeah! Because that's radical confidence, baby. It's about being courageous enough to rock the boat. Rock it even when you already like the boat you're in. Your particular boat could be a yacht that Beyoncé boards when she wants to chill out, but if that boat isn't taking you where you want to go, then it's time to jump. Having radical confidence means making a frikin' splash.

Another thing I did to stab my dream in the heart—which I can recognize now—was not taking the time or energy to define it. I knew I wanted to make movies, but I stopped there. About four or five years in, I realized that when Tom and I talked about our future, "movies" had become "money." We were trying to make money, which was to make movies, but we didn't break it down to see if the end was still going to justify the means. I never dug deeper into my dream to articulate what making movies meant to me, or even which part of making movies I actually wanted to get involved in. Did I want to produce, write, or direct? Why did I have to be in

LA to make them? Did I want to make features, short films, or animations? Because Tom and I never drilled down to the details of what we wanted or why we wanted it, we stalled at our first major roadblock—needing money to fund the projects. We couldn't see beyond that obstacle—we didn't even check the map to see if there was an alternate route. We just stayed there, him working his butt off at a job he hated and me at home, trying to stay busy by organizing our sock drawer: "Do I set them up by color or type?"

To make your dream come true, you have to know what you want, why, and be willing to move in any direction in order to make visible steps toward it. Hazy, foggy-goggled dreams stay floating around up in the clouds. Specific, well-defined ones float down to earth to become reality.

My third dream killer was never giving my dream a deadline. You need a set point where you will reexamine and reassess everything to do with that dream and decide whether it's time to hold 'em or fold 'em on your current approach. At this point in our lives, whenever Tom would come home and say the company needed another twelve to eighteen months, I would agree. I was miserable, but I was like that bleary-eyed gambler at 5:00 a.m., refusing to leave the table because they think that THIS time, my luck is gonna change! I just kept agreeing to another hand, because I felt like I was pot committed. "I've spent thiiiiss long, so I have to keep going because I can't let that all be a waste." Because I hadn't taken the time to really understand the exact details of what I was dreaming about, I was scared to change the game. If I gave up, I was going to lose big. What if it would turn out that I had really just wasted all those years of my life? Because I was so deep into the belief that there was only one way to make my dream a reality, I never realized that all along I had the option to cash in my chips and head to the buffet.

I Can Bet on Myself.

It was time to play No Bullshit again, stripping away all of our assumptions about what we thought we had wanted and what we thought we couldn't do. Trying to make movies within the industry had made us miserable, and trying to make the money to make movies outside the industry had made us even more miserable for even longer. And if we weren't try- ing to make movies anymore, did we even need to live in Los Angeles? The answer was no. Once we realized that the dreams we had been clinging to only resulted in deep daily unhappiness, it was time for something differ- ent! Like a pack up everything and let's move to Greece kind of different!

So we kissed on it. And it was so damn exciting. We started looking at cheap apartments on the beach, and imagining what our days would be like. Tom still wanted to write, but he would focus on books—because it didn't take an entire production company to get a book written—and I'd take care of the kids I assumed we were going to have, and we'd be happy. Because all you need to do is ignore the root of the problem, right? I still didn't really know or think about what would actually make me happy. I just thought that if Tom was happy, then I would be, too. But problems are like shadows—they follow you everywhere.

Looking back now, I was just agreeing to Purgatory of the Mundane: The Sequel (dubbed in Greek). It was the same lead characters, same story line, just in a different location. But I was desperate for a change, any change, that seemed drastic and exciting enough to convince myself it was the right idea. So Tom went in to quit his job, which was a huge deal—these guys had become like brothers to him, and quitting felt like he was leaving them. But for the sake of his happiness and, quite frankly, our marriage, he did it! And called me from the car on his way home. "Babe, I told them," he said. "Boooom! Greece, here we come!"

Then all of a sudden, beep, beep. Call waiting. Literally as he's pulling into the parking garage. "They're calling me on the other line," he said. "I'll see you in a minute." Then, instead of walking into the apartment, he called me back, still in the car. His partners wanted him to come to dinner with them. "I figure I owe them that much," he said. I understood and told him no problem, and that we could celebrate later. After all, I'd already waited this long. What was another hour and a half?

As soon as he came home, I got a sense that the closest we were get- ting to Greece was the bottle of olive oil I was using to make my dinner. But his tone and demeanor were different this time. Doing something he didn't enjoy for all of these years had been dragging him down, and now it was like the weight had finally lifted.

33

"Babe, the guys admitted they're unhappy, too, and want a path to something we can all actually enjoy building. But it doesn't make sense just to walk away. So we're gonna take the next six months to get the company to hit revenue targets, and if we don't, then we're gonna sell it and start something brand-spanking-new. Guaranteed." How could I argue with that? I mean six months seemed like a total steal of a bargain compared to the twelve to eighteen months that I usually got. Tom had already done the hard thing. He had quit. And that was all the immediate proof I needed to see that this time it actually was different.

Six months came and went, and unfortunately (at least that's how it felt at the time), they didn't hit their targets. True to their word, though, they started to build something new while they finally, once and for all, packaged the company up . . . for sale. And just like that, we were taking a new gamble. So, what was our next bet going to be? It couldn't be about money (been there, done that, and all I got was this crappy T-shirt). It had to be something predicated on passion and adding value to people. Something that made a difference. Something we actually believed in. That something was a little protein-bar company we called Quest Nutrition.

RADICAL CONFIDENCE RECAP

- **Know what you're betting on.** Give your dreams the dictionary treatment and define, define, define them. Vague and ambiguous aren't the name of the game here—you need to know exactly what you want. Write it down. Memorize it. Visit it frequently, and make sure everything you do traces back to this dream.

- **Play the game.** Play NBSWWIT? in order to get a clear view of what it will take to achieve your big, audacious goals. Then decide whether you're actually willing to do it. Remember, this is a judgment-free zone, so remove all "shoulds."

- **Kill the squirrel.** There are a million things you can allow yourself to be distracted by. And many of them you aren't even aware you're doing. There was a time in my life where my biggest priority was an organized sock drawer, and all the while I was thinking, "Of course you organize your sock drawer, what kind of crazy person doesn't?"

- **Check in on your assumptions.** Chances are, you hold a lot of beliefs that you've never really examined. Spend time and hang out with some of your big ideas about really important areas of your life (career, relationships, money, family), and see if you really believe these things or if you've just inherited them from someplace else. And not to beat a dead horse, but remember: No. Judgment.

- **Make your timeline as concrete as the sidewalk.** From the beginning, know when you will stop and reassess both your goal and the path you're on. Hitting this deadline gives you the opportunity to pivot or keep going. Either way, you will do it consciously. This is also a good time to dust off the NBSWWIT? box again to help you assess your decisions. I try to do this once every three months now, at least.

- **Eyeball that jackpot like it's a shirtless Ryan Gosling.** Evaluate everything in your life in terms of whether what you're doing day-to-day puts you closer to that big, clearly defined goal, and prioritize accordingly.

MAKE UP YOUR...
MINDSET

Mindset (n): 1. Something you must fix if it's fixed.
2. Something that, when showered with failures and fed with lessons, can blossom and grow.

When we're children, we're expected to learn—we come into this world not even able to hold our own heads up; no one assumes we already know how to write our name, put on shoes, or eat cake without first getting it in our eye. Everyone assumes that we can learn how to do all of these things and more, even though we don't know how to do them from day one. Somewhere along the way, as we grow up, we start to see not knowing how to do something as a permanent state, as a state of failure. But, guys, it's actually the exact opposite. Not knowing how to do something is not—I repeat, not—a failure. It's a goddamn opportunity! When you have radical confidence, every time you're presented with something you've never done before, something you have to learn how to do, you can choose to see it as a chance to grow, change, and get better.

Figuring shit out is what makes life exciting. No one ever says, "Oh my God, you can't have a baby! You've never had a baby before!" to a first-time parent. Can you imagine the horror? In fact, when someone admits their concern about not knowing how to be a parent, the advice I often hear other parents give is, "Oh, you'll learn as you go, and you'll figure it out. Read this book, check out this website, listen to what worked for me, and you'll be fine."

Yet in other areas of life, the idea that you can teach yourself how to do something you've never done before is as freakish as that scene in *Alien* when the creature comes out of that dude's stomach. We've normalized saying "You can't do that, you don't know how" when someone dares to take a leap. What's even more horrific is that we've normalized saying this to ourselves. We start to believe that things we want are "impossible," not even realizing that "impossible" is nothing more than just another bullshit excuse ready to be dismantled.

I first learned about the concept of a growth mindset when Tom interviewed the amazing psychologist Carol Dweck on his show *Inside Quest*. She had written a book called *Mindset: The New Psychology of Success*, and I just remember seeing this really thin, sweet lady who spoke really slowly, but when she opened her mouth, damn! Her words blew me away. She spoke about how a big chunk of your brain is hardwired with who you are and what you're drawn to, but a huge part of it is also totally malleable—meaning you can literally change your brain. She coined the concept of a growth vs. a fixed mindset. Someone with a growth mindset prides themselves on not who they are today but rather who they can become—someone who loves and even actually thrives off hard work and challenges because they believe, believe to their core, that they can change, grow, and expand who they are to improve their lives and achieve their dreams. Aka radically confident. Someone with a fixed mindset, on the other hand, thinks who you are is who you are, and tough luck—you're stuck with it.

When I applied Dr. Dweck's concept to myself, it was a major wake-up call. Oh my God, I, Lisa, she of the Housewife Scalextric and the Purgatory of the Mundane, had a growth mindset. And I'd had one for years, with no clue that it actually had a name. If I'd had a fixed mindset, I'd still be organizing Tom's socks, and not here, writing about how simply believing you can change your life is the foundation for changing your frikin' life. Because I had a growth mindset, I'd been able to embrace new challenges and not be daunted about taking on projects that were waaayyyy above my skill level. In fact, my growth mindset was what allowed me to support Tom when he first brought me the idea of Quest in the first place. Because starting a protein-bar company was a risk—and a big one. I remember the shocker of a conversation we had about how BIG a risk it was going to be, like it was something that just happened this morning in the kitchen, as we were waiting for the kettle to boil . . . .

"Babe," he says with utter enthusiasm, "this new company is going to be different." In hindsight, instead of waiting in anticipation for what he was going to say next, what I really should have done was grab my helmet, because unbeknownst to me, he was about to drop a nuclear bomb.

"It's going to be different because we're going to help fund it this time. We're betting our house and putting it down as collateral."

Yes, dearest reader, you read that correctly. My husband, the love of my life, had just referred to our nest, the home that I had built for us, the home I had envisioned we would start having kids in . . . as "collateral." Even though I was at the end of my eight-year rope, hanging on by my manicured (at home, to save a buck) nails, I was still dedicated to my hubby. My loyalty was to him, not materialistic things. I knew I could get another house. I couldn't get another Tom.

I once read a fire quote from a famous philosopher that said, "Loyalty is doing what you said you'd do even when you no longer feel like doing it." And okay, maybe that famous philosopher was really just a post I saw on Instagram, but it's frikin' true. We're all chock-full of loyalty when times are good, but when they get tough, that's when a lot of people start to hem and haw. "Well, um, you see . . . now, when I said that . . . I didn't actuuuuuually mean . . ."

But I'd married an ambitious man. I knew what I'd signed up for. And to go back on my word just 'cause the house was on the line wasn't the marriage or relationship I wanted or was committed to. You see, showing someone you believe in them only really carries weight when it's not easy. I didn't hesitate. "Baby," I said, "I bet on you."

Tom and his partners were all big into fitness and nutrition. So their idea was to make protein bars that actually tasted good AND were good for you. At this point in time, there was nothing like that on the market. You had protein bar A, which had the consistency of cardboard and the taste of sawdust ("Ooh, what an interesting flavor . . . do I detect a hint of plywood?"), or protein bar B, which tasted delicious because it was basically sugar with protein sprinkled in so they can put the word on the wrapper. (Sure, I guess you could call that a protein bar?) Homemade bars had no shelf life, and they'd start to mold after just a few days. They were high maintenance and had to be refrigerated. But what if this new company could totally change the game, and the market, with an option C? A shelf-stable bar, high in protein and low in sugar, that actually TASTES GOOD?

Tom had never been passionate about the technology industry, but he did care about health. Tom's mum and sister were both severely overweight, and I had watched my own mum struggle her entire life, first with borderline anorexia and then with obesity. Like so many people, they seemed to have just given up on their health. This new idea was much more personal, and something that we could both get behind emotionally because we knew exactly the kind of people we'd be helping. For Tom, this was also different, because this time around, he wouldn't just be acting like a full partner—he would actually be one. The Steve Jobs effect and seven-minutes-to-get-to-work planning was paying off. This was huge. There was just one more thing: This new company was going to run lean. Like Justin Theroux in *Charlie's Angels* kinda lean, so Tom's salary was about to be cut by almost a third.

Over the previous eight years, I'd watched my brilliant, ambitious, enthusiastic husband become miserable as he just went through the motions at a job he didn't care about. I'd become just as miserable as he was, and at this point, I was convinced that if I just had a happy husband, then I'd be happy, too. As he talked about this new company he was going to start, it was like my baby was back. The energetic, hopeful, fiery Tom I once knew had returned, and I could see that spark in him again. Maybe, I thought, this was the opportunity that would make Tom happy. And if Tom was happy, then I'd be happy, too. I feel like a parrot, saying this over and over, but it was truly what I thought. It was sink-or-swim time once again, baby, so we held hands and dove in. I knew I still wasn't happy, but I just told my-self, "Don't worry, you'll be happy when . . ." Oh. My. The dreaded when! There was always a "when" hanging around somewhere, so I want you to take a moment and think about what "when" may be currently stifling your happiness. For me, at this time, it was when Tom and I would finally start having kids. That was when I'd be happy. It just seemed like a good time to do that was never going to come. Despite the common advice I got about "never being ready," when the subject came up, Tom always made a valid point of not wanting to start a family while we were working toward our goal because we didn't have the resources—time and money.

Kids were the natural progression of our marriage, the narrative I'd been hearing my whole life. Ahhh, that wonderful bedtime story we read in childhood, "The Princess and the Great Expectations." Chapter one, get married. Chapter two, have kids. The end. That story had been burned into my soul, and so I didn't question it. And, God forbid, if I ever daaaaared to quiet the idea, my mum (whose dream in life—IN LIFE—is to be a grandmother) generously offered her services to remind me by playing me her number-one hit song, "When Are You Having Kids?" (She'd also occasionally drop a remix like "I can't wait to meet my grandchildren" or "You were meant to be a mother.") And over the years, my answer would change. "When I'm twenty-five," I'd say. "We'll start having kids when I'm twenty-seven." "I'll get pregnant when I'm twenty-eight and have it at twenty-nine." But now I was thirty-one years old. Being Greek and mar-ried with no kids at thirty-one . . . I may as well have been in a geriatric unit. But how can we start a family when we were white-knuckling it on the crazy-fun ride of the entrepreneurship express (though, just like preg-nancy, it comes with plenty of nausea)? So as always, we agreed, another twelve to eighteen months.

Tom and his partners were still trying to get the technology company to a position where they could sell it and devote all their time to the new company, and so they asked me to "fill in." I was happy to help however I could. Soon, I was a go-to gopher for anything and everything—shipping a few bars here, running a few errands there. When they hired a super-sweet and eccentric chemist to help figure out how to make the protein bars shelf-stable, I drove out to her hippie bungalow in Venice to deliver prototypes and sat in her kitchen playing fetch with her dog (one of those breeds that looks like a mop) while she worked.

I packed and shipped finished bars from our fluffy rug on our living room floor. When the orders started to outgrow the living room floor, I started to do the packing and shipping from one of the partners' garages. It'll be quick, they said. Pop in and pop out, they said. Soon, I was working every day, but I didn't mind it. In fact, I kinda liked it. After yeeeeeeeears of stretching a little closet organization so that it filled the better part of the day, an ever-changing to-do list of errands and tasks was practically a trip to Vegas.

I soon learned that shipping out multiple boxes a day wasn't like mailing a letter. You couldn't just lick 'n' stick the postage and put it in the mailbox. Depending on the order and the size of the box, it required its own specific stamp. I wasn't getting paid by the company to do any of this, but I couldn't just NOT ship the boxes because I didn't know how—this was Tom's business and he'd asked me to help and, by golly, I wasn't going to let him down. After weeks of painstakingly weighing packages on my food scale and countless hours at the post office to get each package stamped correctly, one of the partners discovered a shipping-label software system. I'm sorry, a what now? I'd never heard of such a thing, and the more he tried to explain it to me, the more frozen I became. In my head, I was panicking. I didn't speak Techish, and he was clearly fluent, so as he walked me through it step-by-step, I literally wrote everything down. I'm not kidding: Step one: Plug in machine. Step two: Turn machine on. Step three: If step two proves difficult, make sure step one has been completed.

I had a choice. I could let my fear of looking stupid take the lead and keep doing things the way I already knew how to do them. This was a very real option. But this could also mean not filling as many orders, which could mean the company goes under, which could mean we lose our house, but worst of all, I would (no *coulds* here) let Tom down. Nope, no way, no how. Failed Valley isn't a place I wanted to visit, let alone live (can you imagine the plumbing issues in a place like that?).

So, instead, I faced my fears and slowly started to learn the shipping thingamabob. I stared at it, it stared back at me. I pressed its buttons, and oh man, did it press mine. But in a few days, I was translating its beeps and boops with ease, and soon I became a Techish ninja. Until I reached . . . the post office, my own personal kryptonite. No matter how fast I worked, no matter how efficient I was, my productivity slowed to a crawl once I got to the post office. It was like that scene with the sloth in *Zootopia*. I would haul garbage bags full of packed, stamped, and addressed boxes to the post office, where I'd have to stand in line for what felt like an eternity just to hand them over. And you *know* I always ended up behind someone who gets to the front of the line and *then* decides to fill out the shipping label. "YOU'VE BEEN STANDING IN LINE FOR THIRTY-FIVE MINUTES! How are you not ready?" I was screaming and yelling. Only to realize actually I wasn't at all, it was just me in my own head. Phew. There's got to be a better way! One day, I was standing in line, again, just to drop off my packages, again, when those words started echoing in my head—*There's got to be a better way way waaay*—and I remembered something that my mum used to do. Whenever we had anyone working on our house—like a contractor, a plumber, or a painter—my mum would always make them tea and biscuits. It was her little way of letting them know she appreciated what they were doing, and in return, they usually did a better job. Slick mother right there. So what if I could apply that same tactic to my trips to the post office? Who doesn't love free shit? So the next time I went, I took some extra Quest bars. I was thinking, "Oh man, they're going to loooove it! All my problems are solved."

News flash: They did not love it. My problems were not solved. When I offered them protein bars, you would have thought I was offering up a weird Greek dish my *yiayia* had made in the mountains (bowl of unidentifiable mush, anyone? Going once . . .), and they just stared at me. I wasn't sure if it was my British accent, so I held it up and repeated slowly, "Protein baaaaaars."

After a moment of uncomfortable silence, one of the ladies replied, "No thanks." In retrospect, I couldn't blame them—the whole reason we had started making protein bars in the first place was because most of them tasted like inedible bricks at the bottom of a bodybuilder's gym bag—aka like crap. Okay, okay, think. What's the equivalent of rich tea biscuits in America? Then, I got it. Off I trotted to Costco for a huge bag of . . . candy.

I returned to the post office and stood in line with my big bags, but this time, I was armed. Candy armed. As I stood there waiting, and waiting, and—yes, of course—waiting some more, I started to think about what it's like for the post office employees, day in and day out, dealing with customers who are always complaining, customers who are never grateful, customers who compare them to the sloth from *Zootopia* (c'mon guys, who would do that?). So as I approached the counter, I decided to express my gratitude. "You guys are just frikin' amazing," I said to her. "I'm here every day, and you're always helping me out, so I brought you this as a little token to say thank you." And I slid my big bag of candy across the counter. As I handed it over, the smile on her face turned that post office from gray to technicolor. Hell yeah.

After a while, I became their candy dealer, restocking them whenever I thought they were low. Then, one day, I walk in and of course—surprise, surprise—there's a long line. Like always, I get in it. As I start drifting into whatever mindless thought I was having, I hear yelling. At first I thought it was some angry customer (which sadly, wasn't unusual) but then realized it was someone yelling, "Candy Lady, Candy Lady!" At . . . me!

I looked up to the sweet postal clerk waving me to the front of the line. She kept waving me toward her as I kinda embarrassingly passed everyone in line, awkwardly smiling. "You're not cutting the line, Lisa. You're not cutting the line." I told myself just to have enough confidence to make it to the counter.

As I got to the front, she grabbed my bags from me, smiled, and said, "Oh, you don't have to stand in line, Candy Lady." And just like that Candy Lady Lisa was born, and I was in and out of the post office in less than five minutes. I'd always known that you catch more flies with honey than with vinegar in your personal life, but this was the first time I learned that it could work in business, too.

Quest was more than a job—it had become our life. Weekends didn't mean time off, no no no, it was just a different type of work. On Friday evenings, we rented a commercial kitchen where we hand-made bars with rolling pins, knives, and a little pedal wrapping sealer. It would be Tom and I, the partners, their wives, and anyone else we could cajole, bribe, or drag along. Family in town? Oh boy, do we have an exciting Saturday

43

night planned for you! (We did try to make it as fun as possible, though, I promise, and they got paid in bars. Come on now, *that's* a vacation!) But it quickly became obvious that hand cutting bars just wasn't cutting it. No matter how fast we were with our knives (and we got pretty fast), our orders came faster. It was time to level up. We needed our own facility, someplace where we could handle the actual manufacturing and store our ingredients, and an office, where we could handle everything else. We found a place just outside Compton that was big enough for the budget we had and hired a full-time employee. The catch? According to Tom, if we had an employee, then that employee needed a supervisor. Tom and his partners were still working on splitting their time between Quest and the technology company, so who did that leave? Yep, you guessed it. Moi.

"Babe, we need you to go to Compton and supervise this guy," Tom asks like he's asking me to pass the salt. What? I was secretly freaking out inside over the word "supervise."

"We just need someone there so that he doesn't feel like he's totally on his own," Tom explained. "Make sure he's okay. That he's doing his work. You can still ship boxes. You can just do it from there." Ugh, Lisa, you had to bloody ask if you could help, didn't you?

It was another big choice to make. I could choose not to go because I found the situation intimidating and it might be uncomfortable, but that would be letting Tom and his partners down. So the next thing I knew, I was strapping on my radical confidence along with my seat belt and driving to Compton every day to supervise.

Since there were only two of us in the entire facility, and I was "in charge," the buck stopped with me. It was my responsibility to solve all the little problems that came up. Every. Single. Day. For example: "I can pick up a lot more boxes at once if you put them on a pallet," the UPS guy told me one day.

"Great, will do," I responded immediately. Except, what the heck is a pallet, and where the hell do I get one? Thank God for my new bestie, Professor Google. She's a clever gal—she knew everything and didn't mind if I hit her up 17,202 times a day.

Over time, I started to call myself MacGyver, because I was learning how to have a solution to everything. If you've ever seen that hysterical episode of *I Love Lucy* where Lucy and Ethel get jobs at the chocolate factory, then you already have a pretty good idea of what working on the Quest bar production line with limited help was like. We were always barely one step ahead of the bars. It was a tightrope; one wrong step and . . . splat. The bars were damaged before they'd even made it out the door. This was money we couldn't afford to lose, so I handled it myself.

One issue we had at the very beginning was a staffing shortage on the production line. The bars were made, wrapped, and chugging down the conveyor belt, but there was no one to catch them. They just hit the end of the line and sailed off like Thelma and Louise going over the cliff. Bar wasted = money wasted.

So I got creative. I built a cardboard slide for the bars to travel down and a huge six-foot-by-six-foot box to catch the bars, which I made by taping together empty ingredients boxes. I then filled it with packaging foam from the shipping department and covered that with a giant plastic sheet so the bars didn't fall to the bottom of the box and break. It wasn't gorgeous, and my design skills weren't going to land me in the pages of *Vogue*, but you know what? That shit worked!

The only problem now was that the bars piled up in the "kiddie pool" after a while, so I figured out exactly how much time it took for the bars to pile up, and then I would Sha'Carri Richardson it and sprint back there every ten minutes to rotate the gigantic box so that the bars would have someplace to fall.

No big deal, right? Anyone could do it. Except, one day I was sick, and we discovered that no, anyone could not do it. Everyone had given it a go that day, including Tom and our marketing director, and everyone failed. Bars were piling up, bars were falling on the floor, bars were getting dropped, and bars were breaking all over the place. It turned out that no one could keep up with what, from that day forward, we referred to as "the Lucy line." I was Queen Lucy, though I never had to resort to shoving things in my mouth (for FDA reasons, that's my story and I'm sticking to it).

I Can Figure Shit Out.

As the company started to grow, the guys gradually started working out of the Compton facility. There were four of us working out of the Quest office, where we all sat on empty ingredients buckets for chairs and I used a fold-out table as my shipping desk. The company was growing quickly, and even though I hadn't gone to business school, I didn't think I needed an MBA to know that it was hard to be productive and professional while sitting on a bucket (I'm pretty sure numb butt cheeks is high up there on the list of why start-ups fail). Here, I saw a need that no one else was going to address, so in between packing and shipping, I made the rounds to IKEA and Staples, where my coupon-clipping skills came in very handy.

Whereas I'd previously gamified the groceries, now I was doing it with office supplies. "Okay," I'd think, doing mental calculations in the pen aisle, "the cheap pens are three dollars, but those run out in two weeks. The more expensive pens are five, but I know those last a month, if nobody loses them . . ." I bought and built office chairs; when I presented someone with theirs, you would have thought I was delivering the Iron Throne. They were so happy. Having desks put them out of their mind with joy, too. I thought I was on a real roll when I brought in my kettle so everyone could make tea—until I discovered that our American marketing guy, Nick, spent fifteen minutes trying to figure out where the coffee filter was supposed to go.

Soon, we were shipping out so many bars a day that, no matter how fast I moved, I could no longer physically do it all by myself. I would have to hire someone—not to replace me but to help me. And just like your skin after a facial, it became clear this was what I was going to keep doing. And that felt bloody great and exciting because I was thriving off each day being different and not knowing what crazy thing would happen next. Not knowing what new weird and unexpected skill I would need to start learning. It was intoxicating. Tom and I discussed how I no longer wanted to be a housewife, and so we sat down and divided up our household responsibilities. He starts, "I'll take the dogs, and you deal with the grocery shopping."

"Yeh, that sounds good," I ping-ponged. "I'll keep the fridge stocked, but you have to make your own lunch . . ."

And just like that, I had a new job. What was more—I was someone's frikin' boss. Supervising a fairly autonomous employee so he didn't feel alone was one thing, but actually being a manager? Bilyeu Enterprises had been a company of two, and I had no clue how to be a boss. What qualifications did I have to be able to tell someone else to do something? Brighter than a Vegas strip neon sign, the words Impostor Syndrome started flashing in my head. What was I thinking? I felt like a great pretender whenever I tried to exercise any authority, so at first, I went out of my way to avoid it. When I wanted our employee to do something, I would always phrase it as a question—"Do you mind helping out with this?"—as if I was asking him to do me a favor.

Quest had made a promise to our customers that all orders received before 1:00 p.m. would go out that same day. It was a point of pride for us, and a way for us to show people how much we valued their business, but when you're growing at 57,000 percent, it was hard as hell to do. This meant that at 12:59 p.m. every day, you had to refresh the orders, print them, and fill them before the UPS pickup that afternoon. The more orders we got, the more it became *The Amazing Race: Quest Nutrition Edition*. We were racing against the clock, and every second counted. I remember one particularly slammed day when I started to think, "Oh, shit, we're going to miss this deadline."

Our employee had chosen this time to get into a serious text conversation with his girlfriend. I don't know if they were deciding to end things or just deciding what to have for dinner, but he was 100 percent involved with his phone and 0 percent involved with shipping protein bars. Seriously? Now? So what did I do? Did I tell him to step it up? Nope, I did not. Instead, I did a Neo. I worked faster, double-timing it, moving my hands at warp speed so that I could do the work of two people and hit the deadline, not ever owning the fact that, as his boss, I could tell him to do his job. Face, meet palm.

Quest grew so quickly that we soon outgrew our space in Compton and needed a new location. And then, we grew even quicker, so even that wasn't enough, and we expanded and took over the building next door. Shipping had become so mahoosive that we needed more than a room. We needed our own facility. I still remember the day that I walked into my very first office and there was a desk that had been left there by the previous occupants. I opened the drawer, excited to have somewhere to stow all my carefully budgeted pens, and found a dead cockroach. For the record, despite what others say, I definitely didn't freak out. I definitely didn't run screaming. And I definitely didn't say I wouldn't return until someone got rid of it. But dead roach be damned! Little old me—who still often thought of herself as possessing no real skill sets—was thrilled to have her own desk.

I was good at logistics, and when it became obvious that my skills were more valuable and cost-effective when I worked in admin and paperwork—as opposed to being on the floor—we hired more and more people under me. Soon, I was the head of a forty-person shipping department. But did being in charge of such a big operation mean I now knew everything? Hahahaha . . . errr, no. Professor Google and I were still besties, and I was still doing whatever was needed.

Our marketing department was just starting to learn the power of influencers, and one day, our social-media manager came barreling into my now-cockroach-free office, out of breath but excited. "Lisa!" he panted. "I was just in touch with Justin Bieber's cousin, and he's a big fan of Quest. He's going to be with Justin for a few days on his tour, and if we can get the guy some bars, he'll get them to Justin, and maaaaaybe we can get a pic or two. Can you frikin' imagine if we got pics of JB with a Quest bar? That would be huge!"

"Hell yeah," I said, giving him a high five. "Let's do it! What's the address? We'll ship the Biebs bars out today."

"Okay, well, here's the thing," he said, catching his breath as he broke it down. "We have to get them to him in Dubai, and he's only going to be there for the next thirty-six hours."

Dubai? I thought. Surely he can't mean THE Dubai? The one on pretty much the opposite side of the world Dubai? I was freaking out inside, and yet it was weird, I was thoroughly excited for the challenge. This was a huge opportunity for Quest, and it wasn't going to pass us by, not on my watch. No sirree. First thing I did was call UPS and speak to our rep. It became obvious immediately he wasn't going to be any help, so I asked to speak to the manager. "I need to get a food package to Dubai within a thirty-six-hour window," I said, my pen hoverboarding over my pad, ready to take notes. The guy straight-up laughed.

"No way, no how, no can do," he said. "That's impossible." But it wasn't his company. It didn't really make a difference to him if the bars got to JB or not. In fact, my request made his life mooooore difficult, so it was actually easier for him to say that than to try. No one will fight for your dream more than you will, so you have to be willing to step up to the plate, bat in hand, and ask questions until the problem becomes an actionable to-do list.

I've been doubted a lot in my life, and all that doubt led to me feeling really shitty about myself. I got picked on and teased, and if someone thought I was going to fail and then I did, well, gas, meet bonfire. And eff that! I wasn't going to give anyone any reason to think they were right about me. The truth was that the fear of proving someone who didn't believe in me right was WAAAAAY worse than the fear of actually failing (let that sink in for a second). So fail at getting Quest bars to THE BIEBS? Not me, not today! I speed-read Dubai's importation rules and filled out all the forms as best as I could. I even filled out forms that I wasn't sure we needed, and I deliberately overpaid the customs fees and taxes just as insurance against our package getting held up there.

Every time someone told me something couldn't be done, I asked them why not, and they always ended up giving a lame excuse or they went around in circles. And that sure as hell wasn't going to fly here.

After a lot of calling around and a little bit of grumbling from the people on the other end, it turned out that overnighting bars to Justin Bieber in Dubai wasn't so impossible after all. It worked, and whether he liked them or not was totally out of my hands, because I had done my part. Ta-frikin'-dah! (Though Mr. JB's Cousin, if you're reading this, I'm still waiting for that photo, homie.)

I Can Do Hard Things.

Though I didn't recognize it at the time, the fact that I refused to accept that things couldn't be done, that I taught myself how to do things I'd never done before, and that I always looked for solutions whenever a problem popped up were all active parts of developing a growth mindset. Even when I was shit-scared about something and didn't have confidence, I still swallowed my fear and charged into battle. Whether my opponent was new shipping software, complex import-export rules, or good old-fashioned gravity, I gave it my best shot and figured that, even if it took a few tries, I would triumph in the end. That's radical confidence.

If you don't know what kind of mindset you have, consider this a cheat sheet: If you find yourself often thinking or saying any of the following statements, then you have a growth mindset.

- I can figure that out . . .
- Everybody has to start somewhere . . .
- There must be a way . . .
- If she can do it, so can I . . .

If you find yourself thinking or saying the following, then you probably have a fixed mindset, and it's time for a makeover:

- I can't . . .
- It's not possible . . .
- It's not my fault . . .
- I'm so unlucky . . .

Now, if you do indeed have a fixed mindset, DO NOT DESPAIR! Bear with me for a minute, because it's about to get *Alice in Wonderland* trippy up in here, and we're about to go down the rabbit hole. . . . What you need in order to go from a fixed mindset to a growth mindset is . . . yep, a growth mindset. Even if you can recognize that you have a fixed mindset now, believing that you can change this and develop a growth mindset is evidence that you're already developing a growth mindset. I'll pause for a second here so that you can pick up the bits of your brain off the floor, because—oh yeah—this is mind-blowing!

Having a growth mindset isn't about having blind confidence in yourself or thinking that you're perfect. It's about recognizing that you have the ability to grow and change, and that who you are and what you know aren't permanent things. If you ever start to doubt yourself and think, "There's no way I could ever do that," remind yourself of all the things that you used to not know how to do that you probably do now every single day: walk, drive a car, fix yourself lunch, tie your shoe, use a computer, READ. The list goes on and on . . .

But while that's the first step and the foundation, there are things that you can put into practice in your thoughts and in your life to really make the switch from a fixed to a growth mindset.

- **Have your why.** Why do you want to build a growth mindset? What are you looking to achieve? Be specific. And be positive! Instead of "So I don't have anxiety on a date," say, "So I feel good about myself when I go on a date." Instead of saying, "To do better at work," make it, "To feel like I'm making a meaningful contribution at work." Because developing a growth mindset is like taking the red pill. It will reveal the truth and set you free from the Matrix. But first, it will totally suck.

- **Believe you can.** Quest succeeded because we BE-LIEVED it was possible. When we were told by experts, "There's a reason this bar doesn't exist, because it can't be made," we didn't listen. The company never would have started if we had.

- **Watch your language.** Immediately switch the negative language. IMMEDIATELY! Switch "I don't know" to "I don't know yet." Change "I can't" to "I choose not to." Alter "It's impossible" to "I'm unaware of a way right now." And so on and so forth.

- **Watch your actions.** Do they align with what you say? Don't fool yourself. Sometimes the most believable lies we tell are the ones we tell ourselves. Sometimes we can trick ourselves into believing something is true because we merely think it. But you can think it or even say it till you're blue in the face. Ultimately, our actions are a game of true or false. One way or another, the answer will be revealed. You want a promotion and believe you've earned one—but have you asked? You signed up for a gym membership—but have you actually gone consistently enough to see results? Talk the talk AND walk the walk.

- **Surround yourself with growth-minded people.** This has to be VERY deliberate. It's like trying to eat healthy and then going out for drinks with your friends who always want to party hard all night and then hit up Taco Bell at 2:00 a.m. It's bloody hard to resist, compared to a lunch date with your buddies after a Zumba class. You're more likely to stick to that salad. I remember talking to my mum one day a few years back when I already had a growth mindset (after she had lost all her weight and developed a growth mindset as well), and I said something about not being able to do something. She didn't miss a beat. "Well, that's not very growth mindset of you." Like, she totally called me out on something I didn't even realize I was doing. Immediately I was like, "Respect!" Thanks for the reminder, Mum.

- **Rinse and repeat.** Your growth mindset is a muscle, and you have to keep taking it to the gym and training it. If you aren't consistent, it starts to atrophy. You have to keep on practicing and working on it, like the skill that it is. How many people learn an instrument or a language when they're young and then try it twenty years later and have no clue what they're doing? This framing reminds me it's not a one-and-done. So if I slip up (like in the case with my mum), I don't beat myself up. I appreciate the reminder.

- **Celebrate the small wins.** Yeah, it's about the end result, but it's also about the steps you took to get there. You're not going to get it perfect right off the bat. In fact, you will probably never get it perfect at all. So when you do get it right, even in the smallest, itsy-bitsy teeniest weeniest way, give yourself a pat on the back. You're growing, learning, and changing. File this moment away so that you can come back to it the next time you start to doubt yourself. You frikin' did it once; you can do it again.

In those early days of Quest, I didn't feel confident. On a daily basis, I came up against situations and problems (and occasionally people) who made me want to turn and run screaming in the opposite direction, to go home and hide behind the couch with a blanket over my head. But I chose not to accept *can't*. I chose not to pass the buck up or down. Every day was an education in building a business, and I started to see that "I don't know" was nothing more than an excuse. If I didn't know how to do something, then I had to get radically confident and bloody learn. Period. Instead of asking myself, "Can I do this?" I'd ask, "How can I do this?" If the answer to that question involved doing something that I didn't already know how to do, then I knew I was going to have to learn. I was going to have to figure it the hell out.

When you're doing something new, as intimidating as it may be, it's unlikely that you're reinventing the wheel (unless, of course, you work for Firestone). Somewhere, someone has been in your shoes, and maybe, like a caveman drawing pics of fire on the wall of his cave, they've left some clues. Even when you're inventing something that's brand-spanking-new, remember that someone, at some point in time, also invented something that was brand-spanking-new for its time. And when in doubt, ask questions. Ask boatloads of questions—of people and of Professor Google. Read. Listen to podcasts. Watch videos. Research. Find related communities. You may worry that you're being annoying or coming off as incompetent, but fear not! Because you know what's truly annoying? An incompetent person who effs up big-time because they never asked questions. What's not annoying is a person who asks a lot of questions and then nails it.

I Can Get Good at Anything.

Quest's growth wasn't a roller coaster. It was more like a rocket that blasted off into the stratosphere and never looked back, and if we hadn't asked enough questions to make sure we were doing things right, it would have disintegrated on launch. In the first few years, I went from sitting on my living room floor putting bars in a box, to managing an employee, to overseeing a department, to managing an entire ten-thousand-square-foot shipping facility.

Quest put out a call for employees, regardless of their criminal record. As long as they were willing to work hard, we would consider them. And we were true to our word. Soon, the shipping department was a bunch of incredibly hardworking, giant (think 6'5") tattooed ex-cons . . . and little 5'1" me, their boss, who sounded like Mary Poppins. Now I really wish I could say that I was a brilliant, wonderful, amazing leader and awesome manager from day one, but, alas, that was not the case. Am I going to beat myself up about that, though? No, because at the end of the day, you only know what you know. When you find yourself in these situations, where you're leveling up, where you're the newbie, and you're just trying not to fall on your face (in front of forty people), you've got two options: You can be anxious about it, or you can learn.

It can be incredibly humbling to approach a new situation while being honest with yourself about how much you need to learn, but if you're trying to pretend you know something you don't, people can smell the bullshit. If you ask a kid something they don't know, more often than not, they'll just shrug and say, "I dunno." Right? But when we become adults, we internalize the idea that it's bad to not know something. Don't be scared to admit when you don't know something—just get radical confidence and Google that shit.

The one thing you cannot do (seriously, I forbid it) is to wait to do something until you're 100 percent confident in doing it. 'Cause, sweetie, if you do that, you're gonna be waiting a long time. So even if you're scared out of your mind, buy the ticket, jump on the train, and take the ride anyway. Let me be Captain Obvious here for a minute and remind you that you only do something for the first time ONCE. From there, it will only get less scary, and your confidence will only grow.

And sometimes, even after five million and thirty-two Google searches, I learned the hard way that there are some things you're just going to have to figure out through trial and error. Quest was personal for me, and this led me to make a very common mistake. I assumed it was just as personal for everyone else there. Why weren't these people working as hard as I was? Didn't they understand what was on the line? "Come on," I'd yell. "What are you doing? Why is this taking you so long?" I know—shocker!—that didn't work. This was the opposite of a motivation technique, because the truth was that even when our employees loved their jobs, as I think many of them did, it wasn't their company or their house on the line.

So I had to come up with a different way to get my team psyched and working hard. Step One: Go back to the basics. Okay, Candy Lady, what's their equivalent of biscuits and candy to show my appreciation? I realized that everybody really loved Mio Energy water enhancers. So, out of my own pocket, I bought each person their own. Every Monday, I would write their names on them and give them out. The smiles would not only make my heart sing Celine Dion–style but would have been able to power the entire facility each week with all the positive energy it generated.

Now on to Step Two: Connect. I might have been a tiny British chick, and they might have been ex-cons from Compton, but we all loved hip-hop. I'd blast Tupac on the production floor and then bust out the lyrics flawlessly (I mean, *I* did them flawlessly, but sometimes Tupac got it wrong), leaving my team in hysterics and shock all at the same time.

Step Three: Motivation. I had earned an Olympic gold medal in figuring out how to motivate myself to keep going when I was doing something I didn't really care about, like grocery shopping or bulk cooking. I realized that the same tools might be useful for my team—I had to make it fun. Of course, I had to turn it into a game. On days when shipping was balls-to-the-walls crazy and my team was struggling to get it done, rather than just telling them to work faster (which I learned the hard and failed way), I'd roll up my sleeves and walk in, clapping with excitement. "All right, guys, let's *do* thiiiiis. Let's show 'em what we're made of. Shipping is the greatest department of all time. They're going to want to give us medals after we're done!"

I'd sometimes split us into teams to see who could label the most boxes in ten minutes, and the winners would get a reject bar (bars that were perfectly fine to eat but that we couldn't sell for logistical reasons, like the expiration date was only half printed). I'd throw down individual challenges, too. "Okay, you think you can wrap a pallet faster than me? Let's go, then! You win, you get a free box of bars. I win, all your coworkers just saw you get beat by a girl!"

This was my way of showing my team that I wasn't a princess. I was willing to get my hands dirty, nothing was beneath me, and in a lot of ways, we weren't that different after all. Now I could have read a million management books, and I bet none of them would have ever said, "Play Tupac. Play it fuck-off loud," but that's what I did, and that's what worked for me. Using radical confidence allows you to face the problem, and having a growth mindset allows you to believe that, with some trial and error, you will figure that problem out. And when all else fails . . . just turn "California Love" up to eleven and keep going.

~~RADICAL~~ CONFIDENCE RECAP

- **Grow or remain fixed, it's your choice.** If you want to have a fixed mindset, no judgment, as long as you're doing that consciously. But if you want to develop a growth mindset, know that you can learn new things. Keep repeating after me: Not knowing isn't a permanent state. Not knowing isn't a permanent state. Not knowing isn't a permanent state.

- **At first, it will totally suck.** Get ready for some growing pains (and I don't mean the 1980s sitcom). Deciding to adopt a growth mindset will mean taking a long, hard look at yourself and your life, and this can be unpleasant and uncomfortable. If you don't first identify your pain points, then you can't fix them, so just remind yourself that these feelings are a sign that you're finally on the right track.

- **Instead of asking "Can I do this?" ask "How can I do this?"** Start with Professor Google if you have to, but treat each doubt and uncertainty like a task on your to-do list. The world is your oyster of free information, and you can do anything once you figure out how, so tackle that shit and cross it off your list.

- **Call yourself on your own shit.** "I don't know how to do that" or "I've never done that before" are not valid reasons for not trying something. They're just excuses (cough, bullshit, cough).

- **Take your cues from MacGyver.** You don't always need to bring in the big guns. Make problem solving your superpower.

- **Maybe you already know.** We all have areas of expertise that can be applied to other areas of our life. Gamifying menial tasks, coupon clipping, and ~~bribing~~ enticing people with sweets were all things I learned as a housewife that were useful in pursuit of my bigger goals, too.

VALIDATION IS...
FOR PARKING

Validation (n):   1.   The praise, accolades, and respect
                          you get from no one else but yourself.
                    2.   The price you begrudgingly pay to get
                          that mocha.

With the shipping department, I had a major success under my belt. I'd done something that no one would have ever thought I could do. And I hadn't just done it—I had kicked frikin' ass. But I didn't want to just sit around and do stuff that I already knew I was good at. I wanted to keep learning. On the one hand, the thought of moving on and giving up my safety net petrified me. What if I tried something new and failed? Would that become my new story? Would I have to tell my family that I was a failure? Would people stop remembering how successful I had been in shipping and, instead, just know me as the girl who totally bombed as soon as she tried something else? The truth was, if I did something else, I wouldn't be just changing jobs, I'd be changing identities.

Validation Is . . . for Parking

Oh identity. The name of our shackles. Shackles many of us put on willingly, without realizing it. Our velvet handcuffs, if you will. So often, we confuse who we are with what we do and base our identity on how other people see us. If something we do earns us compliments, we pour more of ourselves into that area and shy away from doing anything that might cause those compliments to dry up. For many women, our identities come from who we are to other people: We're someone's wife, mother, or daughter. We become the caretaker, the fixer, the mediator, and we get used to the feelings these roles bring us: We like being needed, feeling valuable, being seen as the one who always knows what to do. But it's important to periodically check in to see whether your identity feels more like a pleasure cruise around the Greek islands or a life raft you cling to for dear life during a thunderstorm. A lot of us climbed on that life raft early on in our lives, when we started hearing that awful word "should." We're praised for things we should be—pretty, nice, quiet, selfless—and shamed for things we shouldn't—outspoken, independent, aggressive (as cliché as it sounds, when I was around ten years old, I actually witnessed a grown man tell my sister that little girls should speak when spoken to). When we let external validation define us, we become dependent on it. We don't know who we are without it, and this keeps us from really, truly knowing who we are, who we actually want to be, and what we're capable of.

I've spent a lot of my life looking to things outside myself for validation and to define my identity, and tearing myself away from that has not been easy. Especially once Quest really took off, I became so identified with my job that I worried that it was the only thing keeping me out of the Purgatory of the Mundane, even when it stopped being as fulfilling as it once was.

I had been so good at my job that I had earned the nickname "the gatekeeper." As head of our shipping department, I was in charge of the bars, and anyone who wanted free protein bars had to go through me to get them. And if there was one thing anyone who came to Quest wanted, it was . . . yep, you guessed it, free Quest bars! So when people came to visit the office, whoever they were visiting, they were always brought over to be introduced to me.

"This is Lisa; she's Tom's wife. She runs this department and is the gatekeeper to the bars. If you want some bars, you're going to have to win her over." I was always conflicted about this. I was still, after all I had done, after all the literal blood, sweat, and frikin' tears I had poured in, I was STILL firstly referred to as Tom's wife, as if it explained or defined my position there. And, truthfully, it felt like a slight shank to the ribs. Now don't get me wrong—I was increeeedibly proud of my husband. Proud of how hard he worked. Proud of the man he was becoming. Proud as hell to be his wife. I was also proud that—yes, yes—I was the gatekeeper. I had earned that title. I had started out not knowing jack shit and had created a department of forty people that successfully handled millions of dollars' worth of product. I reported directly to Tom and his partners, and had an entire team reporting to me. But the truth was, I was starting to feel stuck all over again.

I Can Make My Mission Possible.

A lot of us are familiar with the idea of a mission statement for a business or organization. Having a clearly defined mission helps to keep everything on track and headed in the right direction. But an individual—like you or me—if driven by external validation, can just as easily steer off course if we don't have something concrete to remind us whhhhhy we're doing what we're doing. Without a mission, we can start veering toward a safe place that's cushioned with compliments, but it's actually just a padded cell. Not a place we want to be. A mission can help keep your ego in check and relegated to the back seat instead of letting it drive.

Let's talk for a second about the difference between a mission and a goal, because knowing the difference between the two is a big step toward achieving both. Your mission is why you do everything in your life. It's your North Star that keeps you focused on what's really important and allows you to keep walking past distractions and detours. It's that grand, wonderful motivation that makes you get all teary-eyed and pump your fist and yell "Hell frikin' yes!" when you think about it. Having a mission pulls you through when you're exhausted; it can keep you focused on the bigger picture and throws you a rope when that quicksand shows up again and you start going down, down, down into the mundanity of daily life. Too often, the language of a "dream come true" sounds like something out of our control, like our fate belongs in the Magic 8 Ball of life and we keep getting "Ask Again Later." But reframing this as a mission emotionally attaches you to the cause and puts it back in your power. Unlike craps, it's not up to fate, luck, or chance.

To discover your mission, start with what excites you and drill down from there. What about it excites you? What do you want more of? What is your biggest and highest vision for that area of your life? And, for the love of God, don't think small. It drives me NUTS when people say, "Set the bar low so you can exceed it." That's so the wrong attitude. You set the bar frikin' high and bust your ass to exceed THAT. If you fail, at least you went balls out—and you probably still accomplished more than you would have if you'd achieved your much more modest goal. Just aiming for "good enough" is a toxic mentality that will lead you to believing that in other areas of your life as well. Your mission is your purpose in life, and you deserve for it to be as big, bold, and high as you can imagine.

How you feel about your mission is a gut reaction. It's the thing that gets you all excited, that gives you butterflies when you think of it, like that first kiss on that first date. That thing that, if you were doing it and got in a freakish accident and died right there on the spot, you would be totally content. Maybe there are a lot of things in your life that excite you—and this is frikin' awesome, because it means you're not bored—so which one is your mission? The one you dedicate your life to? You won't know until you try, and that's the catch: You have to try! Yes, you have to risk failure, embarrassment, starting over, and all those things you've been trying to avoid! This is one of those areas in life where you can't take shortcuts. You have to get in there, down and dirty, and see for yourself. This is why you hear so many stories of people who go to school for years to study something, only to spend two weeks in their profession and discover they absolutely hate it. You simply won't know until you try, and you have to try in order to figure it out.

Your mission is your hero quest, and so it should be written out in one to two sentences maximum, for utter clarity. Think of it as the elevator pitch for what you're doing with your life. You're starting at the penthouse, and someone who can legit help you on your mission steps in (turns out they were visiting the penthouse across the hall), and now is your frikin' chance. If you can't explain your mission by the time you hit the lobby, Reese Witherspoon/Richard Branson/The Rock/Michelle Obama is going to walk right out that door.

If you sit down to write out your mission and find that it's more of a paragraph, a page, or even a novella, it's all good, but you then need to break it down. You probably have more than one idea in there. Which one is the big idea, the one that's most important to you? (Ding, ding, ding—tenth floor.) Are your other ideas in service of the big one or totally different? (OMG, we're at the lobby. Dwayne, wait!)

Now, prioritize: Once you have your mission, you can set goals that are in service of it. Is there something that needs to be done first so that you can move on to the others? Goals answer the questions "What?" "How much?" and "By when?" You need utter clarity to know exactly what you're working toward. Let's say your mission is to help people on their health journey, so you work in sales selling Quest products because it directly connects to that mission. And your goal is to be employee of the year. Identifying this tells you how many sales you need to make in a month to get that title. And if you know that your close rate is 5 percent, then that gives you the actionable, clear task of knowing you need to maybe send out an average of twenty emails a day to new prospects to achieve that. Now you set a deadline to reassess. This could be every couple of months or quarterly. When this deadline rolls around, be honest with yourself. Have you made progress toward your goals since the last time you assessed your life and mission? Did you send those emails? If not, why? What can you change so that you can start to make progress? Does your mission still excite you? If not, why is that? Or is it simply time to move on? Maybe your mission is the same but you've realized that you absolutely despise sales. So, what else could you do? Maybe being a chef or a trainer is more up your alley.

The important thing here is to regularly check in with yourself to make sure that you still actively want the things that you used to want. You have to be able to recognize the difference between working hard for a high-stakes goal and being in the Purgatory of the Mundane and losing touch with your goal and mission because of your identity. I know what it feels like to do this, to be sleepwalking without a mission to keep me awake, to let my validation keep me right where I was. I know how it feels to lose confidence because I felt disempowered. I know how easy it is to make choices that don't even feel like choices at the time because I didn't check in with myself before agreeing to something. And it's because I had those experiences that I was able to realize why I needed to start making plans for my next step. Despite the validation I was getting as the gate-keeper, without a clear mission, I risked getting stuck again in the Purgatory of the Mundane, just at a higher altitude.

I Can Let Go.

Something that we had never predicted happened: Quest became a cultural phenomenon. Ryan Seacrest posted about us, Khloe Kardashian was photographed walking out of a gym with a box, and Hillary Clinton even wrote about Quest bars in her book! We started to get letters from people all over the world, telling us how Quest bars had impacted their lives. One mother wrote in to say that her son was a type-one diabetic, and she always felt like such a bad mum at birthday parties, because she wouldn't let him eat the cake and candy that the other kids were able to eat. Then she discovered Quest bars, which was something sweet and fun that he could eat right along with the other kids. Quest, she told us, had literally made her feel like a better mum. Goddamn, that still gets me right in the heart.

We were helping people to eat healthier, and by helping them eat healthier, we were helping them change their lives for the better, and sometimes even actually saving lives. And that shit got real, real fast! But as the company's reputation and glamour started to shine brighter than the sun, no matter how much I tried to convince myself that my hairnets-and-sweats uniform was the "in thing," its shadows reflected back to me the fact that my own view of myself was shrinking and my own glamour level was plummeting and falling into the darkness.

Over the years, I had proven to myself and others that I was actually pretty damn good at logistics. I became a strong woman who could handle my shit, and I didn't crumble like a homemade protein bar when things got hard. But even though I was the gatekeeper who got to hand out bars to all the beautiful, put-together influencers who came to tour our facilities, I felt anything but beautiful and put-together—at work, I perpetually looked like I'd just come from the gym on laundry day. I started to feel bad about myself. All around me, everyone was evolving right along with the company. Tom was being taken seriously in the world of business. People were growing into the jobs they had always wanted for themselves. It was clear to me that I was growing out of the position that I had developed. When I projected and envisioned myself five, ten years down the road, still working in shipping, still wearing that goddamn hairnet . . . shoot me now! Yeah, the shipping department might get bigger—we'd be handling more product, I'd be managing more employees—but I'd still be doing basically the same thing. It was like bulk cooking all over again, and I'd learned that lesson. The bulk-cooking Olympics are still just . . . cooking.

I'd also been so proud of what I'd built with the shipping department, I had ignored the fact that I didn't feel sexy and that my feminine side was slowly withering away. I had been a girl who once didn't get hired for a production assistant job on a movie set because they thought I wouldn't be able to do it in my high heels and acrylic nails; now, even though I still wore eyeliner every day (breaking out the big guns here), I topped it off with a hairnet and flats to comply with food-grade facility rules and clothes that were appropriate for the times big orders came in with a fast turnaround time and I had to jump in and help. While my professional identity was thriving, my personal confidence was taking a right frikin' hook and knocking me to my knees every time I looked in the mirror.

I had gotten used to feeling blah, to not being the put-together Lisa I was all those years ago when we first got married. When I'd see an influencer come strolling through, in a figure-hugging outfit, with her hair and makeup done, oozing confidence out of her perfectly spray-tanned pores from the way she spoke, carried herself, and interacted with people, I started to turn in on myself. As I would be smiling and introducing myself on the outside, I'd start to beat myself up on the inside. "I knew I should have worn that black sleeveless tank top. But nooooo, I had to go and wear this old excuse for a shirt instead. And so what if you have to wear a hairnet? That hairnet doesn't cover your face, does it? Would a little makeup other than eyeliner kill you? Get your shit together, Lisa."

Soon, a not-so-funny thing started to happen: After my mean internal dialogue broke my spirit, it started to turn outward. "Okay, so she's pretty, but her boobs are definitely fake. And could her shorts be any shorter? Any more revealing and she'd need to start charging. And another thing . . ."

Ummm, jealous much? Now there's a big, huuuuge difference between being envious of someone and being jealous of someone. Envy is when you see someone who has something that you want, and you're genuinely stoked for her, even though you desperately want it. You find her success empowering, which can often motivate you to go out and get it yourself. Jealousy, on the other hand, is envy's evil twin; it makes you feel bad about yourself, makes you see someone else's success as nothing more than a reflection of your own failures.

When jealousy hits, it's tempting to grab the brush and paint any picture that makes you feel better about yourself, which in my case meant throwing shade at whoever was making me jealous. Rather than focusing on how proud I was of what I had done or on thinking about how I could reconnect with the parts of myself that had taken a back seat, all my energy and attention was going toward beating myself up for what I wasn't doing. Was this really what I'd worked so hard for? I'd come so far. So why the hell was I invalidating myself and feeling like shit all the time again?

I kept coming up with reasons why I couldn't switch jobs just yet. I would convince myself to wait until our sales got to sixty million. Oh, we hit sixty million? So close to seventy million—why not just wait till then? Well, eighty million isn't that far off. I may as well see it through to that. The squirrel had come back for a visit.

Bit by bit, I started to voice my unhappiness, and soon, Tom and the director of marketing, Nick, had an idea. At the time, Quest had made a few fifteen-second marketing videos that were really taking off on something they called Instagram—it's a social-media platform; maybe you've heard of it?—and if we really wanted to capitalize on that, we needed to build out a whole new media department. How would I feel about heading it up? OMG, me? Hairnet be gone, and cameras here I come! That sounded so frikin' exciting. You would think I'd have moved faster than hearing that Fendi were having a fire sale, right? But the truth was that when an opportunity to change came up, I was utterly torn. I'd be starting from the bottom again, and that Drake song was starting to get reeeeal old. There was only one other person in the media department, and he and I would both be reporting to Nick, which meant that I would have a direct boss for the first time since we'd founded the company. This is the part where the ego swells larger than an MMA fighter's face after losing a fight. Leave my glorious shipping kingdom? What if I fail? What. If. I. Fail?

I felt changing positions would be "giving up" all the pride and validation I'd gotten by looking around and seeing the massive, well-run facility that I'd built. Sure, I was handcuffed to my job, but they were velvet handcuffs, and I preferred to think of them as bracelets—comfy, soft, pretty bracelets. Did I really want to give that up and go back to scrappy territory? Back then, social media wasn't a thing like it is now, and for all we knew, Instagram was just going to be the next Friendster or MySpace—haven't heard of them? Exactly. A lot of people didn't understand what social media was (other than connecting with your relatives and old school friends on Facebook), or how it could be important for a business. I was used to a shock-and-awe reaction when people saw the shipping department: "You built all this?" But with social media, I knew it would be more along the lines of, "I'm sorry, you do what?"

And to top it all off, if I switched departments, I was going to have to leave my desk (aka my tightest handcuff). Yes, the very same desk that I'd found a cockroach in on the day I moved in. That desk. It was a symbol of how much I'd achieved, of how far I'd come. That desk was a reminder that Tom and I had not lost our house, and that the entrepreneurship express had been one hell of a ride. And if I moved to the new media department, I was going to have to leave that desk behind and get used to a piddly little IKEA desk that wasn't even half its size. The kind that didn't even bother coming with instructions because it was basically a board and four legs. Picture Vito Corleone sitting at a piddly little desk—would you be impressed and intimidated? No, you wouldn't. You'd borrow his stapler without asking. And you might even "forget" to return it. My ego took one look at all this and started moonwalking right back out the door. It liked the desk, it liked the accolades, and it wanted me to stay right where I was.

Now, dear reader, maybe you've never been emotionally attached to a piece of furniture that used to be the burial ground for insects, but I bet you can still identify with parts of this story. Take a moment right now to pause and think about the thing in your life that you're priding yourself on, something you wanted for ages, or something you've worked bloody hard for. Got it? Okay, good. Now, don't think, don't intellectualize, just go with your gut and ask yourself if it excites you. No explanations, just yes or no. Make it binary. Because it's imperative that you separate your identity and your desire.

If your answer is yes, and what you pride yourself on excites the hell out of you, then woo-hoo, good job! Pass go and collect $200, because you're on the right path. But if the answer is no, then you have to honestly ask yourself, with no judgment at all, what is more important to you. Is it sticking with what gets you those pats on the back and "Good job"s so that you can continue to feel good about yourself? Or is it starting a new journey, down a bumpy road you've never taken before but that is exciting and thrilling as hell? Even if your handcuffs are diamond-encrusted and from Tiffany, might it be time to start hunting for a key?

Throughout my entire life, even when I didn't like what I was doing, I still took pride in it. I took my role as a housewife seriously, to the point where I sadly will admit that I would judge women who made their husbands do chores when they got home from work. "I can't believe she's asked him to do the dishes," I'd think. "He's been at the office all day."

I took pride in running the shipping department. After feeling bad for so long, I was fiiiinally in a place where I was proud of the value I was bringing to the table (that wasn't dinner). I'd built a mountain out of the shipping department. What if all I could muster in marketing was a molehill? I had zero clue about marketing or social media, so what if everything that I had just spent the past several years learning meant zilch? Would I be totally starting from the bottom? Would I lose all the respect I'd worked so hard to earn? I'd built up my confidence as a manager, but here? What would I be without the pats on the back? WHO would I be without the pats on the back? After all, if I wasn't ~~supreme queen ruler of all that is~~

~~speedy and swift~~ head of shipping, then someone else would have to be. And then what? I would have to ask THEM for permission to get a bar? Hell to the no.

Sometimes this "identity crisis" is a battle others see coming even before we have a chance to reach for our defenses. Take a very recent situation I ran into as a perfect example. One of our employees had an opportunity to go from doing something she was really good at to something she was really passionate about (and no, those two things don't always line up). She's amazing and a frikin' logistics queen. She's the best project manager you'll ever meet, and whenever anyone in our company needs to get something complicated done, they go to her. But I could tell that, while she was amazing, she wasn't excited. We'd been working together on a female superhero story, "WISH Academy," for Webtoons, and I could see that storytelling was what really got her excited. She was consistently bringing ideas to the table, even though storytelling was a totally new world for her. I eventually asked her if she wanted to come on board as an official writer. "The role is yours if you want it," I told her. But even though it was obvious this lit her up brighter than Times Square on New Year's Eve, she wasn't sure if she wanted it.

"I've never done this kind of thing before," she said, hesitating. "I've never thought of myself as a writer. What if I'm not good at it?"

"How many hours have you put in as a project manager?" I asked.

She stared at me for a second and then let out a huge exhale. "Phfff, God, yeeeeears."

"Exactly," I told her. "I bet you knew nothing on day one, right? There's no difference. If you're not good at writing, it's because you haven't put in the hours yet. But you can get there. If you want it." She still wasn't sure, and as she ummed and ahhed, I started to see that it wasn't that different from when I was reluctant to move into media from shipping: She was used to her emotional validation being tied to her identity. She was getting accolades for her current job and was scared to move into a role where she might not get praised. "Look," I told her, "if you don't start writing now, where do you see yourself in five or ten years?"

"I'll still be project managing," she said, "just for bigger and bigger projects."

"And does that excite you?" I asked.

She smiled. "No," she said, the realization dawning on her, "it doesn't."

Handcuffs, meet key.

Then, with radical confidence, she took on the role as a writer.

I Can Validate Myself.

I've seen this happen to so many women. We devote ourselves to the company, the children, the boss, the committee, and it's hard to pull ourselves away from that. Yet, so often, in the end, we end up being everyone's hero but our own. When this happens, it's very tempting to fall into the pattern of waiting for what you want to fall out of the sky, or for someone to come along and rescue you, since you've been rescuing everyone else for years. But, homie, with all the love in my heart, I say this: No one is coming to rescue you. But that's great news because now you can stop waiting. You can stop waiting, and you can stop giving your power away. And the time to do that is . . . *right frikin' now.*

Even after I had agreed to move over to the media department, even though I knew that it was the right thing for me to do, I still kept coming up with excuses for why I couldn't leave the shipping department. "Oh, so-and-so just started. I'll just stay long enough to make sure he learns the ropes." "This huge order needs to be shipped out at the end of the week. I should be here to make sure we hit that deadline." The truth was, I was scared. Watching a horror film at the age of ten alone in the dark—that kinda scared. When I moved departments, no one would compliment me on what I'd built, because I hadn't built anything yet.

As it turned out, my new role in the media department was—quite literally—about building. "Hey, Lisa," my new boss, Nick, said, beaming, "I need you to build us a kitchen set." He was so nonchalant you would have thought he was asking me to make a cuppa tea, not build an entire kitchen. From scratch. And oh, by the way, he needed it in four weeks, on a tiny-ass budget!

"Um, okay, sure . . ." I stammered, and then he sent me on my way.

Now, I have a degree in filmmaking, but I had never taken a class on how to build a frikin' studio. But as I'd taught myself in shipping, I used radical confidence to build my identity not on "Can I do this?" but "How can I do this?" Nick had a problem, and it was my job to solve it. He didn't ask if I was capable. He didn't ask if I could do it. It wasn't a question of "if." Which put me into complete panic mode . . . and yet lit a fire under my ass. I COULDN'T fail.

To start from scratch to build a studio, I did what I did with everything in my life, and broke it down in order to be able to tackle the fundamentals. I had learned in shipping that big, complex problems aren't so intimidating when they're reduced to several small problems that I can solve one at a time. I was supposed to turn this gigantic empty spot in the warehouse into something where people could cook. And where we could film it. And light it. And it had to look good. And real. And it had to be cheap. And fast. And . . . gulp! First things first, I needed counters, a sink . . . you know, a kitchen. And who sold kitchens on the cheap? IKEA. Now that I had a kitchen, I needed to hire someone to build the cabinets. But then I realized, once they were built, we needed something to attach them to. Hmmm, let me think. What do you attach cabinets to? Aha, walls.

So actually I didn't just need to build a kitchen, I needed to build half a room. And since we were in a leased building and might someday move, we had to be able to take it with us—so it had to be on wheels. On the whole, it was a ginormous project, but once I broke it down into a to-do list of tasks that could be completed on their own, it wasn't overwhelming. I now had a game plan.

The contractor I hired told me that what I was suggesting to build would just tip right over, so I went back to the drawing board—literally. Just like sending protein bars to Biebs in Dubai had taught me, just because an expert says it can't be done, doesn't mean something is impossible. I always try to think outside the box and consider all options before stamping something with the big "I" word. I always assume that if there is something I don't know how to do, then that's something I can have radical confidence to learn. (Plus, here I actually had the "inside scoop" a bit: I'd been on a TV set before and knew that the rooms were often on wheels, so it was doable.) I drew up a diagram for what I thought would keep our kitchen from falling in on itself, and the contractor said he'd give it a shot because theoretically it could work. He built it out exactly as I'd drawn it, and ta-da, theoretics be gone. MacGyver is back, baby. It worked.

So now we had a mobile kitchen that could stand upright on its own, but we still weren't finished. The kitchen couldn't look fake. So I had to think, what do real kitchens have? Unless you're living in a basement, a kitchen has windows. Our kitchen needed windows. Who sells windows? Home Depot, here I come! And those windows had to look out on something, so I got a fence panel, but we still needed something else to make it look believable. Plants. But who the hell is going to water them? No one, so . . . aha, fake plants.

Now we were out of money, and we still had no running water. But you can't have a cooking show and not have running water. So we got a hose, ran it from outside through the faucet, and then put a bucket under the sink to catch the water. We couldn't run the water for very long before starting to worry about it overflowing, but on camera, it looked totally legit. Now that the kitchen was up and running (as long as we remembered to empty the bucket), so was our first TV show, *Cooking Clean with Quest*, hosted by the inspiringly wonderful influencer Cassey Ho. An immediate, smash-hit YouTube series was now under our belt. On to the next challenge.

As Quest grew, Tom had become increasingly interested in the idea of mindset and how it shapes personal development. In the beginning, he'd been able to sit around with our employees and share what he was learning (he nicknamed it Quest University), but as Quest grew, that became harder and harder. The intimacy had dissipated, and Tom wanted a way to reconnect. So he decided that one way to do this was to produce an hour-long talk show on YouTube where he would interview guests about their mindset. It sounded like a crazy idea. What was the protein-bar guy doing talking to people about the mind? And who would want to watch it on YouTube? At that point, the videos on YouTube mostly fell into three categories: cats, people falling on their faces, and cats falling on their faces (or, now, add cooking shows), and he had never been on camera.

This last part didn't really bother him, because Tom really wasn't imagining it as a big thing—it was just a way to help bring and maintain positive thinking into the company and keep his promise of passing on any and all of his entrepreneurial knowledge as well as preserve the employee relationships that he had poured himself into building. As Tom got more and more into mindset—reading about it, and enthusiastically diving into anything he could get his hands on that even rhymed with mindset—I had seen an incredible change in him. His love for life was intoxicating. He would always suggest certain books he thought I would enjoy, and he wanted to be able to share this with people beyond just our family. So many of the people who worked on our line came from tough environments and bad neighborhoods, and Tom had read an article that said the most determining factor for your future success was not, in fact, your IQ but rather the zip code you grew up in. Could a change in mindset change that? This really influenced what he was trying to do, and Tom thought that the same information that was helping us grow and change could help our employees. Tom really cared about everyone who worked for us, and wanted to show them how powerful a change in their mindset could be. So he came to me and asked me to construct a talk-show set where employees could sit in the audience and watch the show taped live whenever they wanted. As a bonus, we would put the videos on YouTube and send the link around to employees to watch whenever they wanted. Simple enough.

I got to work building a talk-show set right next to the kitchen set. Every week, we would tape a new episode of *Inside Quest* in the warehouse, and we would put it on YouTube. I was developing and executive producing behind the scenes (aka getting shit done and handling problems). When we couldn't get an audience, I ran around to departments and persuaded employees with sample recipes, like protein cupcakes and donuts, from the media kitchen. "Hey, come watch this show. You might learn something, and you will definitely get a snack." (Candy Lady strikes again.) The videos started racking up numbers of views that made it obvious their reach was much wider than just our employees. Quest Nutrition was in the content game.

We were starting to see that social media could be a powerful platform, and our following and the number of comments we were getting were growing insanely by the day. Instead of worrying so much about how I was feeling about myself all the time, I was getting lost in how other people were feeling in their lives. People were always sharing stories of their personal transformations. We had a series called *What's Your Quest?* where people would post pictures of themselves eating a Quest bar on top of a mountain, or in the desert while riding a camel, or some other crazy-ass place. We were getting real-time feedback on what people liked and didn't like. Our "Transformation Tuesday" posts, where the community shared their radical, life-changing transformations, were a huge hit, so we decided to produce a *Transformation* series of inspiring stories from the Quest community on our YouTube channel. Our videos were getting tens of thousands of views; what was more, we were helping people change their lives and had built a community where people could learn and grow and connect with each other. It was an incredible feeling.

In the media department, I was able to get back to my first love, which was filmmaking. My dream had always been to create content that impacted people, and while I thought my path was going to be through film, the off road I took still landed me in the same destination.

The more I tuned in to this bigger picture of what I was doing in the media department, and what Quest was doing on the whole, the less I depended on external validation, like compliments from other people or scary nicknames. My motivation had evolved from a goal—build a company so I don't lose my house—to a mission: Help people change their lives. Our employees were always coming up to me to tell me about how something they had heard on *Inside Quest* hit them so hard they couldn't stop thinking about it, and they had been inspired to make changes because of it. The same was true for our customers, who loved our content and our product. I'll never, ever forget a letter we got from a young woman who had gone from being hospitalized for anorexia to being severely obese. My mum had similar struggles with her weight, so this really resonated with me. Quest had helped save this girl's life, she told us, because it had helped her find a community of people who would hear her story without judgment, and the bars helped her learn to love food again and want to value her life. Holy frikin' shit, indeed. (Her name is Brittany Burgunder, and she's a woman I'm truly honored to know. We're still in touch today, and she was even a guest on my show.)

I Can Be Wrong.

When I first went over to the media department, there weren't a lot of companies who were focusing on content the way we were, and people hadn't really yet picked up on the idea of working with influencers. It felt like the Wild West, though no one was challenging us to a duel because we were the outlaws *and* the sheriff—we really didn't have anyone to compete with. The number of followers, views, and comments we were getting told us that people were really into what we were doing, and there wasn't another nutrition company out there that could even come close to having the kind of audience we had.

But as anyone who has ever posted anything to social media knows, looking for lasting validation there is like trying to find the golden ticket in a bar of chocolate.

When our videos did well, I got so excited. I felt amazing, like I was on top of the world. When they tanked, I took it very, very personally, and my ego would fall to its knees.

I wish I were as good as Professor McGonagall and could concoct a magic potion for making it so that I could create and post content and not care about how it did. I'd call this spellbinding potion Don't Give an Eff Eau de Toilette. I don't know about you, but the truth is that, even now, I still get that double-sided sting: I don't know how to get rid of the glee when something does well or the disappointment when it tanks. So since I can't make it magically disappear, I do the next best thing: I make these feelings work for me.

When a video does badly now, I don't try to brush it off immediately. I allow myself to feel the sting and the hurt. But instead of letting it make me feel bad about myself, I use the ouch to teach me something. "Why am I so bummed about this?" I'll ask myself, and then I'll break it down. Maybe I'm bummed because everyone's complaining about a certain part of the video, and I bloody knew it but didn't listen to the warning signs. Or I thought I was so right that I didn't listen to other people's opinions; my team told me that photo of the bar wasn't going to resonate, but I loved it. Then when we posted it, it tanked like the *Titanic*. And after a few of these, I eventually realized the error of my ways and sent my ego packing on a dinghy with no life raft. If I focused on my validation being tied only to successes, then I wouldn't have learned some pretty surprising things, like how a crappy cell-phone shot of a coffee with a bar on a blah table way outperforms a high-quality, studio-lit professional shot of the same bar. Say what? Having studied photography and loved the art form, this was utterly mind-blowing to me. It was like people saying that *The Blair Witch Project* was better than *Citizen Kane*. Totally crazy making! But I could protest and argue all I wanted, the results were staring me right in the face. People wanted the real shit, not the fake. They wanted authenticity. Another mind-blowing revelation. These were things I never would have seen had I not then been open to hearing why I was wrong.

The flip side of this, though, is that if you're going to be willing to weather the sting, you have to be equally willing to be able to do the same with the things that do succeed. What did I bring to the table that made this so kick ass? Successes and failures are exactly the same—they're tools providing information to get the results we want next time.

I've learned that your value will never depend on whether one thing succeeds or fails. Or what you're good at. Or how many pats on the back you get. Or what your title is. Or what your identity is tied to. As long as you learn and grow from everything you do, it's a win. Period.

RADICAL CONFIDENCE RECAP

- **Identify your "bug in the desk."** What are you priding yourself on? Is it something that truly excites you? Or is it just something that you're used to and comfortable with? If it's the latter, it might be time for a change.

- **Beware the velvet handcuffs.** When you find yourself procrastinating on making a big change, take a good look at your excuses. Are they legit? Or are you just too comfortable, and it's a bunch of BS?

- **Keep your ego from feeding on external validation like a parking meter feeds on quarters.** Are you basing your worth and validation on the things you're good at? Things you get praised for? While the pats on the back may feel great, take a good, hard look and be honest with yourself to see if they're keeping you from trying something new and getting after it.

- **Tie everything back to your mission.** The more you can tap into the bigger picture of why you do what you do, the less you depend on the little things—like titles, compliments, or perks—to make up your identity.

- **Successes and failures teach the same lesson.** When something fails, examine it. Ask yourself why. Is there anything you can learn from it? When something succeeds, do the same thing and get your validation from being the person who does both.

EMBRACE THE ICK...
OPEN UP THE CAN OF WORMS

The Ick (n):   The messy truths and shitty situations that you have to deal with in order to live out your dream.

For a lot of us, it's hard to identify the things that are holding us back and keeping us from being happy. They're often ingrained in us so deeply that we believe they're nonnegotiable. For me, I silently suffered through eight years in the Purgatory of the Mundane in part because I thought that having children was the thing that would finally make me happy. There was so much expectation (and shame around not meeting this expectation) wrapped up in this idea that for a long time, I didn't even question it. I didn't even know that I was allowed to question it.

Greek women always did what was expected of them, and for many of the women that I grew up with, marriage was like the 26.2-mile mark.

The finish line. The endgame. While they might, like my mother, have had jobs and even enjoyed them, such things were just a stopgap until they found a husband. And a husband was a prize that made life worth living. Even as a little girl, when I would fall and skin my knee or something would upset me and make me cry, my *yiayia* would come rushing to comfort me. "Don't worry," she'd say in her almost unintelligibly thick Greek accent. "You be okay by de time you getty marrrrried." As if my life's mission was to make it to marriage.

I heard variations of these sentiments so often, and from so many different people, that I just assumed they were true. First comes love, then comes marriage, then comes Lisa with a baby carriage—THAT sort of thing. I never stopped to examine if I actually believed this, and most importantly, if it was something I actually wanted for myself. It just seemed that it was a given, and so when Tom and I got married, I assumed that kids were right around the corner. That was how it worked with Greek marriages: You have the wedding, and then within a year, the kids start popping out like Whac-A-Mole.

When I first expressed this idea to Tom, though, he responded in a way that was right in line with his true, romantic self. "Babe," he said, "I married you because I love you. I didn't get married because I wanted to have kids. I got married because I want to spend time with you." Once again, this man of mine was challenging my assumptions and blowing my mind. I'd never thought about it like that before.

When Tom and I had decided to get married, he asked for my dad's blessing. My dad's answer was immediate and, despite his thick accent, required no translation. It was a big, fat, Greek *no*. My dad knew that we were in love, and he liked Tom and always treated him with kindness and respect, but those things didn't matter much to my pups. My entire life, he had worked incredibly hard for his family; to him, a husband was, first and foremost, a provider, and in that sense, Tom, with his lofty movie dreams, didn't fit the bill.

My dad was as traditionally Greek as one could be. He met my mother when she was working at a bank, and as soon as they were married, like Greek clockwork, within a few years she quit her job to stay home and have her first child—even though my mum was actually making more money than my dad. That was just the Greek way, and years later, it broke my heart when my mum confessed to me that she hadn't wanted to quit at all. She'd liked what she was doing, and was good at it—she was the first woman there to ever authorize a million-dollar check—but she left anyway, because that was what was expected of her.

For the first two years of our marriage, even my Greek family didn't pressure us. When I'd bring up having kids to my dad, he would always shock me by downplaying the idea. "Oh, there's plenty of time," he'd say. "You're still very young." Looking back on that now, though, I can see he just assumed that Tom and I wouldn't be able to withstand the struggles of our cultural differences and I wouldn't be able to withstand being away from my family, and so we'd inevitably separate. Once it became clear that we were in it for the long haul, his tune changed. "Lisa, enough with the dogs! Where are my grandchildren? You won't understand the true love of a child until you have one." Sheesh, people, give a girl a break. Ha! A break was not how the Greeks rolled.

I Can Challenge My Assumptions.

Tom and I knew we had a good marriage, and neither of us wanted to risk changing this, so we started to talk, really talk, about whether or not we wanted kids, and what our lives would look like if we did, or didn't, have them. It was time to play No Bullshit, What Would It Take? all over again, and the stakes were higher than ever before. I needed to examine some of the base assumptions that I had about my life. I had always just assuuuuuuuumed I would have kids, but did I actually want them? And if so, why? So that's where we started—with the big question: Why did we want kids in the first place? The instinctual answer to this was "our legacy." That was what my pups would always say: "Who is going to take care of you when you're old?" or "If you don't have kids, who are you going to leave your money to?" (And that was before we even had any!) Tom was technically the third Thomas Bilyeu, so we had already decided that if we had a son, he would be Thomas Bilyeu IV to carry on that legacy—Tom had also started learning Greek so he could speak it with our hypothetical kids.

That thought excited me, so I had to acknowledge that I would be giving this up if we didn't have kids.

Time was another huge part of the conversation. Marisa Tomei was constantly stomping her foot in my head, reminding me that my biological clock was ticking, and so I knew that if I decided not to have kids soon, the one thing I was taking off the table for myself was the ability to have my own babies. Because I didn't want to remove any option before seriously considering it, I thought about freezing my eggs. It was like a safety net so that in five or ten years, if I changed my mind, they'd be there. But I was already dealing with health issues at the time, so I had to be honest: Was I willing to put my body through something that would not be good for it, just because I was worried about future regrets I miiiiight have? Let that question sink in for a second. That answer was a big fat no.

Sure, there were always things like surrogacy and adoption, but while I have increeeedible admiration for people who choose that path, I had to be honest, with no judgment, that it just wasn't the life I saw myself having. If I was going to raise children, I wanted to feel what it was like to be pregnant. Part of what excited me was the thought of feeling the little thing inside me, kicking, so that thought went on the "PRO" list. To see little Tom in them as they were growing up and running around—another PRO. OMG, I could literally melt faster than a snowman in the Mojave Desert, even now, at that thought.

We had to open the can of worms. We had to be brutally honest and ask ourselves some questions that were really frikin' hard to answer. For example, what if we decide not to have children because we want to prioritize each other, but then Tom dies early? And then I'm alone, without the person who was number one in my life? My biggest fear in life—and I don't mean that hyperbolically, I actually mean my biggest fear IN LIFE—is losing Tom, so you can imagine it wasn't super fun to think about this, but I knew that, when making a decision this big, I had to look at it from all angles. And having radical confidence means that no matter how hard it was, I could give myself permission to take off the blinders. Little Tom, my fear of losing Tom, our legacy, and not wanting to die alone were, in all honesty, in serious contention, but when I started to look at the nitty-gritty reality of it, I saw a different picture.

I never wanted to permanently close a door without first looking behind it, and from where I was standing, there were three doors in front of me. Cue the announcer and game-show music . . . Let's see what's behind thessssseeeeee dooooooooooors!

Door Nuuummmmmmber One: You don't have kids.

Door Nuuuuuumber Two: You have kids, and you're a stay-at-home mum.

And the final door, Dooooooorrrrr Number Three: You have kids and you're a working mum.

Now, before I made my pick to see which life I'd won, I had to really delve into what life was like behind all of these doors. So I started to look at what an average Wednesday would be like with each of those scenarios. I picked Wednesday because it's hump day, right in the middle of the week, and absolutely nothing special—the day we most loathe.

I knew that I had to take Tom's truths and put them in my buckets. In all of our conversations, he had always been very clear and honest with me about what I could expect from him. "Babe," he said, "I will love those kids with all my heart, but you need to know that I'm not going to be the guy who's home every night by seven to have dinner with you all, or who gets up in the middle of the night with the baby. I know I'm ambitious, and if I wasn't able to be true to myself, I would start to resent you and the kids." Okay, that's uber clear, and they were all fair points. Now I know that, with all of my buckets, the bulk of the day-to-day responsibility for raising kids would be on me.

So, to recap before we cut to commercial: Door Number One: We don't have kids, my Wednesday stays the same.

Door Number Two: We do have kids and I'm a stay-at-home mom. I give up the career I love and what I've worked so hard for, and I have to know that, from Monday to Friday, I'm basically a single mother. Okay, but then what do our weekends look like? Again, I know Tom, and while he's incredibly driven with work, I also know that he's a big pile of mush (seriously, you should see him with the puppies). He was very clear that he didn't want to be an absent father, so whenever he wasn't working, the kids would be his number-one priority. Okay, great, that's super sweet, but then where did I fit in? And it went both ways. No judgment on anyone who doesn't do this, but for me, if I had kids, I would want them to be my top priority in my life on a day-to-day basis. Nature relies on you putting their needs first, but would I be okay with what this would do to my relationship with my hubby? Tom and I were ALWAYS each other's number-one priority. So not only did I need to ask myself if I wanted Tom to be my number two but was I actually willing to be bumped down on HIS priority list? I have four words for you: Hell To The No.

Now, Door Number Three, me as a working mom: This was totally a possibility, and tons of women do it, but was it for me? I had to look at my options on how I would do this: I know myself and know that when I'm at work I LIKE to go all in. I don't want distractions. So I would need help, and a lot of it. But seeing as my mum, no matter how much she says she wants to help, lives in the UK, I turned to the idea of a nanny. That's entirely possible. I also know I love my sleep, so I personally have zero problems hiring someone to get up with my kids in the middle of the night and change diapers and all that (literal) crap. But thinking through the reality of that thought, if we were going to have someone who got up with the kids, then we'd have to have someone live with us, and that's a big no-no in my book. I'm a girl who likes her privacy (aka likes to walk around topless from time to time).

I'd be getting up with the kids in the middle of the night, since Tom has already said he won't do it. But then who's taking the kids to school? Who's making them lunches? Is it the nanny? What if they're sick and I'm dealing with a crisis at work? What if they need a last-minute doctor's appointment but I have an important meeting that took me a month to get? Even if we had a full-time nanny, there'd still be plenty of stuff that I would have or want to do, so I'd inevitably have to take time off work, because if I didn't, then how much time would I really be spending with my kids? Not a whole frikin' lot. And if I'm not going to spend time with my kids, then why am I having them in the first place? No shade at anyone who decides otherwise, but I knew what kind of mum I would want to be, and that wasn't going to be possible as long as I was working.

And I didn't want to quit working, because I loooovved what I did. It was more than just a job, after all. It was my mission. I loved my Wednesdays, just as they were, and what I loved most about my life was that I had the ability to go all in. I love giving 100 percent, going hard after my goals, and challenging myself every day, and would I be able to do that with kids? No. Absolutely not. Every working mother I've ever spoken to says that having kids is like the British carnival ride the Mary Rose. One day, you're swinging hard in their direction, and the next day you're swinging hard toward work. And the guiiiiilt! On both sides! I would get dizzy just hearing about it.

I had now peered behind each door and filled my buckets with that info. I had to admit that the only bucket that got me excited, the only bucket I felt really good about, was the bucket I was already in. After years of thinking being a mum was what I wanted, after telling Tom when we first met that I wanted four kids, I had now come to the conclusion that I didn't really want kids after all. Not even one.

Holy.

Fuck.

I Can Get Uncomfortable.

I'd opened the can, and now I had to deal with the worms. For almost a year after I'd come to this conclusion, I still didn't say it out loud to anyone other than Tom. I was too ashamed. Ashamed that "people" will say I'm not a real woman if I don't have kids. That "people" will say I'm not maternal. That I'm selfish.

And the guilt! Oh, the guilt! Especially the guilt when I would tell my family. Some of them, like my mum and dad, would be personally affected by my choice, and I needed to be confident in my decision before I began to have these conversations. So I took baby steps to process the idea. I'd whisper it to myself in my head (yes, I see the nonsense in whispering in my own head, as if someone else would hear it, but often the things you don't want to admit do start out more like external radiation than an explosion to the face). "I don't think I want to have kids," I'd whisper, and slowly, I grew more confident that this was the right decision for me and Tom.

The first person I told was my sister, and it felt like we were little again, sneakily staying up late past our bedtime, sharing our secrets as we hid under a blanket—"Lul, I don't think Tom and I want to have kids." She was, of course, being the best sister on the frikin' planet, there for me. Then I opened up to my mum's life partner, An, who is one of my favorite humans on earth. These conversations were incredibly supportive and understanding, and helped me prepare myself for the ones that might be, um, let's just say a little different. By far, the hardest conversation I had was with my mother. She had sacrificed her own career to raise kids, and she has given her children everything, and always wanted to be a *yiayia*, and let's just say I didn't handle it as well as I could have. I didn't go into this conversation the beeeest way possible, and I didn't totally acknowledge that, while it was my decision, my mum was going to have her own feelings about it. Instead, my defenses went up (as often they do when we feel like our decisions are being "attacked"), and I tried to persuade her to see it my way, and just tried to shut her down when she tried to say anything different. Eventually, I realized that I needed to give her space to grieve the idea she had for me, and I also realized that I actually needed to grieve, too. This was a huuuuuge light-bulb moment for me. Choosing to do what was best for me could be the right decision AND a bittersweet one at the same time.

I think this is something that's so important when making hard decisions, and it's something that's so often overlooked: Even when it's the right decision, you can have radical confidence to allow yourself to grieve the person you thought you were going to be. Deciding not to have kids meant that I would never know what it was like to be pregnant and to feel a baby growing inside me, never be called mummy, never see little Toms running around, never have a daughter whom I could raise with a different mindset than the one I had growing up, and that's something I'm truly sad about. But does being sad about that mean that I regret my decision? Hell no!

Choosing one thing will always mean leaving something else behind, and when you acknowledge this, and are honest about any mixed feelings you have, you're a lot less likely to regret your decisions. Unprocessed emotion is like putting a lid on a pressure cooker only to have it explode in your face years later (and, let's face it, that ends up being a way harder mess to clean up). If you want to do big things, you have to—I repeat, you haaaaave to—get comfortable with being uncomfortable. I wish it weren't true, but there's no way around it. When I started working full-time at Quest, there was a period of time when Tom had to adjust, and even mourn, the fact that I was no longer a stay-at-home wife whose primary responsibility was making sure his needs were met. It was important to me to show him that I understood my change was impacting him, as well as myself, so I geniusly suggested, if I do say so myself, that we "wean" him off my responsibilities to make the transition easier. Instead of cooking seven days a week, I'd cook five, and then four, and then three. To this day, I cook on the weekends because that's how I like to take care of him. It makes ME feel good, and I have yet to hear of any complaints from him. But because now I was only home on the weekends, just like him, if Tom woke up and found he didn't have a clean pair of underwear, he was shit out of luck. "Babe, I guess I'm going commando," he'd joke (but not really joke, because he'd actually head to work without underwear).

So yeah, we had some uncomfortable days (he maybe more so than me, what with his man parts and all). But he often, without hesitation, said that it was worth it and would gleefully comment that a happy and fulfilled wife is waaaaay more important than clean underwear. If you have to go commando to get there, then commando you go.

I Can Ask the Hard Questions.

The very first step in embracing the ick is giving yourself permission to open the can and have radical confidence to ask the tough questions. The tough question that you need to answer might be, "Am I happy in my marriage?" or "Is this really the career I want to pursue?" Even just saying something like that out loud, to yourself, might feel like a punch in the gut, but it's like ipecac. Yes, it makes you throw up, which sucks, but it also gets rid of the poison that was slowly killing you on the inside.

Now that you've given yourself permission to ask the question, you have to actually ask it, and then, dadarada . . . you have to answer it. This is where it gets really terrifying for a lot of us, because it starts to reveal all of the work that needs to be done. Say you asked yourself, "Am I happy in my marriage?" and the answer is no. That's a whole lot of ick, and a whole bunch of other questions. Are you willing to work on the marriage? Can you articulate the specifics of what you want and need to see change? Is your partner willing to work on the relationship? And what if the answer to any of those questions is no? Does that mean you have to think about divorce? What does that mean for the kids? Who gets the house? Will you be alone forever? When you start to break it down like this, and look at it in a No Bullshit kind of way, you can see why it's very tempting to go "Aw, fuck it" and bury those questions in the desert like an old Las Vegas gangster getting rid of a snitch. But that's the tricky thing about worms—they don't stay in the desert for long. Once they're out, they're out, and it's going to be very hard to get all of those suckers back in. So you'd better deal.

Embrace (or just tolerate) the idea that if you want to truly change your life, sometimes you will have to go down before you go up. This is a choice you make. A mindset you frame. When you have a growth mindset, you know that setbacks are just like training bras—temporary. Life will get messy. You will have to have hard conversations. Things will have to change, and for a while, they might seem worse before they get better. And this is all goddamn hard, hard, hard.

I've had countless therapists and psychologists on my show, and they've all told stories about how so many of their clients will come in and say, "I knew this marriage was over years ago." A fight happened, or it was something their partner did, that was a total deal breaker for them, but they stayed because they thought it was easier to just live with the status quo than shake things up. But it's noooooot. Okay, I'm not actually an expert, so I can just simply speak for myself and you can take it for what it's worth . . . it wasn't for me. When you embrace the ick and know things will get messier before they're clean, you will probably find that the things that once terrified you actually turn out to be the things that thrill you, because that's the thing that signifies you're growing and changing. That's what having radical confidence is all about. Being terrified and doing it anyway.

A while back, my sister got divorced. A few years after she'd said I do, she embraced the ick and realized that she hadn't gotten married for the right reasons—she'd felt like it was something she should do, as opposed to something she wanted to do. She'd been with this guy for ages, and they'd had very traditional roles at home (she cooked, he took out the trash kinda thing), and there were so many things that she'd never had to do before or navigate on her own.

One day, not long after she'd gotten divorced, she called me breathless but happier than Carrie Bradshaw walking down Fifth Avenue wearing a new pair of Manolos. I know this woman so well and we're so close that the joy in her voice was oozing from my headphones the second I answered the phone. "What's going on?" I asked. "Did you just get laid or something?"

"No, better," she answered. "Li, I just mowed the lawn!"

She had just slayed her dragon. This one tiny thing, the fear of mowing the lawn, had become a giant monster that had held her back from making a change in her life, and she had just conquered it. Which meant that the next time something started fire-breathing down her neck, the beast was easier to slay.

Challenging beliefs that have been with you your entire life might leave you quivering in your Uggs, and admitting them to yourself and to others might leave you even more petrified. I get it. I felt the same when I had to face the kids question. But in doing so, I can honestly say that it's a decision I've never once looked back on and regretted. Not. Once. So, girl, get the can opener, because if you can embrace the ick, then you too can start to slay some dragons of your own!

RADICAL CONFIDENCE RECAP

- **Give yourself permission to ask.** The very first step to answering the tough questions is asking them, which can be bloody hard when they challenge some of the deepest beliefs you have about yourself and your life.

- **Talk to yourself.** Whisper your answers. Write them down. Say them to yourself in the mirror. And then LISTEN. Get comfortable with talking to yourself before you start talking to other people.

- **Go commando.** You can tolerate a little chafing—aka being uncomfortable—while you move toward something that's truly meaningful and fulfilling.

- **Mourn the life you have to give up in order to create the life you want.** This is a necessary step in order to move on without regrets.

- **Recognize that other people are also only human.** Give them space to have and feel their own feelings. Recognize that they don't have to agree. Don't try to change their mind, and give them the grace to be human and have an emotional response. But remember, you aren't there to persuade. Your decisions aren't up for debate. This isn't a presidential election, so other people don't get to vote.

- **What does an average Wednesday look like?** The "big" answers to tough questions are often very emotional, but answering the little, practical ones will reveal what's really excitingly sustainable long-term.

5

LIFE IS NOT A FAIRY TALE...
SAVE YOURSELF

Fairy tale (n):   1.   Once-upon-a-time tale in which
women are the damsels in distress
and do a lot of sitting around waiting
to be saved.
2.   A total crock of shit.

For years, I dealt with horrific, unimaginable, wouldn't wish it on my worst enemy kinda stomach issues. I can honestly, hand on my heart, say that my health issues were one of the best things to ever happen to me.

Yep, you heard me right: I'm supercalifragilisticexpialidociously grateful for my years of painful stomach problems. It showed me that money and success truly mean nothing when you can barely get up, and that there is zero sense of pride, accomplishment, or satisfaction when you ignore your body, turn a blind eye to warning signs, and try to pretend that everything is fine when it's SO NOT FINE. But, more important, it taught me the life-changing idea of ownership. The powerful lessons I learned the hard way here shifted my mindset not only about my health and the importance of taking ownership over my self-care but about relationships, business, and every single thing that I now do. Taking ownership of your life means you take the good, the bad, and the ugly. And the ugly part of this was realizing how my problems were actually all my own doing. Yep, you heard that right. I was 1,000 percent the person to blame. Now you may be thinking, "But isn't blaming myself just gonna make me feel even shittier about myself?" And the truth is, yes, it absolutely can . . . if you let it. But when we have a growth mindset, we want things to be our responsibility. And why? Because then we can frikin' fix it.

I grew up surrounded by people who worried about their weight. No, wait. Scratch that—I grew up surrounded by WOMEN who worried about their weight. In the Greek way of thinking, if the men happened to put on a pound or thirty, it meant your wife took good care of you. But the women that I knew approached calorie restriction like it was a competitive sport. And everyone was going for the championship belt.

When I was a teenager, my mum, whom I idolized, was borderline anorexic. None of us would have used that term at the time, of course—we just thought she was watching her weight—but on an average day, she would eat a yogurt and two pita breads. Now, just to be clear, not a pita bread sandwich or a pita bread with anything on it but a plain, dry-ass, paper-like toasted pita bread, and that was her dinner. When my older sister, whom I admired because she was everything I wasn't (popular and pretty), was sixteen, she embarked on her own womanly dieting rituals and started replacing meals with diet shakes. After I went through puberty, I started to notice my body was changing, and—what a surprise!—not at all in the areas I wanted it to. It didn't help anything, either, that other people treated my weight as fair game for comments and unasked-for suggestions, and if you've ever met a Greek, you'll know they're brutally honest. They have zero shame to call you fat to your face. The same people who had used to tell me, "You're so lucky" that I was skinny had now changed their tune to a less-preferable beat called "You'd better watch out!" Sadly, I did.

The real kicker for me, though, was a moment that's still burned into my brain over twenty-five years later. My first boyfriend (a real piece of work) pinched my waist and said, "Oooh, gettin' a bit fat, are we?" While I should have done the classy thing and kneed him in the balls and told him to get lost, I didn't. After years of being picked on for my looks, I finally, finallly felt validated by having a boyfriend, so of course I didn't want to lose him. I mean who would validate me? (The irony being he actually did nothing but INvalidate me.) So I took his words as truth. At that point in my life, my entire sense of self was based on external validation, and I felt like being skinny was one of the few things that people admired about me. I was terrified that this was going to go away, so when someone lobbed the word "fat" at me, I went into a panic. Defcon 1 panic. For most of my life, I'd seen the women around me go to extremes to avoid being "fat," and so I couldn't imagine anything worse. From the moment he said that, I decided that staying as skinny as possible was going to be my class major.

I started out by trying to stick my finger down my throat. People had talked about it, and it seemed so simple—eat whatever I wanted, and then just throw it up!—but I couldn't do it. I just ended up poking myself in the esophagus, which was equal parts painful and ineffective, so I started to just restrict my calories as much as I could by only eating one meal a day. After about five or six days of this, I'd be absolutely starving, so I'd binge on an entire packet of biscuits. People would see this and be impressed. "Oh my God, you're so skinny and you can eat whatever you want. You're so lucky." If only they knew. My relationship with food became unhealthier than my relationship with my boyfriend. But everyone around me was doing something similar. Okay, as I write that, I realize it's a lie. Because if I really thought it was okay at the time, then why did I pretend that I'd eaten breakfast? When someone saw me binging on biscuits and said, "You're so lucky," why didn't I tell them the truth—that I'd been starving myself for days and was now as hungry as a horse with the munchies? I think, subconsciously, I knew that what I was doing wasn't actually something to be admired, and that's why I lied about it and kept it a secret: I worried people would stop praising me for being skinny if they knew everything I was doing to get there.

When Tom and I went on our first date, I was starving by the time we got to the Chinese restaurant. The food was good, but I didn't let myself eat more than a few bites. Women were supposed to be delicate little birds who survived on a few lettuce leaves and lemon water, right?—so I thought—so even though my stomach was screaming "FEED ME," there was no way I was going to inhale the Orange Chicken in front of him. Later that night, when we went to the after-party for his friend's film premiere, I was overjoyed to see there was a buffet. But I didn't want to come across as having an appetite. "Be a lady, Lisa, be a lady" (a lady meaning to eat as little as possible so I don't bloat), I told myself as I picked my hors d'oeuvres as carefully as if I was playing a game of Operation. Tom later told me he thought I was a nut. I didn't recognize my own behavior and didn't think I was doing anything that he would even notice, but he pointed out how hilarious and endearing he thought it was that I walked through the buffet line in front of him, putting something on my plate, then getting a few feet down the table and seeing something else I wanted more, so I put what I'd had on my plate back, as if an extra shrimp was going to permanently tip the scales out of my favor.

As Tom's and my relationship progressed, my relationship with food kind of morphed from whitewater rapids to a lazy river. Between being in love, getting to know the man of my dreams, having that man totally accept me just the way I was, and puzzling through the Rubik's Cube of transatlantic dating, I had plenty of other stuff to focus on. But when Tom and I settled in LA, and he went back to work and I struggled to adjust to life as a housewife, hello ups-and-downs and wild spins—calorie-counting moved front and center in my life again. It was a distraction that gave me a sense of purpose and accomplishment in my otherwise boring day-to-day—aka squirrel.

I started each day by weighing myself, but that absolutely came only after I peed and totally stripped down. I mean, I wouldn't want that sip of water I had at 3:00 a.m. or my G-string throwing off my numbers. My breakfast was a mouthwatering five scrambled egg whites with a metric ton of salt, and a calorie-free butter-flavored pan spray (because a girl needs some flavor). After that, I hit the gym.

Now, I love working out, but back then, my daily gym trips were more self-punishment than self-care. I pushed myself hard, and exactly how hard was determined by how "bad" I felt I had been the day before. Bad being, of course, how many calories I had taken in. For example, if I was a girl gone wild who'd eaten two sugar-free popsicles, then I added extra cardio. I'd run in fifteen-minute increments, and then when that fifteen minutes was up, I'd decide to keep running until I rounded off my run at an even number of miles. But sometimes, that even number of miles will be a weird time. I mean, who stops at two miles if it's twenty-four minutes and seventeen seconds? So then I'd keep running until I hit thirty minutes. But if thirty minutes turned out to be just 2.67 miles, well, then I had to keep going until it's an even three miles, right?

The carrot on the stick as I ran my ass off was a brownie that I always had stashed in the pocket of my gym bag. Well, let's put "brownie" in quotes. I made the brownies at home from a special recipe I'd perfected myself: egg whites, chocolate protein powder, and sugar-free chocolate chips. Doesn't sound that good to you? Well, wait until you eat one after you've just spent one hour on the bloody treadmill, running as fast as you can to stay in the exact same place. Then, sugar-free chocolate chips might as well be Ghirardelli!

Over the years, the list of foods that I ate had gotten narrower and narrower. When I was still a teenager, even before I began to restrict calories, I cut out oily foods because my brother told me they caused acne. Later, I heard cheese was bad, so I cut out cheese. Nuts were high in fat, so goodbye nuts (back then, it was believed that eating fat meant you got fat). I have a very addictive personality, so when I get into something, I go all in. This is great when it comes to working on a project that I'm passionate about, but not so great when it comes to things that are self-destructive, like excessively monitoring my diet.

I don't half-ass anything, so when it came to making sure my own ass didn't get any bigger, I treated it like a full-time job with unlimited overtime. I was always trying to figure out how I could eat the most food while consuming the least amount of calories. It was like a complicated game of nutritional Jenga as I removed fat and carbs, and stuck with protein and veggies, while trying to go entire days without consuming a single gram of "wasted" calories (as you will see, this does not make for a very stable tower).

I ate shrimp, chicken, and egg whites with broccoli and green beans. I wouldn't even allow myself a carrot, because carrots had sugar. I'll always remember how flabbergasted I was when a friend of mine told me she ate a Fudgesicle every night. "Wow," I thought at the time, "she must not care about her weight if she's that indulgent with what she eats." To be clear, it was a sugar-free Fudgesicle that has forty calories. And just to state the obvious here: My mind wasn't healthy, and an unhealthy mind leads to an unhealthy body, which in turn leads to an even unhealthier mind. It's a vicious cycle, like the teacup ride at Disneyland. You want to get off, but it just Keeps. Bloody. Spinning.

I Can Admit I'm Not "Fine."

I was literally starving myself, and I was wrecking my gut in the process. Approximately 70 percent of your immune system is located in your digestive system, but my immune system was barely functioning because I never gave my digestive system anything to chew on. My body basically became a five-star resort where the wrong bacteria could check in for an extended stay. If a cold came to visit, it would stay for weeks, and my chest infections became VIPs with frequent-flier miles. Each time, I would go to the doctor for a prescription for antibiotics, never having any clue that this was only making my problems worse. It got to the point where I wasn't even going to the doctor anymore; I'd just call the office for a prescription every time I felt a new chest infection coming on. One time, my doctor said, "You know, I really shouldn't be giving you more antibiotics." But he still wrote the prescription—and I still took them.

After years and years of this "antibiotic abuse," followed by not eating what I needed in order to replenish my gut flora, I got to the point where I was no longer able to digest anything outside of my normal, very restrictive diet.

But despite it all, I lived for celebratory dinners. When you're restricting calories like I was, forget fantasizing about sex. You fantasize about food! I would spend a literal month planning where we were going to go and what I was going to order when Tom and I got a rare night off to go on a date. I would go extra hard on the treadmill and on food restrictions for the weeks leading up to it (no way I was "slipping up" on an extra sugar-free Popsicle), which put my gut in even worse shape. One year, we were going out to dinner for a special occasion, and I thought through everything. What I was going to wear. What restaurant we would go to. And we would end the night at the Grand Lux Cafe in the Beverly Center, and I was going to eat some motherfucking double-fudge chocolate cake with some extra motherfucking hot fudge.

With this in mind, I wanted to make sure that where we went for dinner was someplace healthy, so I picked Fogo de Chão, a Brazilian steakhouse known for their delicious, giant hunks of meat. The reason these giant hunks of meat are so delicious is because they're bathed in herby sauces, spices, and marinades. As you can probably imagine, herby sauces, spices, and marinades were murder on my stomach, and I'd barely finished eating before I had to run to the bathroom.

I was in there for what seemed like an hour, while Tom sat at our table alone. By the time I was able to leave the stall, I headed back to our table. "I'm so sorry, babe," I explained. "My stomach was hurting so bad."

Tom was very understanding. "Baby," he said, "don't worry about it. I paid the check already, so we can just head home." Record screeching to a halt right here. Did he just say we'll go home? We can't go home. What about dessert? I told him as much, and Tom looked at me as if I had been possessed by a demon.

"Babe," he said, "you're doubled over in pain. You can't even stand up." Which I couldn't, but I could still stand my ground. I'd been looking forward to this for weeks, but he had a point—I could barely breathe, let alone eat chocolate cake. Oh, but thaaaat caaaake. There must be a solution. There must be a solution. I've got it. Pepto Bismol! So my patient, loving husband drove me to a CVS, where we bought some Pepto Bismol, which I chugged on our way to the Beverly Center to eat dessert at the Grand Lux Cafe.

Homie, can you believe I still didn't think anything was wrong? At the time, getting Pepto Bismol seemed like a great solution (so quick, so easy), but as I type this now, I'm really disturbed by what I did to myself. At this point, the red flags were straight-up whipping me in the face, but I was so determined not to pay attention to them that I just shut my eyes and commented on the wind—"My, strong breeze today, isn't it?"

Even if you haven't ever bought Pepto Bismol on a date, you've probably been in a situation like this at some point in your life, where it seems easier to keep making excuses than to face up to the enormity of the problem. Maybe it's with a relationship ("He's just really stressed with work right now, and that's why we're not getting along") or a job ("Once this project is over, I won't have to work so much"), but it's amazing how we can convince ourselves that things are "just fine." Admitting that something is wrong means that you have to deal with it, and dealing with it means that you have to take responsibility for creating change in your life that can often feel difficult and scary. And because of that, many of us do what I did for so many years—ignore the problem and plan around it.

Looking back at this time in my life, I think often about what made me keep pushing through my pain rather than examining it to figure out where I needed to make a change. We're so often taught to just hold on, push through, and white-knuckle it, if we have to, so that we don't seem weak or—God forbid!—inconvenience anyone else with our pain. Actually, I'm not sure if we're taught to do that or if we just really, really hate how it makes US feel to be the squeaky wheel. At least I can speak for myself: I hate the feeling of being a bother or a burden. It makes ME feel guilty. Who wants to be around someone who is always complaining? I mean I wouldn't want to be around me if I was always complaining, so why would anyone else? So if I can be utterly raw with you, keeping quiet was actually for my own sake, so that I would feel less guilty that I might be bothering Tom or my family with my problems.

Quest was bonkers busy, and we worked constantly, nights, weekends, and holidays. Some days, I couldn't help but have those "What the hell are we doing?" moments, and for motivation, Tom and I would take a break and go drive around Beverly Hills, talk about our mission, and fantasize about what we'd do if the company ever became hugely successful. Our car at the time was a Ford Focus with a hole in the exhaust, and the car started to rattle and the steering wheel shook if we drove over 60 mph. We never got it fixed, because any extra cent that we could save went right back into the company. So we'd cruise around Beverly Hills in our Rattlemobile (it's amazing no one called the cops) and got into serious debates about which mansion we were going to buy when we got wealthy. I preferred Mediterranean-style villas, while Tom always went for more of a classic Cape Cod look. "Ugh, but I hate that look," I would protest, as if he'd said he wanted to make an offer on it there and then. The one thing that we agreed on was that our future house was definitely going to have a pool, and that pool was absoluuuuutely going to have a waterfall.

I was a '90s girl who loved hip-hop, so in my mind, "cool" wealth looked like a rap video. If I ever got rich, I liked to joke, I was going to put on a bikini, stand under that waterfall, and twerk my behind for my hubby while showering myself with Dom Pérignon—you know, keep it classy and understated, like a proper woman should.

Then something crazy happened: We, along with the other founders, decided to sell a small percentage of Quest. These things took a long time, so we didn't tell a soul because we didn't want to count our Quest bars before they were wrapped—aka until it actually happened. For months, Tom and I would talk about it, still not sure whether to believe it or not.

Then finally, one morning, Tom and I were working out in our garage. We had heard "rumors" from our advisers that today was going to be the day. Tom had his phone open to our bank account and just kept hitting refresh in between reps. Refresh, refresh, refresh. All of a sudden, there was our portion of the proceeds, just sitting in our account. Eight figures. Holy. Frikin'. Shit. Our lives had just changed in an instant.

We hugged, we took a couple of selfies to mark the occasion, and then Tom nonchalantly got up and started to walk into the house. "Wait," I said, "where are you going?"

"It's Tuesday," he said. "I'm going to get ready for work. We're not done. We've got people's lives to change."

That day I was as giddy as a seven-year-old on Christmas morning, but I didn't tell a soul (except my immediate family). I called my dad on the way to work to tell him, and he just kept repeating with utter pride, "That's unbelievable. I'm so proud. That's unbelievable! I'm so proud." Then I called to tell my mum, and I thought for a second we'd lost reception when there was dead air. But no—she was just speechless! Tom and I would smile or wink to each other if we ever passed each other in the hallways, but we were still too shocked to even whisper about our secret. I felt like I'd been holding my breath all day, and when we finally finished up at work, I could exhale: It was really frikin' happening. It was time to celebrate. We went to Cartier, where I had planned to splurge on a piece of jewelry, but instead I ended up balking at the prices. I would pick something up and then freak out at the price and set it back down so quickly you would have thought it had singed my fingertips. "Fifty thousand for an earring? An eeeeeearing?" But Tom insisted. "Babe, come on, you've worked so hard." There is only so much a man needs to do to convince his wife to buy jewelry. So I finally settled on the cheapest ring they had. Now look, it was still frikin' Cartier, so it was still the biggest splurge of my life. Are you kiddddinnnng me? I couldn't believe that I—ME! Lisa!—was now the proud, slightly stunned owner of a Cartier ring.

We were on Rodeo Drive in Beverly Hills, and as we exited the store, Tom asked me where I wanted to eat. "We're celebrating, babe, so wherever you want to go, we'll go." I didn't hesitate . . .

"The Cheesecake Factory, obviously!" (Isn't that where everyone goes after going to Cartier?)

Shortly thereafter, we started looking for our dream house, and found a Tuscan-style villa with a pool and a waterfall, in none other than, yes . . . BEVERLY FRIKIN' HILLS! When we moved in, I honestly felt like I was dreaming. Like a kid playing dress-up, pretending to be in someone else's shoes. But I wasn't. We didn't just come close, we had actually done it. There I was, with a booty-enhancing bikini on and my bottle of Dom in hand, about to live out my ultimate fantasy. Cue bass, drop the beat, and warn Snoop that Lisa B is in Cali. Tom gets into the perfect photo-capturing position, as I step under the waterfall and navigate the fine line between water seductively pouring over my body and drowning. Now with us both in position, I'm ready for my close-up, Mr. DeMille. I toast the camera and take a swig, purposely missing part of my mouth so some of it pours down me. In that moment, the very second the champagne hits my stomach, it felt like my gut . . . exploded.

There was no twerking.

There were no sexy, come-hither looks.

I scrambled out of the waterfall and bolted to the bathroom, totally in shock. What was happening to me? I knew I had gut issues. I knew that if I indulged today, I'd pay for it tomorrow, but I'd always had a little bit of a buffer. But now it was instantaneous. I hadn't even eaten anything. All I'd done was take one bloody swig of champagne.

When I could finally leave the bathroom, I hobbled back out and got straight into the pool. I didn't want to ruin the occasion, so my plan was that I could better hide my pain from Tom if I was mostly underwater. But even the gentle pressure of the water felt like a Mike Tyson punch to my stomach. Abort the plan. Abort the plan, I screamed to myself! This dream moment that was supposed to be my fairy tale turned into a Stephen King–scripted nightmare—only I was already awake.

I had spent too long totally ignoring all the stop signs and red lights my body was signaling. And so in that moment, the moment I had worked hard for, in that moment of my dream actually coming true, my body was no longer crying out for help. It just out and out pulled the emergency rip cord.

And after that, nothing returned to "normal." My gut was so painfully distended that I couldn't even wear a bra, and Tom couldn't touch me without my wincing in pain. I couldn't even cuddle, much less have sex. And for someone who can proudly admit that she loves to feel admired by her husband, you can imagine how utterly heartbreaking this was. I loved feeling sexy. It made ME feel good. But even though I wanted to jump his bones, all I could offer was a good-night kiss. And while Tom was the most understanding husband and never, not once, complained, on top of battling crippling health issues, I was now battling my own guilt about the situation as well. And guilt is one hell of a crippling disease.

I Can Rescue Myself.

Something horrible began to dawn on me: This situation had been years in the making. My body had been sending up distress signals, which I had shot down like I was playing a game of Duck Hunt. Severe pain ripping through my gut? Ignore it! Low-functioning immune system? Ignore it, and gimme the antibiotics! Hours spent locked in the bathroom? Break out the big guns, and ignore that shit, too! But you can't ignore your body forever. Money doesn't buy health, and when you can't stand up, when you can barely breathe and feel like shit—let me tell you, it doesn't matter one damn bit if you're in your dream house. Because feeling like shit in your dream house . . . is still just feeling like shit.

Even when I finally realized something was wrong, I tried to downplay it. Lots of women had stomach issues, I told myself; mine just happened to be worse than others. I just needed to find the right doctor, and someone would fix me. With the right pill, I figured I'd be fine in a week or two. I started to make the rounds in Beverly Hills, visiting some of the "best" doctors in the world—aka the kind of doctors that charged an arm and a kidney, whose office walls are lined with celebrity photos. Each new doctor I saw was confident they could fix me. "Try this," they'd say, handing over a new prescription. But nothing I tried worked. If I ate anything other than beef, chicken, lamb, salt, or coconut oil, I was instantly in gastrointestinal hell. I couldn't even eat a Quest bar. I became wafer thin, my hair was falling out from malnutrition, and I started to think that no one was going to be able to fix me at all. Finally, after about two years, I met with a doctor who had a different approach. I had my food diary out, ready to read her my detailed catalog of every crumb that had crossed my lips and an equally detailed record of how it made me feel, but as I started to read it off to her, she stopped me.

"No, don't tell me what you eat," she said. "That's not the problem."

"But it's my stomach," I told her. "Of course it's related to what I eat."

"I'm more interested in *how* you eat," she explained to me. "Tell me what you *do* when you eat. How do you eat breakfast?"

"I eat breakfast while I'm working," I said.

"And lunch?"

"While I'm working."

"And dinner?"

I thought, "Doesn't this chick get where I'm going with my answers?" Out loud I said, "While I'm working . . . "

She didn't even hesitate. "You must stop working when you eat," she said. "That's the absolute first thing you must do."

"Sure, okay," I said, agreeing just so we could move on to what I eat. Then she dropped a bomb on me.

"And you must stop working out," she said.

Wait, what? Noooooo! I loved going to the gym. I NEEDED to go to the gym, because working out was a huge part of who I was.

"Your body needs time to rest," she explained when I protested. "Right now, it's always struggling to repair itself, and it's failing."

I let this sink in: Going to the gym had always made me feel better about my body and how I looked, but now I had to ask myself what was more important, my health . . . or my appearance? Damn. That question was brutally honest. When I stopped and really looked at it with that type of clarity, it was obvious that I had been letting my health come last for most of my adult life. I decided to begrudgingly give it a go. What did I have to lose?

My addictive personality had a new challenge, so I started to follow her advice immediately, and began to sit down and eat meals by myself without multitasking. I took up yoga (the soft, gentle kind, not goat yoga) and acupuncture. Within a few weeks, I started to notice that I actually did feel better, and then something pretty major dawned on me.

Once upon a time I wouldn't have believed it, but maybe, just maaaaaybe, all along it wasn't so much *what* I was eating as *how* I was eating. Maybe my health problems weren't the result of something being wrong with my body but something that I had created with my lifestyle and my attitudes toward food. "Oh shit," I thought. "Did I do this to myself?" Taking this type of ownership about my problems could have made me feel bad about myself, but by this point, with all the work I had been doing to develop a growth mindset, I tried to see how it could serve me. And here was my aha moment (my girl Oprah would be so proud): If I had brought this problem on, if it was all myyyyyy doing, then maybe *I* was the one who could make it go away. As heaven opens up and the angels (who look a lot like Destiny's Child) start singing, it dawns on me:

I didn't need someone to fix me.

I could fix myself.

I Can Trust My Gut.

The more I started to process this, the more I realized that I had been giving my power away for years. Instead of listening to my body, I pushed through the pain, convinced that it was normal. I blindly listened to "experts," assuming that of course they would know more about me than I did. Even when my doctor said, "I shouldn't be giving you any more antibiotics," I assumed that if that was really the case, he wouldn't give them to me. I didn't ask questions, I didn't ask why, I didn't ask him what the consequences were. I just kept on thinking that the experts were in control and not taking any ownership over the outcomes.

For instance, as soon as I started to try to figure out my issues, I kept meticulous food diaries: what I ate, when I ate it, if I had a bowel movement, what that bowel movement was like (I said detailed, didn't I?), what time, how I felt afterward, how I slept, and how I felt the next morning. Yep, nothing went into, or came out of my body, without being thoroughly examined and recorded in a little book (and by book I mean my Evernotes app). From being this precise, I had learned that one of the few things that never seemed to cause an upset stomach was fatty beef. However, when the results of one of the allergy tests I took suggested that I should stay away from fatty beef and instead eat mostly raw vegetables, yep, you guessed it, that's what I did—even though I kneeeeew that raw vegetables were Jack-the-Rippering my stomach.

But slowly, I started to listen to my body for the first time in my life, and found that when I paid attention to the signals it was giving me, it would usually lead me in the right direction. For years, I had always wanted to be skinny, and what's the trite saying—be careful what you wish for? Even I had to admit now that, with my gut issues, I had gotten too skinny. So I shifted my focus from the number on the scale to how I felt. It took my health going to shit to make me realize that I didn't actually care about being skinny. I just wanted to feel frikin' good. This was a MASSIVE shift for me. You know how they say that the grass is always greener on the other side? Now I would have given anything to be a bit on the heavy side and just be able to eat meals, and enjoy them, like a regular human.

To do this, I had to change how I'd been thinking about my weight, so I trashed the scales in our house and made a conscious effort to look in the mirror at my naked body less. For three months, I didn't set foot in the gym, not even a toe. I actively sought out and developed a new routine, where I'd swim, or just sit and read during the morning time that I had previously been devoting to the gym.

When I was finally ready to start adding exercise back into my life, my gut was still in bad shape, so I couldn't do anything from the waist down. The treadmill had always been my go-to, but that was a big ixnay, so I focused on lifting weights. When I did that, I was drawn to it like a moth to a flame. My body loved the feeling of actually getting stronger, and I let that feeling guide me. I'd ignored my body for ten years, so now I made a point to listen to it every chance I got. If something felt good, I kept doing it. If it didn't, I stopped—no matter who or what told me otherwise. I continued to see and try different doctors, but it got to the point where sometimes I didn't even try their suggestions, because my body would have such a visceral reaction, just hearing what they were proposing I do, that I knew in advance it wasn't going to work.

I Can Accept That It's All My Fault.

I began to see my gut issues in a new light: No longer were they problems that just "happened" to me. Now I saw them as problems that I had created by making a series of small choices, over and over again, for decades—and that I could solve by repeatedly making a series of small, different choices that were finally informed by what felt good rather than what I thought would bring me external praise. So many women I knew practiced extreme calorie restriction, but I still made the choice to do it to myself. Because it seemed like what everyone else was doing, I had chosen to push through the pain, no matter how awful I felt. I had made the choice to believe that it was someone else's responsibility to fix me. The most freeing realization on the entilllllllllre planet for me was when I realized that my health problems were All. My. Fault.

Now, when you say something like "This is all my fault," you will see utter shock and horror on people's faces.

They will try to reassure you: "None of this is your fault. It just happened to you. You did nothing wrong! It was those doctors." And while, yes, there is some initial comfort in this, the reality is that if something isn't your fault, then it's also out of your control.

Now, I would just like to take a moment to emphasize that this framing doesn't pertain to everyone. If you've experienced abuse, mistreatment, or tragedy, this thinking in no way applies. And if it does apply to you but you find the word "fault" even remotely triggering, you can use whatever word you want—"ownership," maybe, or "responsibility"—so long as you use a word that will spur you into action. And that's exactly what the word "fault" did for me: It spurred me into action. Four years of action. And now, over the past year, my gut has flared up twice. To give you perspective, it used to happen two to three times a day (in case you're counting, that's a reduction of 99.8 percent). And who did that? *I* did that.

When you have a fixed mindset, it's easy to point at a problem in your life and say, "It's not my fault." But declaring that something isn't your fault frees you from the responsibility of having to fix it. Also, let's not forget that we've been conditioned our entire lives to believe that "fault" is a bad thing. If, when you were a kid, you ever had an angry, red-cheeked adult up in your face screaming at you and asking you if something is your fault, then you know exactly what I'm talking about. We've been taught to see accidents, mistakes, setbacks, failures, and vulnerability as bad things, so taking on fault might feel like taking on shame and guilt. And who willingly wants to take on shame? No one.

But having a growth mindset and radical confidence means that you can approach these same things without shame, because you know two critical things: 1) they're all temporary, and 2) they don't define you. You can take responsibility because you believe in your ability to change as a person, and you can use radical confidence to change the circumstances and situations that you're in, even if you don't yet have a clear plan for how. Ownership implies agency, and a person with a fixed mindset doesn't want agency, because then they have to do something about it (or feel guilty and anxious about not doing anything about it).

Again, there is no shame or judgment here if you have a fixed mindset and want to stay that way—just be conscious of the decision you're making. It's very hard to move toward your goals without taking ownership. In fact, screw that, I'm just being polite. The truth is I don't see how in the bloody hell you will achieve your dreams without taking ownership. A fixed mindset turns up its nose and says, "That's not MY fault." A growth mindset accepts fault, then rolls up its sleeves and, with radical confidence, dives in.

Now, when something is going wrong, whether in my business or my relationship with Tom or any other area of my life, one of the very first things I tell myself is "Okay, Lisa, if this was all your fault, what would you do to fix it?" This is an empowering way to frame it for myself, and it helps to change my perspective on whatever issue I'm facing.

You have to learn to listen to you, you, and only YOU. What do you really want? How does something make you feel? What have you learned from your experiences? When you take ownership, you have the opportunity to make fully informed decisions and take into account whether or not you choose to accept the consequences of those decisions. Sometimes things will go wrong. Sometimes you will have to pick yourself up, dust yourself off, and get out the lint roller, but no matter what happens, you have to truly believe that you know what's best for you. In other words: Homie, you gotta trust your gut.

RADICAL CONFIDENCE RECAP

- **You don't get brownie points for pushing through pain.** It's okay to push yourself occasionally, but you cannot ignore your distress signals. There is no material goal that's worth the sacrifice of your mental or physical health. Success on its own won't make you happy. Whatever the "crap" in your life is, it will still be there even if you reach your goal.

- **Follow this famous Greek dude's advice.** Socrates said, "Know thyself." Pay attention to how things make you feel, physically, mentally, and emotionally. You know what's best for YOU, and don't let anyone else convince you otherwise. You are the only one living your life.

- **Homie, it's all your fault.** Accepting responsibility can feel like a gut punch at first, but if you're choking, that gut punch can act like the Heimlich and save your life. As long as you're blaming your problems on other people, you need other people to fix them, and that's like setting up camp on Disempowerment Drive.

- **Raise your goddamn hand!** Stay open to other people's opinions—not all advice is bad—but question EVERY-THING. If something someone tells you to do doesn't feel right, sit with it and figure out why. Then it's trial and error until you find something that does feel right and works for you.

6

MAKE YOUR
NEGATIVE VOICE YOUR BITCH...
AND YOUR BFF

Negative voice (n):   That bitch inside your head who
comments on everything, who never
has anything good to say, and who is
occasionally right.

I've never learned how to shut off my inner negative voice. I've tried oh, how I've tried. I'm not a defeatist, though, so I just kept bloody trying, telling myself all the while that one day she'll shut the hell up. But what's that Einstein quote? "The definition of insanity is doing the same thing over and over and expecting a different result"? When "one day" never came, I realized I could choose to keep making myself insane, or I could make that bitch work for me.

Making your negative voice work for you is frikin' key to stopping self-sabotage. When you try over and over to shut your negative voice off but fail, it just becomes Cruella de Vil cruel, because your inability to get her to shut up just becomes another failure to add to your list. "See, you're so lame," she starts taunting. "You can't even get me to shut up, and I live inside *your* head." I spent years trying and failing to shut her up, turn down the volume, or straight-up kick her out, but she always found a way back in. And she just got louder! Nothing worked, so it was officially time to change my strategy. What if she wasn't my kryptonite but rather my superpower? If I couldn't tune her out or turn her down, could I at least use her to my advantage? What if I could use my negative voice to actually help me to achieve my goals, get what I want, and be a better version of myself?

Your negative voice is ultimately an extension of your ego, so she shares your ego's goals: She wants you to do nothing. Why nothing? Because nothing is safe. As long as you're doing nothing, you don't risk embarrassment, failure, rejection, and all those other things that terrify your ego but that ultimately lead to growth.

I once heard a story about Arnold Schwarzenegger, the Governator himself, from back in his bodybuilding days. He'd always been praised for his bulging biceps and Godlike upper body (okay, okay, I added the Godlike, but come on, for Pete's sake, have you seen the man's photos?), but he still had these scrawny little chicken legs that he was always trying to hide. So he'd stroll into the gym, shirt off and guns blazing, all while wearing long pants so that no one could see that his legs were less tree trunk and more twiggy. Finally, he had a realization: He'd never be able to strengthen his weaknesses if he constantly hid from them. He had to stare at them nakedly. Literally. He started covering up his upper body and put his legs on display. In his autobiography, he wrote: "I knew if I exposed only my better body parts—my arms, chest, or deltoids—all I'd get from my peers would be wonderful comments and I'd soon forget about my horrid lower legs, so I continued to wear the cutaway sweatpants that invited ego-bruising pain."

Now if you're wondering whether it worked or not, the man went on to win Mr. Universe five times, and Mr. Olympia seven. So, yeh, I think it's safe to say it did. If your negative voice is always pointing out your flaws, maybe it's time to listen. I've learned to treat my negative voice as a helpful, slightly rude (okay, VERY rude) friend who is always pointing out places in my life where I can do better.

This journey really started for me when I was working on *Inside Quest* and having my mind blown daily. One of our early guests was motivational speaker Lisa Nichols, who went from being a single mother with twelve dollars in her bank account to being a CEO and a frikin' global powerhouse. I'd never heard of her before this, but as word spread through the company that she was coming, you would have thought Lady Gaga was visiting and our employees had a VIP ticket to the meet and greet. I could see that many of our female employees were incredibly excited—they loved her. And when I sat in the audience to listen to Lisa's interview, I could see why. This woman was fire, and there was literally not a dry eye in the crowd as she spoke. And I was sitting there thinking, "I could never be as good as her. She's so amazing, she's so amazing, she's so amazing." Then she said something that has stuck with me to this very day: "Don't make me extraordinary to let yourself off the hook."

Daaaammmmmmmnnnnn. That hit me so hard. Here I was, putting myself down while putting her up on a pedestal and not even realizing that, by doing so, I was giving myself a free pass to not even try to be as amazing as she is. Her words were eye-opening, and I could now see that this was an opportunity to see successful people as motivation instead of intimidation. Could I make my goals and my mission even bigger? She was living proof it could be done. And sometimes, that's all we need to make us realize it's actually possible.

I Can Start—Small.

With *Inside Quest* and interviews like the one with Lisa Nichols, Tom and I began to realize that our mission had grown beyond just protein bars. The bars were great for people who could make the choice to live a healthier lifestyle, but what about the people who suffered from too much anxiety to even step foot in the gym? Or people who were too depressed to believe that they were worth it in the first place? Tom and I now truly believed that the power of the mind was just as important, if not more so, than the power of the body. Mindset was the true ticket to really taking ownership and living a fulfilling life.

Now, at one point, if you had asked, Tom and I would have said that Quest was going to be our forever company. We believed in the mission and were looking for more and more ways to introduce storytelling and go beyond just helping people with issues of the body. But trying to expand a brand's meaning within the minds of the consumer is as pretty frikin' hard as you might imagine, and it represented a vision for the future of the company that not all of the partners agreed with. So, given the mahoosive success that the company had achieved, and the amount of money that Tom and I had saved, we spun the studio part off into a stand-alone company. And *Impact Theory* was born.

By the time Tom and I left Quest, I had built the media department to a team of twenty-one. We had producers, directors, editors, a project manager, assistants, and a ten-thousand-square-foot soundproof studio with air-conditioning (you don't know how much of a get this is until you've had to record in an un-air-conditioned studio). And with *Impact Theory*, I was back to square one. That square being: moi. We were a start-up yet again, but by now, I knew that if there was one thing I was good at, it was figuring some mother-effing shit out. I stayed up late reading instruction manuals for our new equipment and was almost relieved when I had to build another new studio. Been there, done that, right? Well, kinda. This one ended up being built in our home.

Over time, we opened our studio audience to a few fans that we trusted, who had been following us since *Inside Quest*, and I remember one particular fan who always told me that people wanted to hear from me, too. I'd never even thought about that—people wanted to hear my story? Frikin' nuts! Even at this point, I was still keeping my health struggles a secret because I was so ashamed, but as I started to share little bits and pieces about my own life—whether that was my relationship, my health, going from housewife to Tom's business partner, or deciding not to have kids—I was flabbergasted that people were always incredibly receptive and just asked me more and more questions. It seemed like my story was actually impacting them—which was the whole purpose of our company.

When you have the support of a community, and you can hear stories similar to your own, like the magic carpet ride, it can lift you up and keep you motivated. And actually sharing my own steps toward a growth mindset helped spread our *Impact Theory* mission even further, because now we had a whole different group of people—namely, women—who saw themselves reflected in what we were doing.

Even though I wasn't sure I wanted to stay behind the scenes forever, I was still hesitant about sharing my story on camera. Lights camera . . . ANXIETY! But a growth mindset and radical confidence had taught me that just because I had never been on camera before didn't mean that I could never be on camera, and finally, after much badgering from Tom, we decided that we would do a special Facebook Live for Valentine's Day. Except, I was way too terrified to record it live. So we compromised. I agreed to shoot it, and he agreed it didn't have to be live. And so on the day we shot, I actually made the entire team stay home so that I could have complete privacy. "Babe," Tom said, "I'm your safety net. If you get stuck, I gotchou." Then he goes all Phil Jackson on me. "You can do it! This is just like the conversations we have all the time about our relationship. There just happen to be cameras, which you'll soon forget are there anyway. You got this."

And I didn't choke. I didn't freeze. I just sat there, talking to my husband about the kind of stuff we always talked about, and . . . I had the best time. So good, in fact, that we lost a lot of our conversation, because we were so deep into it that we didn't even notice the camera had stopped rolling and we had no one there to tell us.

But aside from that technical difficulty, it was frikin' awesome, and we started doing them more. But actually live this time. To be entirely honest, it's not easy for me to watch those early videos now and not be critical of myself, because I wasn't confident in myself, and I didn't have the passion that comes across now. ("Look alive, Lisa," I always want to shout at the screen when I watch those videos now. "Have conviction!") But I had to start somewhere, and I showed up to those first shows determined to learn, grow, and get better, and over time, I was definitely becoming more comfortable being on camera and telling my story.

I Can Stop Beating Myself Up.

The wonderful influencer Cassey Ho had been a good friend of mine ever since *Cooking Clean with Quest*, and I was always badgering her to start a podcast and share her brilliant brain. She even had a podcast room that she never used. Her comeback? "Lisa, YOU need to do a podcast." Finally, she texted me one day. "Can we talk?" I immediately called her to make sure everything was okay, and then she hit me with it: "What if we did a podcast together?" Wait, whaaaattttt? It sounded frikin' awesome, but I didn't think I was even close to being on her level. What was she talking about? But I admired Cassey so damn much, and I trusted her, and if she thought that I would be a good cohost, then I was going to do everything in my power to live up to it. Tom was incredibly encouraging as well and was always the first to grab the megaphone and be my hype squad whenever I started to doubt myself.

Cassey and I released our podcast, called *The Sheroic Podcast*, and we darted straight to number frikin' one in our category within twenty-four hours because she was such a big-name influencer and her announcement spread like wildfire. Every so often, we would have guests, but mostly, we would do episodes where it was just me and Cassey, hanging out and talking. It became easy to build my confidence with the safety net of having my girl Cassey there.

Eventually, Cassey got so busy with her company and brand growing that there just physically weren't enough hours in the day for her to also keep up with the podcast demands. She knew she had to step away, but she was so encouraging and urged me to keep going. At that point, I still thought of my own wings as puny and didn't know if I was strong enough to fly solo without Tom or Cassey as my copilots, so in the end I decided to stop *Sheroic*.

Except—I missed it. I missed sitting down with women and having these real, no-bullshit talks about how we, as human beings and as women, struggle. I wanted to get back to that, but I didn't truly believe in myself. So I tried to downplay it when talking to Tom about the idea of launching a podcast of my own. "You know, it'll just be over Zoom," I said. "Very cheap, and I'll just talk to my friends." No big deal, right? I didn't want the pressure, so I figured that if the podcast wasn't that big of a deal, then it wouldn't be that big of a deal if I failed. So I decided to launch my no-big-deal, sort of just an after afterthought, very-frikin'-big-deal podcast. But Tom wasn't having any of it. "Babe, we have cameras just sitting there on set. Why on earth wouldn't you film it and put it on YouTube?" Well, damn. The man had a point.

"Okay," I said to myself, "I don't want to get in front of the camera on my own because it doesn't make me feel good. But what's more important: trying not to feel bad about myself, or impacting lives?" As I started to think about my next step, it felt like these two things were in competition: Helping people meant that I had to keep pushing myself and putting myself in more situations where I felt uncomfortable was scary. But the more I thought about it, the more I realized it was also a little thrilling.

But what did my life look like if I decided that it was more important to protect my ego? If I did that, I stayed behind the scenes, working to support Tom. There was nothing wrong with this, but if I didn't speak out, then I wouldn't be helping the people who could benefit from my particular story. I had to ask myself what was more important: my ego or helping people? Frikin' helping people was my mission, after all, so I concluded that no amount of shit talking from inside my own head was going to keep me from my mission.

I was still nervous, though, so I wanted to start with my comfort blanket . . . yep, you guessed it, the one and only Cassey Ho. Having Cassey on would feel just like *Sheroic*, except on a set with pink cushions and neon lights. This would make it easy and casual, I figured, and even though this would be my first time hosting a show solo, since Cassey was such a good friend, I didn't really think things through. I didn't prepare . . .

A door creaks in the night. A tumbleweed blows down an empty street. The phone is dead, and there's a thump in the basement. Are you scared now? Good! Because have you ever heard three more ominous words than "I didn't prepare"?

In my case, no. I knew the episode was going to be about friendship, and I had conversation points, so I tricked myself into thinking I was prepared—but I had no idea how to start the interview, and no idea how to end it. I had produced so many pieces of content that I thought I was going to be good with just a few talking points ready to go. Big mistake! And that was when I had the realization: Leveling up was humbling AF. In those moments, I could have strapped on the gloves and gone in on myself. "Lisa, you don't know what the hell you're doing. Seeeeee, I told you that you would embarrass yourself." Instead, I fell back on my growth mindset and chose to give myself the grace to grow. "All right, Lisa, my homie, you can quit right now, or you can embrace the fact that this is page one of a new chapter, and that you can get better if you're willing to look at what the hell you did wrong and improve. You can swallow your bloody ego and say, 'Okay, you came in with some fake cockiness, and you're never going to do that again. Lesson learned. Don't ever think you've got your shit together when you haven't done anything to earn it.'"

You can't expect to walk into every new situation feeling confident. But you know what you can do? Bust your butt and walk in overprepared. When I started hosting my show, *Women of Impact*, I noticed that I would start to get anxious as soon as I started feeling like I didn't know something or that I was stuck. But when I was overprepared, no matter what came my way, I could duck and jive and avoid getting punched in the face by the thoughts of how badly I was messing up.

When I sat down and was really honest with myself about how and why I'd messed up in my interview with Cassey, I saw that I hadn't wanted to assess my level of competence because I didn't want to give my negative voice a mic and a soapbox to make me feel bad about myself. I feared that if I was honest about all the ways I was unprepared, I would realize what a crazy thing this was for me to attempt and then, you know, not do it.

Let's be real: When you're getting ready to try something new and start thinking about all the ways in which you might TOTALLY SUCK at it, you're definitely not going to feel too good. None of us actually want to point out our flaws when we're already feeling like a total bucket of nerves and unconfident, but trust me when I say it's waaaaay better to be aware of all of this beforehand, rather than finding out in the moment—like, for instance, when you're on set with a whole crew, a polished guest, and the cameras rolling.

I Can Get Better.

My ego would have been perfectly happy if I never hosted another video again. However, the rest of me would not. So I took all of the self-criticism I was facing and tried to listen to what it was directing me to try to improve.

I also knew that my inner bitch was standing in my way. She was full-on chanting, "You're no good, you're no good, you're no good" with backflips and all. And if I got those negative lyrics stuck in my head, I knew that they were going to be frikin' crippling.

But the thing was: The bloody cow was right. I wasn't any good because I was a total beginner. Back when I was in film school, I gave myself the grace to not expect myself to know everything about filmmaking on day one, so why on earth would I think I'd be an expert here already? Tom was so good at being on camera and conducting interviews that I told myself people had high expectations for me, but looking back, I can see that this was just the expectation I put on myself. This had noooooothing to do with other people: I just admired Tom a lot, so how could I use this information to serve my goals instead of holding me back?

When it comes to your negative voice, the most common advice you will hear is to shut it down and don't listen, but I do the opposite. I treat that bitch like she's my bestie. I put my arm around her. I give her a big squishy hug, invite her in for a cuppa tea, and get us all prepped and comfortable for a nice heart-to-heart. "So, homie," I say, "talk to me. What am I doing wrong?" And then, when she starts to talk, instead of trying to shut her down, I listen.

It takes radical confidence to address your weak spots, but it's an essential part of growth and change; once you find those weaknesses, you can then use them as Band-Aids and extra padding, so that when you do show up, all your weak spots have become unbreakable. What I realized was that by addressing my inadequacies, by actually looking at what I was shit at, by acknowledging my weak spots and giving them a voice, I was actually making myself stronger and more competent.

The first thing I learned from my negative voice was that I needed to figure out how the hell to open an interview. I spent hoooooours writing my introductions, so that I didn't have to worry about how I was going to introduce each guest on the fly. I also prepared a final question—"What's your superpower?"—so I knew what I was going to say in advance and had a preplanned way to transition out. Then I practiced. I would say my prepared lines on camera and then replay them, and each time I watched, I let my inner bitch run wild and took notes on what she said. "I felt like I was slouching, and yet noooooo, I didn't adjust. The Hunchback of Notre Dame could teach you a thing or two about your posture." Straighten up, homie. "No one can understand me. OMG, I'm so squeaky!" I made a note to speak up and squeak lower. "Why do you keep touching your hair like that? Do you have a tic?" Okay, watch out for nervous habits and don't do them on camera.

When I acknowledged how much I stumbled with my outros, I came up with the line "Be the hero of your own life," and wrote it on a giant whiteboard and put it right under my main A camera. That way, when it came time to wrap up the episode, I'd turn to that camera and, in case I froze or forgot what to say—booooom—this kind of prep gave me confidence, because I would be gut-wrenchingly tense as the episode came to an end. But I now had a game plan to get out of my own head, and I developed that game plan by listening to the voice in my head telling me "You're shit at outros!" I knew that as long as I was faking the confidence, then I was faking being a host, and that was the opposite of what the show was about. But by being willing to put in the time and effort and an ungodly amount of prep work, I could actually be confident as hell, all thanks to that bitch—I mean *friend* in my head. When I position my negative voice as a mate, then even when she's saying things I find hurtful, I can recognize that she's just trying to help me. I had to take everything she said as a potential truth that could help me move forward. Because that, my friend, is the goal. Never lose sight of that.

As a result, it becomes possible to listen to that voice without being beaten to a pulp by it. Now, of course there will be times when something happens and you decide that the most important thing in that moment is to protect your ego and listen to her in the hope she shuts up. Homie, give yourself a break. This is human nature. We're wired to move toward pleasure and away from pain, which is why most people eat ice cream and watch *Iron Man* instead of training for one. There's absolutely nothing wrong with choosing to take it easy, just as long as you're aware that you're making that choice.

You have to live the life YOU want, and sometimes eating ice cream is the thing that's going to make you happy. So frikin' enjoy it! Go HAM! Just don't beat yourself up for it, saying, "You pig! Of course you're choosing Ben and Jerry's over bench presses and jumping jacks. You're never going to get in shape." Instead, savor those bites. Dig out all the chocolate chips and bits of cookie dough, if you want; offer to share it with your negative voice, and own the fact that sitting on the couch with a spoon in your hand and *Big Little Lies* to binge on is exactly where you need to frikin' be right now. The most important thing is to be aware that you're choosing to be there, and that you can choose to be anywhere else you want to be when you're damn well ready.

I Can Think Differently.

It can be very, very hard to listen to the lessons your negative voice has to offer without giving in to the demons. Your voice grows those evil horns not when it points out your flaws but when it convinces you that you can't do anything about them. A lot of this comes back to the language you choose to use, because that can 1,000 percent impact how you perceive yourself and what you're capable of. I'll never forget the time I was on vacation and got to talking with a lovely woman while waiting in line at the omelet station. You know, the typical talk—Is this your first time here? How are you liking the hotel? That kind of thing. Then she asked me what I did. I beamingly started talking about Quest, *Impact Theory*, and *Women of Impact*. Realizing I had been talking a lot, I asked her what she did. Her reply completely horrified me, and I literally, for a split second, was speechless. What did she say? . . . "I'm just a mother." JUST? The woman had three kids she was homeschooling, for God's sake! Dealing with my pup Wookiee this morning as I was trying to cook and get back to writing this book was a complete undertaking, so being a full-time mum AND homeschooling is increeeedibly time-consuming as well as bloody admirable. She was helping build society one kid at a time. And what she was doing should never be underplayed or downplayed by using the word "just."

And every single time she said the word "just" out loud or even to herself, it was discounting all her effort. And I told her that. She looked a bit shocked at first (I don't think she expected me, a total stranger, to call her out on using the word "just"). But by the time our omelets were ready and we had trashed the word "just" in the garbage along with the eggshells, her entire demeanor had changed. By changing her language she was able to change her thoughts, and, as a result, how she saw herself. By the end, she was raving about the techniques and methods she had developed and the new procedures she was researching to get her kids more engaged in certain subjects.

As women, we're always discounting ourselves and what we do by using language that diminishes us, thus fanning the negative flames. But discounting is for Black Friday sales, not for your accomplishments and triumphs. So, when going after your goals and dreams, you have to start reframing the words in your head in order to empower yourself. Here are some to get you started:

Instead of that . . . Say this.

*"You never have
your shit together."*

**"You need to make a plan
and be prepared."**

"You are shit."

**"I was shit at that.
How can I do better?"**

*"You have no frikin' clue
what you're doing."*

**"I've never done this before,
so I'm going to have to learn."**

"You're so lazy."

**"You need to find a way
to motivate yourself so
that this doesn't keep
happening."**

"You're not good enough."

"What does good enough actually look like, and what do I need to do to be good enough?"

"You don't deserve it."

"I need to put in more work."

"Congrats, you effed up! That was seriously embarrassing."

"Congrats, that was a great lesson. How can I avoid making the same mistake in the future?"

"Everyone thinks you're stupid."

"Everyone else is too busy thinking about themselves to care. But I do care, and that's okay. I need to learn, prepare more, and communicate better."

Perhaps you're noticing a pattern here: Get back up. No matter how hard you front-face smack the ground, no matter how many people are watching, learn from it. And try again. When you position yourself as someone who's growing, your negative voice can land a few uppercuts and right hooks, but it won't knock you out. When you get back up, failure is something you can actually be proud of. And the one thing that's absolutely bulletproof and that your negative voice will never be able to penetrate is whether or not you showed up. If I do something half-assed and know I didn't give it my all, then my negative voice is going to kick my ass when I fail. And rightly so. But if I work my butt off and pour my heart and soul into something, then if it doesn't work out, my inner bitch—who almost always has an insult ready to go—is frikin' speechless.

I Can Sabotage My Self-Sabotage.

If you wonder why your negative voice has a tendency to show up at the WORST TIME, like when you're about to do something important, it's because you care. When you care about something, you want it to go well, you want to do good, and caring isn't a bad thing. And don't ever tell yourself otherwise. If you only ever did things where you didn't care about the outcome, then your negative voice could get the gold watch and retire right now and move to Florida. But what kind of a life is it when you're only doing things you don't care about? Trying to convince yourself that you shouldn't care so that you're protected from your negative voice can be a form of self-sabotage, because remember, your negative voice doesn't want you to try anything new. And self-sabotage is just a way of rolling out the red carpet for your negative voice and then giving her the VIP treatment when she arrives.

When we think of self-sabotage, our mind often goes to extremes, like drugs, alcohol, or self-injury. But what about the type of self-sabotage we may not even be aware we're doing? The death by a thousand cuts. When you tell yourself you're gonna start eating healthy: "Come Monday . . . it's on! But since it's Friday, I may as well spend the next three days stuffing my face. After all, I don't start till Monday, right?" Boom, self-sabotage! Or what about when you find someone you like, but hang on—they don't check all your boxes, so what's the point? Your expectations are so high that they just can't be met. Boom! Self-sabotage!

Self-sabotage can also be so subtle that we don't even recognize it. "There's no way it's going to work, and everyone is just going to say, 'I told you so,'" your negative voice says when you're first excited about a new idea. So you don't even give it a shot, even if you want it really badly. You're basically saying, "I told you so" to yourself before anyone else even has a chance. You might feel like you're just playing it safe, but BOOM! self-sabotage strikes again. This kind of self-sabotage will ring true with a lot of us, and it's this kind of stuff that gives our negative voice a big-ass stage, a megaphone, and frikin' confetti cannons so we can't ignore her.

To prevent self-sabotage, you have to first recognize it, and then take steps to break the pattern in order to get to your goal. Get ready to stare nakedly at the truth. It might be a little uncomfortable being this bare, but radical confidence is all about a little bit of pain for a whole lotta gain.

- Get a piece of paper, and something to write with.
- Write down your goal, in big bold letters, at the top.

- Underneath that, write down where you are right now. Maybe you're close to your goal, maybe you're miles away, but you have to be honest with yourself so you can clearly see the road that's ahead.
- Now, one by one, write the steps you need to take to get you to your goal.
- Beside each one, be honest about why you aren't there yet.
- Now read over your reasons and brutally scrutinize them—are they valid reasons? Or are they excuses?
- Then write out the steps you need to take to get past them.

Take me as an example:

My goal (today): To create content that empowers fourteen-year-old girls to believe in themselves so they don't have to spend the next twenty years of their lives working to unwire that negative and destructive mind-set that I had when I was their age.

Am I there yet? Not even close.

Why? Because to reach fourteen-year-old girls on a global scale will take time. My calendar says five years, to be exact. I've given myself five years. So while I'm not there YET, you'd better believe that every single day I bust my butt to work toward that. I mean, the hooooooours I've put into writing this book are all in service of THIS goal.

Reason or excuse? Reason, homie!

Now, contrast this with how I used to think and go after my goals when I was stuck in the Purgatory of the Mundane.

My goal (then): To make movies.

Am I there yet? Not even close.

Why? Because we need more money. Because we need more time to make more money. Because we haven't met anyone who will finance our dreams. Because Tom works all the time. Because I need to do the frikin' laundry.

Reason or excuse? Excuse. Excuse. Excuse. Excuse. Definite excuse!

No judgment if some of your reasons are excuses. But if you notice that a lot of them are, it might be time to play the NBSWWIT? game to see if you're actually willing to do what it takes to reach your goal. It might be that you're not, and that's fine. Then it's time to reevaluate what new goals might actually give you the life you want.

To sabotage your self-sabotage, you have to be prepared, because it's a lot easier to get your negative voice to stay quiet than it is to get her to shut up once she's already started running her mouth. Do the work in advance so that, when the time comes, your excuses are left out in the cold. Say, for example, your goal is to start waking up in the morning and going to the gym before work, but day after day, you forget to set your alarm, so you don't go. Or you spend fifteen minutes looking for your shoes and you're now running too late, so you . . . don't go. First, be real with yourself: Do you really want to go to the gym in the morning? Or would you rather get more sleep? NO SHADE. If you want to sleep, then go to bed earlier. If you hate that idea more than you want to train and get healthy, theeeeeeeen noooooo shaaaaaade. Don't let your negative voice come at you with a list of why you've failed and what that says about you. Instead, just say, "I would rather go to bed later and not set an alarm than train and get healthy in the morning." Done. Donezo! In this case, examining your self-sabotage told you that your goals weren't actually aligned with your priorities. But if you really do want to train and get healthy and you know that the best time to do it is in the morning, then ditch the bloody excuses! Do what's needed. Set that alarm. Set two, if you have to. Go to bed early. Fill your tank up. Put your trainers by the bed. Thank your negative voice for the clarity, and give the middle finger to your self-sabotage.

RADICAL CONFIDENCE RECAP

- **Be BFFs with the bitch.** Reframe your negative voice as a well-meaning friend who is just trying to help you do better.

- **Translate that shit.** The bitch can be harsh, so learn to dissect and interpret what she's saying. If she says, "You're not good enough," ask, "What does good enough mean? What can I do to get there?"

- **Get. Back. Up.** Getting back up renders your negative voice speechless because she can't argue with it. As long as you're picking your self up and climbing back in the ring, failing is something to be proud of because it's making you stronger and better.

- **Hone your superpower.** Let your negative voice be your Phil Jackson. It will identify your weak spots, and those are the areas where you need to go extra hard with the preparation. Overpreparation might not make your confidence bulletproof, but it will make it a lot harder to ding.

- **Choose your language.** Negative language (and f-bombs) might not serve everyone, and some people might find it hurtful and triggering. The point is to find a way to talk to yourself that works for you. That's exactly how I came up with this method: Everyone always told me to "talk nice to myself all the time," but that didn't motivate me. It just put me to sleep like Ambien.

- **Kick self-sabotage to the curb.** Here, awareness is your most powerful weapon. Take a cold, hard look at the "reasons" you're not achieving your goals. Are some of those reasons actually excuses in disguise? If so, prepare yourself and be on the lookout so your self-sabotage can't ambush you when you're not paying attention.

7

LEAVE THE LOSER ...
CHOOSE YOURSELF

Loser (n): 1. A person who is incompetent, constantly fails, and is destined to disappoint.

2. Someone who wrecks your confidence and keeps you from finding the person who actually deserves you.

"**Y**ou're never going to find anybody who loves you as much as I do." These manipulative words came out of my first teenage boyfriend's mouth during a super heated argument. If this had been the Relationship Olympics, we would have won gold in all the screaming matches we competed in together. But as painful as his threatening words were, at the time, they seemed actually, twistedly . . . romantic. I can see how damn insane this is with hindsight and all, but at the time, I was young, totally insecure, and certain that a boyfriend was the ticket to fitting in and feeling better about myself. And so I chose to see this threat as more of a compliment. I mean, he DID love me after all, right? But that isn't even the worst part. The utterly heartbreaking thing was that, even though he was extremely toxic and verbally abusive to me, I believed him. I was determined to make our relationship work, no matter the cost. Because what was the alternative? What if no one EVER loved me that much again? Oh, dear Lord . . . would I end up being one of those women on the news who was found dead in her apartment, half devoured by her twelve cats? I can see the headline now: "Crazy Old Cat Lady Dies Alone After Finally Leaving the ONE Guy Who Ever Loved Her."

Nothing—and I mean *nothing*—will shatter your confidence faster than a bad relationship. It can dim your light, knock you down, keep you small, and make you doubt the deepest core of yourself. Sometimes I think back to that ex-boyfriend—to whom we'll affectionately refer from here on out as "The Asshole" or "The A" (capital T, capital A) for short—and wonder how differently my life would've turned out if I hadn't broken free of the grip that relationship had on me. I was in deep, homie, and it took a lottttttttt of mental gymnastics to vault me out of that dark place. I can see now that I was trapped in a textbook toxic relationship, one that poisoned my understanding of who I was, how I saw myself, what I deserved, and how I saw the world as a whole. Those four letters—L-O-V-E—can, with the right person, make our lives even more magical. But I don't want you to just find any old love, especially if it looks anything like my ex. I want you to find the most kick-ass, supportive partner who helps elevate you, your dreams, and your confidence. You may be thinking, "But, Lisa, that will never happen for me—'nobody's perfect,' 'I'm unlucky in love,' or 'all of the good ones are taken.'" Trust me, I hear you. I felt that way once, too, and as a result I thought I had to accept whatever scraps of attention came my way.

Back in high school I had some guy friends who allowed me to kick it with them—I loved soccer, hated skirts, and wasn't "prissy"—but they never seemed to see me as girlfriend material. Maybe it was the tomboy look. Maybe it was because I had zero game and the closest I came to flirting was to tackle them in the penalty box. I tried to pretend that I didn't care when they talked about the popular girls in a romantic way, but oh man did I care. I was dying inside from constantly feeling unwanted, so when I heard through the grapevine from mutual friends that there was a boy who fancied me, well, stop the frikin' presses! A flat chest, a unibrow, and frizzy hair were apparently no longer my kryptonite, and I was sure I'd found my hero. His smile lit up the room, his laugh was infectious, and he certainly knew how to "schmooze" my mum. This was it! I would no longer have to be the third wheel on my friends' dates, I had someone to kiss at midnight on New Year's Eve, I had someone to take care of me when I was sick—*this* was gonna be the love story Disney promised me! Never mind that he belittled my moviemaking dreams. No matter that, over time, he put me down. Forget about his insensitive critique of my weight, pinching a bit of baby fat around my middle. (Yup, this was the real piece of work I mentioned back in Chapter 5.) He said he loved me, and if he said it, then he must mean it, right? And wasn't that all that mattered? Although some of the things he said hurt my feelings and shook my confidence, I finally felt "worthy" enough to be validated by somebody. This is reason number 915 why external validation is a trip to Nowhere Land! If he has the power to give you a ticket and invite you aboard, then he also has the power to rip up that ticket and throw you over the side.

I dated The A for four years, off and on, even though our paths started veering in very different directions. At first I just ignored it because I had no idea who I would be without him. I was following my dreams and studying film at university, but I would drive back to my hometown every week to see him, where he was busy delivering pizzas for Domino's as a cover for his side gig as a low-level drug dealer. I'm not throwing any shade on The A's work—somebody's gotta deliver those ultimate pepperoni pies and stuffed cheesy breads, and we were still young and figuring ourselves out. But I had massive ambition and lots of goals, and he had . . . zero. Okay, I'm actually being generous, because he had less than zero! He was perfectly content to smoke weed, hang with his boys, and rip to shreds anybody who wanted more from life. Any mention of my dream to go to LA would be quickly shot down with mockery. Over time, just like water dripping on a stone can change its shape, I, too, started to change mine. And it was a shape I could no longer recognize. I made myself smaller and smaller and argued back less and less just to keep the peace. And even though I became just a little blur of a Lisa that you had to squint hard to see, I persisted, convinced that this was just what "love" was.

Think about this way: when you're starving, like utterly ravenous, a dry, unsalted, bland-as-ass cracker will do the trick. It fills you up, and you're just grateful you have food to eat. Well, that's what being young, insecure, and finally getting a boyfriend feels like. You have *no clue* that you're just one aisle or maybe even one shelf away from a bounty of other options! When you're this hungry for external validation, you don't realize that you can wait for something that truly nourishes you. It's so tempting to just settle for what's given to you and never ask for more, or for better. But, homie, doooooooon't! Ritz crackers *do* exist! Sure, you can survive on the frikin' dry crackers, but once you get a taste of the good stuff, you'll never look back. And, most important, to continue our cracker analogy for a second, you can feed *yourself*. You don't have to be dependent on the lame, bland crumbs someone happens to throw your way. There's a whole grocery store out there for you, I promise. You just gotta start saying no to the things that don't nutritionally fill your heart!

Maybe you're stuck in a relationship that you know in your heart of hearts probably isn't good for you. Maybe you're single and trying to figure out which of the mismatched dudes hitting you up on the apps are worth a date. Maybe you're happily partnered up now, but remember being in a bad relationship, like I was, or have a friend who's struggling. Wherever you are, homie, when it comes to matters of the heart, I think many of us have had the confidence rug pulled out from under our feet by someone. I'm focusing on romantic relationships for now, but a lot of this applies to anyone in your life who may be toxic and bringing you down, from the aunt who "tsks" over your career path at the Thanksgiving table to that frenemy who's always trying to passive-aggressively one-up you. You may not be able to cut them all out, but at least you can recognize toxic game when you see it.

One of the biggest and hardest things about being in a toxic dynamic can be the way it slooooooowly but surely chips away at your confidence over time. Toxic comments are like teeny paper cuts that sting at first, so you just slap bandages on them and move on with your day. If you treat them quickly and properly, you can heal from them. No biggie. But toxic relationships are like paper cuts that get infected, and a week later you look down and realize that, holy smokes, your poor hand is dripping with pus. Maybe you ignored those cuts for so long that they've turned into gaping, infected wounds, and you need to go to the doctor for some antibiotics and a stitch or two. You didn't mean for it to happen; it wasn't a big deal at first, and now you've been suffering for so long that you don't remember how everything even started. Well, homie, this is your wake-up call. It's time to rip off the metaphorical Band-Aid!

I Can Spot the Red Flags.

When I was at university, I lived in a shared dorm with five other women. We each had our own bed and bath suite (this sounds fancier than it was—in reality it was the size of a sardine tin and you had to squeeze sideways to get into the shower), but we shared the common areas. One day I was in the kitchen on the phone with The A—remember, this was the late '90s, when phones were still attached to walls. We were chatting about some random thing that had happened that day, and just then one of my roommates and her guy friend came giggling into the communal kitchen. The A, hearing this, asked me who else was there. Ugh. This was when my stomach started tying itself in knots. You see, this wasn't the first time he'd showed signs of jealousy and utter insecurity, so I just brushed it off, quickly changed the subject, and defused the situation. Or so I thought. A few hours later, as I was relaxing in my bedroom watching *Friends* on VHS for the 564th time, there was a knock at the door. I open it to find The A standing there. I swooned! Woooooow, he just drove for hours to come and surprise me! And for a split second, I was overwhelmed with such joy. "See," I thought to myself, "he *DOES* love you!"

But aaaaaas you may have guessed by now, he hadn't come to visit as some sort of grand romantic gesture. He hadn't brought me chocolates or flowers, nor did he serenade me because of his uncontrollable desire for me. Nope. He was an insecure shit who didn't trust me and was out of his mind with jealousy. The A stormed into my dorm and started ransacking the place like Joe Pesci in *Home Alone*. He headed straight for my closet—

empty. Then to my bathroom, where he pulled back the shower curtain and—nothing. He didn't find a mystery man hiding anywhere, but he did eventually emerge triumphantly with a pair of my dirty knickers from the laundry hamper. Holding them up victoriously like a fisherman with his catch of the day, he pointed to a bit of discharge on the gusset. Finally, he had proof, he said . . . that I had indeed been cheating on him! The bloody fool was ignorant enough about normal female bodily functions that he thought it was semen. But here's the even twistier, more effed-up part: He was so adamant that I started to question myself. Wait, was something wrong with me? *Was* it normal?

At this point, you may be thinking that this was surely how our relationship ended, and that I quickly dumped The A on the spot after this insane and inappropriate behavior, but noooooooope. We had a few more rides on the merry-go-round of love. I rationalized his actions by telling myself that it was because he loved me *so* much that he was heartbroken even thinking about me with another guy. After all, he must have really cared about me to make this huge effort to drive all the way here and make sure that everything was okay. Somehow, some way, I justified this crazy act as "love" and saw it as my "duty" to show my love and appreciation back. So I doubled down on my efforts to never, evvvvver have a male voice anywhere within earshot of our phone calls again. You know, the totally reasonable thing to do to fix a problem that didn't exist outside of The A's control-freak imagination.

Bending over backward to people-please is no way to live your life. Staying quiet and succumbing to the triggers of a toxic person is *no way* to live your life! Now, maybe you haven't had to deal with a guy sniffing your underwear (I sincerely hope not!), but if you've ever had a partner act out on you, you miiiiiiight be in a toxic relationship. Do they call you names and then say they're only joking? Do they mock you in front of other people and call you too sensitive when you bring it up later? Do they violate your trust and say it's just your imagination? Do they threaten to leave you if you try to stand up for yourself? Do they use your vulnerabilities against you? A toxic person will manipulate your vulnerabilities to gain power over you. They don't care if it's a deep cut. Oh, wait—actually that's a lie. They *do* care. The deeper the cut, the more painful it is, and the more likely it is to get infected. And *that's* what they actually want, because it gives them the power. They'll do whatever it takes to make you doubt yourself and keep you down, and, as a result, stuck with them.

Shitty Things People Do
That Break Your Confidence.

- **Manipulation:** Controlling by unfair or insidious means in order to obtain a personal advantage. Emotional manipulation occurs when someone tries to direct your feelings in a way that allows them to gain, or maintain, influence over you. Aka: Doing dodgy shit.

- **Gaslighting:** Psychological manipulation of a person over an extended period of time that makes them question the validity of their own thoughts and perception of reality. Making a person think that a little discharge on their undies is a sign that something is wrong with their body and they should be ashamed about it. Aka: A dick move!

- **Bread Crumbing:** Stringing someone along with juuuuuuust enough affection and attention to keep you on your toes. Classic signs include lack of commitment (both to you and any plans you make), sending mixed signals, and unreliable communication. Aka: No one loses their phone charger that often, trust me.

- **Ghosting:** Ending a relationship suddenly and without warning, including abruptly cutting off all contact. Yes, this is purposefully designed to make you feel absolutely, certifiably crazy. Aka: Just be glad you saw through them.

- **Codependency:** A relationship dynamic in which one partner is "the giver" who sacrifices their needs and well-being for the other partner, "the taker." This often enables some sort of destructive behavior. If you regularly find yourself playing caretaker instead of paramour or thinking that you can "fix" your partner with just a little more effort, you might be stuck in a codependent rut. Aka: Get out now!

- **Love Bombing:** When someone you don't know very well yet showers you with all sorts of attention and affection with the intent of influencing you. This could look like wanting to spend all their time with you, constantly checking in, lavishing you with unnecessary gifts, and saying "I love you" early and often. Aka: If it seems too good to be true . . . yep, you know the rest!

Now, I can't talk about signs you're in a toxic relationship without talking about—*dun dun dunnnn*—the red flags! My dorm fiasco was a huge one, of course, and that was partially because I kept ignoring the red flags that had come before, determined to keep my head down and turn a literal blind eye to any issues. When I was around seventeen years old, two years into my relationship with The A, he broke up with me totally out of the blue—like, one day he was saying "I love you" and the very next day we were over. I had no idea what had happened! Heartbroken and utterly confused, I was desperate to get him back. I mean, who would I be without him? The "why" of it all had me spiraling downward, and I became . . . let's just say a little "stalkery." I would do drive-bys past his house looking for his car to see if he was home; if he was, I would call him, sobbing, begging for answers, and pleading for him to take me back. And yep, you guessed it—the more he refused to talk to me, the more desperate I got. I was so distraught and couldn't focus on anything else that was going on in my life at the time. After about a week of what felt like waterboarding, he finally broke his silence. Sitting in a freezing parking lot at midnight, he confessed that he had cheated on me. Ten times. *Ten times!* Now, we were just seventeen at the time, so he wasn't sleeping with all of these other women, but he'd been making out with them at clubs when he was out with his boys, which was still an utter betrayal. When I went clubbing without him, I never even glanced at anyone else, so it didn't occur to me that he could be out on the town doing his best Leonardo DiCaprio impression with every woman he met.

Was I naive to trust him? Yes. He showed me so many signs that he wasn't trustworthy, and I kept ignoring them. But I refuse—*refuse*—to feel bad about trusting someone. I believe trust is an imperative part of a long, happy, healthy relationship. Where I went wrong was choosing to trust the wrong person, and that led to my making more horrific decisions. Here's the craaaaaazy thing, though: I was so heartbroken by his betrayal, and yet so relieved to have him back in my life, that I just said I was fine with it. I'm horrified to write it, but the truth was that I was so upset he'd broken up with me that I didn't care about his indiscretions. I forgave him, and we moved on. Yup—as if nothing had happened. It was such a genius manipulation tactic that I hadn't seen it coming and *totally* fell for it, hook, line, and sinker! He had so completely twisted my emotions with his shock-and-awe breakup technique that when he confessed (which he probably did only because he got worried that someone else would tell me first), I took him back rather than dumping his ass like I should have. And unfortunately for me, it worked like a charm. So on this one, not only did I look past the red flags, homie, I straight-up ignored the frikin' ten-alarm fire!

Of course, not all red flags are as glaring as that one was; the more subtle ones are often even worse. Here are some ways you can identify them:

Do you swallow your thoughts and worry about speaking up because you think that your needs are a bother? An imposition? And so Gooooood forbid you ever ask for something or take up space, so as a result you dull your light? I had no idea how dim I'd gotten. You see, we often bury our needs and wants just to keep the peace, and what we don't realize is that we've buried them six feet under, never to see the light of day again.

When I first met Tom, I told him I didn't care about flowers. Now, the truth is that I looooooove flowers. Nothing makes my day more than a lovely bouquet, but I'd been disappointed so many times by my ex that I'd come up with the idea that if I didn't ask for what I wanted, then I wouldn't be disappointed when I didn't get it. At the time, it actually seemed like a smart strategy. If I wasn't disappointed, then we didn't have to argue about it, and if we didn't argue about it, then we could just maintain the status quo rather than addressing the fact that my needs had gone unfulfilled. Damn; even now, this belief saddens me. But I learned the lesson that with the right person, your desires can be greeted with open arms. And so, a few years into my relationship with Tom, I finally told him that flowers were actually meaningful to me—and you'd better believe he gets me the most epic arrangements now. So listen up! You have a right to ask for what you want. It doesn't mean you're materialistic, it doesn't mean you're too demanding, and it doesn't make you a bother. Your partner might not be able to deliver all the time, for whatever reason, but asking for what you need—or even just want!—doesn't make you a nuisance. Having needs doesn't make you needy. It makes you human! It's dangerously easy to lie to ourselves about our desires and to suppress our wants so we can appear easy and low-maintenance. We all want to be the cool chick, right? It can feel like a subversive act to say what you really want, but when you deny your desires, guess what? You end up living someone else's life instead of your own. You deserve—yes, deseeeeeerve—someone who wants to make you happy even when . . . actually, scratch that, *especially* when you tell them exactly what you want.

Now, there's one other big red flag I want to mention, but you need to bear with me, because you may not like it (but I have to say it for us to really change). This red flag is . . . *your* red flag! Yes, homie, you may be waving a flag without even realizing it. How do you talk about your relationship to your friends and family? Yes, *you*, not them. Do you find yourself hiding your partner's iffy behavior from them? Would you tell them if you were upset about something your partner did, or do you avoid mentioning it because you know they would tell you, "Girllllllll, kick that loser to the curb"? I get it, I really do. Without even realizing it, I kept my mouth closed about all the paper cuts The A inflicted on me over the years and never gave anybody a chance to help me see what was happening. I mean, my own mum had no idea The A was *such* an A until I came clean decades later on social media. You see, when you're with someone toxic, it becomes second nature to cover for them. You want everyone to like them, right? And you've already convinced yourself that they're going to change because you saw a spark of possibility one time ages ago at that one party, so why tell others about that bad incident? If you just ignore it, then you can just forget it ever happened. And if you do tell someone, then you may feel ashamed that you're not actually with Prince Frikin' Charming. You may have seen this toxic behavior modeled as a child and feel like it's actually normal—and comfortable—even if you have a feeling in your gut that something isn't quite right. Maybe saying that there's a problem out loud would feel like saying you're not the strong woman people thought you were because you're sticking around and accepting it—because you know, deep down, that no badass woman puts up with this crap.

Phew . . . my homie, it can be a lot to unpack, but take a peek deep inside if you find yourself making up justifications and editing your stories about your love life. Remember, the excuses will feel real, so don't let them trick you into staying!

Now, I do want to make a caveat here: When I'm talking about toxic relationships and leaving them, I'm talking about people who are bringing you down and messing with your confidence, *not* domestic violence or sexual assault. That's not my area of expertise, and so please, please, please, I *strongly* encourage you to reach out and seek help, because you deserve more. If you or someone you know is dealing with abuse, look for a number you can call for your area's confidential National Domestic Violence Hotline.

If the red flags are flying high, it's likely you've got a toxic partner on your hands. *But*, let's not fall for the BS that's out there these days and slap everyone with a "toxic" label just because they behaved badly. There's a big distinction between *actual* toxic behavior, which is when someone deliberately looks to manipulate your feelings in an effort to control you, and the behavior of someone who's simply going through a bad time and maybe not bringing their best self to your relationship. And, sadly, we often lump this all into the same bucket, call it toxic, and go about our merry day. But we've gotta stop! This is a massive disservice to you, your potential relationship, and your future together.

So, how do you know the difference between a paper cut you can treat and one that's infected all the way down? You need to take the time to assess what's truly toxic and what's just bad timing, and then have the ability and the radical confidence to make that next move. Start by asking yourself, was there some obvious trigger, like a job loss or a death in the family that coincided with a change in behavior? Is there a health issue that might be causing a chemical change in their personality? An emotional distraction that might be impacting their ability to show up the way they have in the past? Do they seem to be at least a littttttttle self-aware of their situation and able to talk to you about it? If so, there's nothing wrong with giving someone grace and trying to support them through the rough days, especially because we all have them. Of course, you're under zero obligation to white-knuckle through this turbulence if it's simply not working for you anymore, but I don't want you to jump straight to, "Well, hmm, my boyfriend snapped at me last week and I read an article that said that was a red flag, so I guess I need to dump his ass, label him toxic, and permanently give him a bad reputation." No, no, noooooo!

If you're still unsure, then I want you to do a little thought experiment with me that might help you figure out whether you're in a relationship that you've gotta bounce from. Think about your goals, your dreams, and what you hope to accomplish in your life. Write them out, and then think about where you'll be in one year, five years, and ten years if you take this journey with your current partner. Add details next to your goals! Is this partner sitting in the front row and cheering you on as you take the stage for the first time? Are they lifting you up and boosting you to that next level toward your future and your dreams? Or do you find yourself diminishing your desires in order to keep the peace, not ruffle any feathers, and take care of *their* priorities and needs?

Here's what I imagine would've happened if I had stayed with The A: I probably would've finished university. Within five years, I would definitely find myself back in North London, married to him, trying to fix up a shabby flat on marijuana income, and tending to our first little bundle of joy. Maybe I'd be pregnant with number two. The A probably would've become more controlling, more emotionally abusive, and more jealous, and our fights would definitely have escalated. Sure, we would have some good moments here and there, just enough to keep me in place, but everything little Lisa had dreamed of would stay just that—dreams. Ten years out, I would be unhappy, with a gaggle of kids and my former confidence buried in the couch like a lost Binky.

When I think about the difference between that vision of the future and my actual life—in which I did spend several years serving my husband rather than focusing on my own dreams—I can put my finger on some important factors that, for me, meant the difference between years of positive hard work versus toxicity in my relationship. As you know, I spent a good deal of time at the beginning of my marriage with Tom as an unhappy housewife. But, unlike The A, Tom fully supported my dreams. We talked constantly about what we were working toward, what we were building, and how we might evolve together to make our crazy schemes a reality. And Tom listened and adapted when I told him that I wanted to change. When it was time for us to really take off, Tom was literally the wind beneath my wings (picture Patrick Swayze lifting up Jennifer Grey). He always knew we were equals and pushed me to own my full power.

So, let's rewind to what *actually* happened in that ten-year span: I did eventually break up with The A, and it was far less dramatic than the dorm-room showdown. I spent my last two years of college single, going to parties, going on lots of dates, nailing my film studies, and generally building up my confidence and having a blast. When the once-in-a-lifetime opportunity to go to the New York Film Academy came up, I jumped on it. If I had still been with The A, there's no way I would ever have moved abroad, even for a short stint. Five years later I was married to Tom and, even though I was biding my time in the Purgatory of the Mundane, we were crazy happy in love and talking constantly about the future that *we wanted to create together*. And now, more than twenty years later, we've started Impact Theory, made a difference in the lives of more than half a billion people through the content we've created, and . . . you're holding my frikin' book in your hands. Talk about achieving my wildest dreams!

A partner can be a heavy anchor around your ankle that pulls you down to the bottom of the deep, dark ocean as you gasp for your last breath, or they can be a life raft that keeps you afloat and saves you from drowning. The way your partner shows up for you can make or break you.

A relationship can make or break your confidence. It can make or break your future, your dreams, your goals, and the person you can become. Being with the right person can make a huuuuuuge difference in how you see yourself and how confident you are—not because it's a partner's job to make you believe in yourself but because a partner can double (or halve) the amount of energy that you bring to your own life. When that energy is soul-sucking, it becomes ridiculously exhausting to fight for yourself; when the energy is positive and uplifting, it's like strapping a jet pack to your back, giving you double the momentum. And let's be honest: There's nothing sexier than being with someone who wants to see good things happen to you.

I Can Choose to Leave.

There's another thing I realized (in hindsight, of course) when I was with The A: Dating someone toxic makes *you* toxic. Yup—you get dragged down to their level. As embarrassing as it is to admit that it happened to me, this is an important part of the toxic dynamic that we must address here. You should've heard some of the epic fights The A and I used to have. We're talking all-out, dirty, Kardashian-style screaming matches. And you better believe I gave as good as I got. I knew how to press his buttons, and so whenever I felt threatened, I'd press the hell out of them to defend myself. I've since learned that my behavior—which haunted me for a long time because I felt so ashamed for also sinking that low—was actually a natural response to feeling powerless in a relationship. It's a survival mechanism more than anything else. If you're getting mauled by a tiger, you have two choices: eat or be eaten. Predator or prey. And a predator stays alive. This is about maintaining whatever power you can in the relationship, even if you're hanging on to it by a thread. In a healthy relationship, you'd be confident enough to set a boundary when conflict rears its head (see more on boundaries in Chapter 8), but in a toxic relationship, you just slide down, down, down to their level. This is how you assert yourself in the relationship and justify staying.

A really important reality to acknowledge is that a toxic dynamic may even in fact feel exciting, because the heightened emotion of fighting is easy to mistake for passion. And let's not forget about the appeal of makeup sex. Yeah, baby, there's a reason this is a thing! If you're caught up in this type of pattern, a nontoxic relationship may actually feel boring to you. Where's the heat? Where's the desire? Emotional turmoil can feel exhilarating, and it can even be fun—in its own sick, twisted way—to egg on the drama. But real growth, and real confidence and connection, isn't going to happen when you're wrestling down and dirty in the mud all the time. A healthy, safe partnership fueled by mutual care, love, and support helps both of you bring out the best in each other. And not to mention that this kind of prolonged nastiness can compromise your own morals and values. Do not *ever* let someone influence you into acting in a way that doesn't make you proud of yourself.

When The A and I finally broke up for the last time, it was literally one of the most boring endings you've ever seen. No Hollywood director would ever have scripted it this way. We were back together once again after a few months off, and once again we were bickering about the fact that we were going out for dinner. You see, he never—like, evvvvver—wanted to take me out. His idea of a good time was staying in (he lived with his mum, so when I say staying in I mean staying in his bedroom like kids), getting high and blowing the smoke out the window so his mum didn't smell it, and having sex in silence so his mum wouldn't hear (you know, real grown-up and classy). Anything other than that was just a bother to him. Just like toxic clockwork, on the way to the restaurant (that I had booked and was driving us to, of course), The A bitched and moaned. The whole. Way. There. From the moment he got in the car, he started going off: "Why are we going out to dinner? It's so expensive and never worth it. I don't even like the food there. Blah blah blah," and on and on and on he went. And for some reason, that's when the light bulb finally turned on. In an instant, I was done. I turned the car around. I didn't need to be there anymore. I didn't have to listen to him complaining and devaluing my company for another damn second. I deserved better than that. I could choose better than that; I could choose something different for myself. Without explaining, I quietly and unemotionally dropped him off at his house and told him this was my final goodbye.

He had just placed the last straw that finally broke my back, and it was goodbye for good.

Life is frikin' short, my homie, and there's no need to waste another second on people who don't light you up. Radical confidence is knowing when it's time to go. Now, sometimes it may not be as easy to walk away as it ended up being for me, but, maaaaaan, did I waste a lot of years not knowing my worth. I came to that conclusion after far too many scars on my heart. I wish I'd realized all this sooner, and so, to save you more wasted time, let me just say it as clear as day: *You* hold the power. I mean it! You, and you alone, get to choose how you spend your time and who you spend it with. And good frikin' riddance to anyone who doesn't deserve the gift that is you. If they can't appreciate a dinner out with you, they certainly won't celebrate building a life with you. Or care for you when you're sick. Or help you when you're struggling. I know this is easier said than done—yes, this shit is haaaaaaaaard, or otherwise so many of us wouldn't find ourselves giving our toxic partners just one more chance—but the sooner you get these people out of your life, the sooner you can move on to the partner who's truly worthy of being with you.

I Can Get Over Him.

Okay, so you've made the decision to leave. You gathered up all your courage and told him that you were done, once and for all. You did the hard thing. You holed up with a copy of *Eat, Pray, Love* and a pint of Ben & Jerry's. You blocked him on every social media app. You called your bestie and cried about all the awful things he said and did. So why do you still feel so frikin' terrible? I can hear you thinking, "Lisa, you promised me bold, badass confidence once I dumped the loser, and I'm over here puffy-eyed and feeling worse than I have in a long time."

Here's the deal, homie: You need time to heal. Toxic relationships give the heart a real beating, and yours needs some true R & R. Remember that paper-cut-to-gaping-wound analogy we used before? Well, you're just now bringing yourself to the doctor and getting a few stitches. That skin is going to be tender for quite a while as it generates new cells and closes up the fissure. And even once it's better, you might have a scar. Post-breakup, you are literally growing in all sorts of new ways to heal yourself and come out stronger on the other side. This is a process, my friend. This may sound extreme, but I recommend that you take a year (yes, like twelve whole months) before jumping back into the sweet embrace of a relationship. And no rebounds! Even if the sex was amazing, grab a vibrator, but do not—I repeat, *do not*—rebound even for just a night. The wound that's healing is super-duper sensitive, and you've got to nurse it back to health, not keep ripping it open. In my experience, this is the only way you can truly restore yourself from the inside out, put up some strong boundaries, and build your confidence back up. This is your phoenix time, but you've got to do the work under the ashes before you can rise and soar to even greater heights.

Even though you know you did the right thing by leaving, you're not instantly going to be happy. You're going to grieve the relationship. You're going to grieve whatever future you thought you two were going to have together. You're going to grieve that there's no more "we." You're going to grieve the change and evolution you're going through, necessary as they may be. So, crank up some Celine Dion and know that [Your] Heart Will Go On, eventually. Give yourself some grace and just ugly-cry it out. One thing I discovered through my own grieving process that I found incredibly helpful was to remind myself that everything awful I'd endured wasn't personal. I needed some distance and space before I could really see that, but it was true. What happened to me, what was said to me, what I did in reaction to all those paper cuts building up over time—none of it really had anything to do with me and who I was as a person. The truth was that The A would've treated *any* girlfriend the same way. There was nothing wrong with me. Losers gonna lose, no matter who they're with.

It might feel a little uncomfortable to be alone. After all, you previously thought you enjoyed the company of a toxic asshole more than that of your own sweet self, so this will be a shift, to say the least. Being alone can sound very scary, and it can *be* very scary. There might be a voice in your head telling you all kinds of bullshit lies: Alone means you're not attractive. Alone means you're not good enough. Alone means no one wants you. Alone means [fill in the blank with your own personalized fear]. There's probably a story you're telling yourself or a belief system you've inherited that says being single is a bad thing, and that being in a toxic relationship is better than not being in a relationship at all.

Say what?!

Homie, this is a biiiiiiiiiiiig frikin' lie. A lie, lie, lie, I tell you. This is shame ringing you up and delivering a judgment call that's totally false. No man (or woman, for that matter) is worth losing your mental health, well-being, and sense of self. *Never!* And it's up to you to pull up your big-girl panties and stop taking the safe route to nowhere. I get it; in the moment, it can actually feel easier to stay where you are. Sometimes toxic behavior can feel more soothing than the negative voice in your head. But let me tell you: Gaining radical confidence means developing the ability to know your worth and to walk away. Even if you don't believe that right now, trust that the proof is coming.

Another common side effect of toxic relationships is losing your connection to who you are, and to what you do and don't enjoy. You've spent so long molding and shapeshifting yourself into what they want you to be that you don't have a bloody clue what you actually like. Did you really love watching football or debating the downfall of the Roman Empire? Maybe you did. Or maybe you were just expressing interest so that it seemed like you and your ex had more in common, and so he would think you were hella cool. It's time to drill down into your own desires. There's a phrase I've heard used as shorthand for when someone is totally lost: "She doesn't know how she likes her eggs." Do you *really* like over easy, or did you just go along with what your ex wanted for brunch even though you're actually more of a scrambled type of woman? If your whole personality changes every time you date someone new and you find yourself bouncing from soft-boiled to poached, chances are you've lost a lot of yourself along the way. But fear not, my homie, because it's time to take the first step, and that means going on a date with yourself! Yep, now is the time for recovery and rediscovery. Are you an introvert or an extrovert? Do you like to stay up late or greet the morning sun? Is there a new hobby you've been curious about trying but you knew your ex would say was dumb (i.e., it would take time away from him and his needs)? Maybe a pickleball league is calling your name! Maybe you've always wanted to try your hand at gardening or learn Chinese. This is also a fantastic time to rebuild relationships with friends and family, especially if one of your ex's manipulation tactics was to keep you away from anyone who threatened their status. Zero shame! It happens to the best of us, and now it's time to make it right again. And if at a moment of loneliness you find yourself getting weak and are just a fingertip away from calling him again, just remember that nothing is lonelier than being in a relationship with someone who doesn't really see you and doesn't support you. It's time . . . to get reacquainted with the smart, funny, badass woman you really are.

I'll be honest—this part really sucked for me. I didn't like my own company when I was younger. That little voice in my head was mean and constantly reminded me that I wasn't pretty, I wasn't smart, I wasn't good enough; so you can imagine that being alone was the equivalent to buying a one-way ticket to Cruelville with no chance of an exit ramp. I needed all the distractions I could get to ignore that voice, and while some people turn to alcohol or drugs to quiet it, or sleep around to avoid intimacy, little Lisa turned to someone toxic who could drown her out. Because when you're alone, there's nowhere to hide. And so I realized that the only resolution and antidote to this mean voice was to consciously start to cultivate a nicer relationship with myself. With radical confidence I had to sit down and do the hard work of figuring out 1) who I really was, 2) who I wanted to be, and 3) what I had to do to get there. If Stella could get her groove back, well, by golly, so can the rest of us!

The week before Tom and I were to be married back in my hometown in North London, The A called me out of the blue. Even though we hadn't been in contact, we knew people who ran in the same circles, so I had a feeling he'd heard I was about to get married. When I answered, I just cut to the chase, told him I wasn't interested, and called it a day. It probably ticked him off, but I was done, and had been for a while at that point. I was about to say "I do" to the love of my life, and I didn't need anyone raining on my wedding parade. Then, the evening before our wedding, "someone" threw a brick through my car window. Yep, that's right, a brick! Coincidence? Well, I don't know for suuuuuuuure that it was him, but my stereo wasn't taken and no one else had a V for Vendetta against me. It was a pretty insane thing to have happen, but to be honest I was too happy celebrating to be bothered. The most thought I gave it was marveling with pride at how damn far I had come. The old Lisa, who bent over backward to protect The A's feelings and keep the peace, was long gone, and in her place, in the wise words of Cardi B, Lisa 2.0 was "unbothered, moisturized, in her lane, well-hydrated, and flourishing."

Here's the thing: When you start to realize your value and worth, you can't be as affected by a toxic person anymore. When you feel fully confident in who you are, this type of negativity can roll off you like water off a duck's back, and you won't feel the need to lower yourself to their level. Yes, The A may have broken my window, but you'd better believe he could no longer break my heart.

I Can Trust Again.

Once the early, intense stages of the breakup are behind you, it's time to take stock and be brutally honest about the red flags that were liiiiiiikely there all along. You may have recognized some of these before the breakup, but now it's time to examine all of them up close and do the deep work. You cannot build back trust—in yourself or in someone else—if you aren't willing to roll up your sleeves and do the work. And yes, be prepared to see flags that were so obvious that they almost gave you whiplash and you *still* consciously chose to ignore them. So embrace the pain a little, because those flags are there to remind you to make better choices next time. You're not Marty McFly and you can't go back in time, but you can take a long, hard look at your mistakes so you can make sure never to repeat them again. The burn bloody hurt, but it sure taught you never to touch the hot stove again, am I right?

And there's a good reason to revisit these red flags! Once you've laid them all out, you can turn your attention toward the green flags. Yes, let's now focus on the positive! What traits would make you say "Hell, yeah!" when you saw someone who had them? What attributes would make your heart flutter? What behaviors would make you feel seen, heard, and appreciated? What nonnegotiables are you going to have in your next relationship? What boundaries are you going to stand by? This is the kind of wisdom you can glean when you take the time to heal before jumping into something new, so give yourself a damn pat on the back for getting here. It sucked, yes, but you made it in the end, and—let's be honest—the alternative is being stuck in toxic la-la land. So, time to stop beating yourself up and time to start smelling the green (flags, that is). Some of these green flags are likely baseline expectations: no cheating, no physical abuse, no name-calling. Honestly, this is the bare minimum you should expect from anybody, and it's a little crazy that in this day and age we have to even say they're deal breakers. But having gone through the "snogging ten women in the club" debacle, I wasn't going to leave anything to chance. By the time I met Tom I had built my radical confidence, and so I swore that I would be very clear about my boundaries and needs.

Now, what other qualities are important to you in a relationship? What are *your* values? Establishing these before you start dating again is imperative, and they can become a cheat sheet, if you will, for what and who are right for you. Do you want your partner to check in often, or do you prefer to fly solo? Are you a foodie who's into trying every new restaurant, or are you happy ordering Postmates? Do you crave intellectual stimulation from your partner, or are you a social butterfly who likes to get jiggy with it and is looking for a party cohost? (Not that these examples are all mutually exclusive—you can want both!) What else would really allow you to thrive in a partnership? For example, what sort of life do you envision having together? Where will you live? How will you navigate spending time with friends and family? Career demands? Do you want kids? How much sex do you want? Will you share your finances? These are all conversations to have with your future partner, but know your preferences now so that you'll be equipped. This way, when you see red flags, you can slam on your brakes in time and avoid a head-on collision. Or, when you see green flags, you can put the pedal to the metal and find yourself yelling "Let's Frikin' Go!"

I Can Be Me.

The most devastating part of being in a toxic relationship is losing yourself. Your identity and confidence can take a real frikin' hit, and you can find yourself subsumed by your partner's negativity. But waiting ahead of you is freedom. This is one of those rare times when the grass actually *is* greener on the other side. When you break free from a toxic partner, you'll regain the ability to discover who you truly are (warts and all), know what you really deserve from a relationship, and accept *nothing* less. Leaving a toxic relationship kinda reminds me of that classic scene from *The Shaw-shank Redemption* in which Red is reminiscing about his friend escaping from prison through a literal sewage pipe: "[Andy] crawled through a river of shit and came out clean on the other side." Yep—that's exactly what it feels like if you've dragged yourself out of a toxic shitstorm and are now free. Go live your best life loud, proud, and damn confident!

Your whole journey of building radical confidence in a relationship starts with two things: First, you have a choice. And second, it's never too late. A few years ago, I was at an event and a woman came up behind me and tapped me on the shoulder. I turned around, and she just started bawling—like, uncontrollable sobbing. And through her tears I heard her say, "Lisa, you saved my life. I know this is very heavy for me to say, but you actually saved five people's lives." She went on to explain that she had been married for nearly thirty years and had had four kids with her husband. He was both extremely verbally and physically abusive to her and would use the kids as ammo by threatening to harm them if she ever "stepped out of line." Now, to him, stepping out of line meant singing or dancing, among many other "offenses." He used their kids as a manipulation tactic to keep her in check and to control her, and it worked. For yeeeeears she thought she was stuck. She explained to me that she thought she'd "made [her] bed with him, and now [she] just had to lie in it." But then she came across some of my content, and it planted a seed. A seed that would slowly blossom over time. That seed made her believe that maybe, just maybe, she could have a different life. That maybe she didn't have to suffer through this terrible situation. Some of my content about narcissistic personalities especially resonated with her, and she realized how much of her marriage was about doing whatever it took to keep her husband calm and happy. And what kept him calm and happy? Well, it was keeping up external appearances, despite what was happening behind closed doors. Her husband needed their big house and fancy cars to feel important, but she didn't. She couldn't care less about materialistic things when every minute of the day was spent living on such a razor's edge. And that was the moment—the moment she finally believed that she didn't have to settle. The moment she packed up her kids and rented a one-bedroom apartment. Although all five of them had to squeeze into a teeny-tiny place, she told me the story with a giant smile on her face. "Lisa, do you wanna know the first thing we did when we got the apartment?" she asks. "We square-danced!"

Daaaaamn; this still gives me the chills! I hope you never find yourself in a situation as horrific as this (and if you do, please, please, please reach out to someone—this can be very dangerous, and there are people who can help!), but this story is also a beautiful reminder that we can make different choices. That we can speak up. That it's never too late. We can say what we want, need, and deserve. We can build back our radical confidence and never let it go again. We can choose to leave. To find better. To never, ever settle. And if you ever find yourself in another situation where you're trying to leave a toxic partner and he replies with, "You're never going to find anybody who loves you as much as I do," an accurate, Lisa-approved response is . . . "Thank God!"

RADICAL CONFIDENCE RECAP

- **Be a mystic and peer into your crystal ball.** Think about what your life will look like with your current partner one year, five years, and ten years from now. Write it down, and add details! Are you thriving and living your dreams, or has your confidence and ambition withered like a neglected houseplant?

- **Leaving is *always* a choice.** You choose who you spend your time with, and no one else can do this for you. It's never too late to change your circumstances and create a new future for yourself. You hold the power!

- **Rip off the Band-Aids.** Breaking up really is hard to do, and when you finally get the courage to leave a bad relationship, you're going to need to recover. Give yourself the gift of time and space, get to know yourself again, and rebuild your radical confidence so when the right person comes along, you're whole, healed, and ready to *go*!

- **Let your green flags fly.** You know what those toxic red flags look like, so now flip them upside down and keep an eye out for their positive opposites: green flags. What are the signs that someone sees the real you, supports your dreams, and will be a kickass companion?

- **Folk-dance the night away.** A toxic partner keeps you small and dims your bright light. You deserve to shine (and sing), homie, and don't ever forget it! Seek out whatever brings you joy and happiness—and always, always choose yourself first.

TOUGHEN THE FUCK UP ...
BUTTERCUP

Buttercup (n): A kick-ass person who can take a licking and keep on ticking. She goes after her goals and knows how to roll with the punches, and she's embraced her vulnerable, insecure side and uses it to her advantage.

One of the most common questions I get whenever I do Q&As is "How do I stop caring what other people think of me?" And you know what my answer to that question is: I have no clue. I've never learned how to not give a fuck, and I probably never will. Because I *do*. In fact, I give lots of them. I care what other people think, and I can't shut that off. It's part of my personality, and an important part of what makes me who I am. If my mission IN LIFE is to help people, then how on earth would I be able to do that if I didn't care what other people thought? So I realized that trying to shut off the part of myself that cares is actually a way of trying to be someone I'm not. And that's not the radical confidence way—we're all about embracing who we are here. Flaws and all. Knowing that I'm always going to care, to differing degrees, what other people think of me and what I'm doing, I don't let other people's expectations or opinions affect how I show up. I keep going No. Matter. What.

Now, believe me, I know what I'm saying sounds less than pleasant. And I know what you're thinking is even worse—how on God's green earth am I supposed to break free from the expectations that others have of me if I still care about every complaint and criticism they make? But guess what? Ignoring those voices doesn't make them go away. It's just like with your negative voice—trying to drown her out just makes her louder and meaner. Since you can't control the voices, what can you do? I'm glad you asked. It's a two-step process. Step one: Find the constructiveness in the criticism. Step two: Toughen the fuck up, buttercup.

I Can Face Criticism.

I once received a comment on a YouTube video in which a lady wrote in totally dissing my bright pink leg warmers. She hated them so much; they distracted her from the video's content soooo much that she had to turn it off. That's right. My leg warmers were so offensive to this woman's eyeballs that she couldn't watch the show.

A lot of people would have done one of two things: laughed at this, said, "Eff that!" and moved on; or taken it to heart and never worn them again. But I couldn't do either one of those. The whole point of doing these videos is that I want to share something with people so that they can learn and grow and make their lives better. So I decided to explore whether she had an important life lesson for me. I had to listen to what this criticism had to teach me. What if she was just one of many that were turned off by those same awesome, stylish, hip, fashionable leg warmers? If I changed my look, would more people be willing to listen to me? I dress the way I do because it makes me feel a certain way—looking badass on the outside leads to feeling badass on the inside—but were there people out there who were missing my message because they couldn't get past what I was wearing? Was there a compromise I could make in how I dressed to send a signal to a wider audience that I had something valuable to offer?

On the other hand, I reeallllllllyyyyyy liked my bright pink leg warmers. They made me happy when I wore them, and I did my best, most authentic interviews when I was happy. Plus, *Women of Impact* is all about celebrating radical authenticity and honesty, and me being my radically, authentic, honest self comes with bright pink leg warmers and all! And if I were to shove my totally awesome, rad, pink leg warmers in the back of a drawer with my mismatched socks and never wear them again, then I really wouldn't be staying true to myself or the mission of *Women of Impact*. No matter how I dress, I believe in what we're doing and that the message can change your life. So, I decided, viva la pink frikin' leg warmers. This was exactly the type of situation where I could care what someone thought, but also keep right on going with what works best for me.

When people who know you and who are important to your life criticize you, there can be value in acknowledging and listening to that (maybe you ARE always late to every family gathering and need to make more of an effort to get there on time. Your sister's just sayin' . . .). There's also value in giving yourself a minute to consider criticism that comes from people who don't know you, especially if it's about something that relates to your goals, like me and my leg warmers. For example, maybe you're trying to launch a business and you keep getting negative feedback from your customers. Do they know you? No. But should you blindly dismiss it because of that? Um, not if you want your business to stay in business.

But there are also a lot of times in your life when paying too much attention to criticism will hold you back. If this is NOT what you want (because no judgment at all if you decide that what other people think of you is more important than your goal—that's your decision), then you have to take some steps to correct that. First, ask yourself who are the people you're worried about pleasing. Actually get out a piece of paper or open up the notes app in your phone and make a list. Is it your mum? Your dad? Your friends? Your partner? The Starbucks barista? Whose comfort and happiness matters so much to you that you've been putting it above your own?

Once you have your list, ask yourself how the people on it would respond if you did X, Y, or Z of the things you really want to do. And here's the hard part: These responses may not be pretty. Maybe they'll say negative things to you, tear you down, or try to get you to change your mind.

When I introduced Tom to my dad, I knew that my dad wasn't going to approve of our relationship. It was nothing personal against Tom. It was just that I was the first person on my dad's side of our family to marry someone who wasn't part of our culture, and Greeks—especially the Greeks in my family—are known for their stubborn streak. You've never seen a sweeter and more loving woman than my *yiayia*—God bless her— until she's scorned! I remember when I was a teenager, she received a birthday card from a family member. She was so happy they'd remembered, until she saw there was more than one name signed on the card. And this was the name of someone she'd refused to talk to for yeeeeears. All of a sudden, she stormed over to my mum's desk, grabbed some Wite-Out, and started furiously blotting out her name.

Since I knew that stubbornness was encoded in my family's genetics, I also knew that if he didn't want me to marry Tom, he wasn't going to easily change his mind. But what was more important to me? Living a life that would make me happy? Or living a life that would make my dad happy? Because it really does boil down to that. And when I could see it in terms that clear, it was damn easy for me to answer it. ME, obvi! Now I'm not going to pretend it was easy. I'm not going to pretend there weren't nights I cried my eyes out. I'm not going to pretend that, after a huge argument I had with my dad about the wedding, I didn't suggest to Tom that we jump on a plane and get married on a beach in Hawaii. But Tom guided me off the eloping ledge and helped me reframe the situation.

He reminded me to first go to the base fundamentals. And that base is my relationship with my dad. Initially, I was just seeing and focusing on him being super negative toward my relationship with Tom. But getting out of my emotions and looking at "facts" started to help me see things differently. So what do I know about my pups? That the man loves his children more than life itself. Knowing that, and replaying the situation with that in mind, why would he be so negative? Because he cares. He frikin' cares A LOT. Okay—if he cares, then he believes his concerns are valid.

So before dismissing him, maybe I should listen because maybe one or more of his concerns ARE valid (because as I already established, they come from a genuine intention). I sat down with my dad and listened, straight-up actually listened, to what he had to say. And just like that, we went from ugly crying (at least, me) to having a heart-to-heart and building an even tighter bond. Did he change my mind? Nope. Did that stop me from marrying the man of my dreams? Nope. But because we talked through it and cleared the air, my dad from that day on was super supportive—major props to that man; he paid for the entire wedding, cried when he saw me in my wedding dress, walked me down the aisle, and danced with me at the reception. And since that day, he's been incredibly supportive and has never said a negative word about our relationship.

There's nobody who's more of an expert in what you need to live your life than you are. If what other people expect of you is holding you back, you have to use radical confidence to first decide it's not okay. You have to make it clear to yourself that this is not bloody okay. I'm here to tell you straight, homie: You must first DECIDE it's not okay that your life is being steered by others. You have to first demand a better life. Then, and only then, can you move on to the next step—taking action!

Start small. Do one little thing that you've always wanted to do but haven't out of fear of what "they" might say. And you don't even have to tell "them" either. Maybe it's that top you've always wanted to wear but have been too concerned about people thinking you're trying to look too young or cool or dope. Or maybe it's that hip-hop dance class where you know everyone there is way better at pop and lock then you are. I mean, you can barely pop. Now it's time to make a plan to do it, regardless of the naysayers. Maybe you try out that new top by wearing it around the house. Or maybe it's that dance class, so you strap on your radical confidence cape and . . .

- Sign up in advance, and put it on your calendar. Now you know that this Thursday at 7:30 p.m., you will be getting your *Step Up* on (fingers crossed the instructor looks like Channing Tatum).

- Plan what you're going to wear. You may not feel ready to put on those booty shorts and flat-brim hat just yet, but you also probably won't feel ready to shake it to Megan Thee Stallion if you show up in the sweatpants you usually wear to bed.

- Get there early. Introduce yourself to the teacher, if you can, and tell them it's your first time. Find the spot in the room where you will feel most comfortable. Maybe that's in the back. Maybe it's in the waaaayyyy back. Maybe it's actually in the front where you won't be so tempted to compare yourself to everyone else. So long as it's not in the bathroom behind closed doors, find the spot that works for you.

- Focus on what matters: You. Remember, everyone else is there for their own sake, so stop focusing on other people because they sure as hell aren't focusing on you.

- Have some frikin' fun. Be totally present. Sweat your ass off while you shake your booty, and know that next time, it won't be so intimidating.

You need to practice, practice, practice doing things that make you uneasy without having the added pressure of other people's opinions. This is your wax on, wax off moment, and I'm your Mr. Miyagi. This will prepare you to eventually show people who you are, who you've decided to be, and what you're frikin' made of. And over time, people will respond in one of two ways. They'll either show you that they respect—or at least accept—this part of you. Or, yep, you guessed it, they won't, or they don't. And radical confidence is saying that that's okay. That it's not under your control. But what *is* under your control is how you react to it. Do you tap out when Johnny breaks your ankle? Or do you get back up like Daniel San and crane-kick them in the face (metaphorically, of course)? Either way, you get to choose, because you've been training for it since you put on that rhinestone-encrusted crop top and did the dishes. It's tough, but so are you, buttercup.

I Can Set Boundaries.

A lot of us think that we have no idea how to set boundaries, but in reality, we've been setting them our entire lives. When you were seven years old and told your brother, "Oy, you have to ask before you play my Mario Brothers"—that was you setting a boundary. And when you screamed and yelled at him and threw him out of your room when he ignored you—that was also you setting a boundary. And when your mum told you, "Share with your brother," that was renegotiating your boundaries. We just didn't think of it like that, because we were kids. It's like one of my favorite stories, which comes from David Foster Wallace's 2005 commencement address at Kenyon College: "There are these two young fish swimming along, and they happen to meet an older fish swimming the other way, who nods at them and says, 'Morning, boys. How's the water?' And the two young fish swim on for a bit, and then eventually one of them looks over at the other and goes, 'What the hell is water?'" The fish were always surrounded by water, so they didn't even realize they were living in it! Best. Story. Ever.

You're frikin' swimming in boundaries that you already have. So if a relationship isn't working right now, that means you need to reexamine and reframe the boundaries that currently exist in that relationship. With every interaction, you have a chance to reframe, tweak, spin, and mold those boundaries into shape (if you need to imagine a shirtless Patrick Swayze sitting behind you to get motivated, then by all means . . .). You've always had boundaries; like the water in which the fish swims, they've surrounded you for your entire life. It's just time to start taking an active role in setting them.

A few years back, when I was in the middle of dealing with my health issues, I had to set boundaries with my mum. My mum and I are really frikin' close, and we talk a lot, but every time we'd speak, we'd have just said hello when her tone would change. She would immediately get this note of pity in her voice and ask me, "So, how are yooooou? How are you feeling? Are you okaaaaay?"

Now, I appreciated my mum's concern, but her doing this always made me feel crappy. I spent almost every waking moment trying very hard to stay positive and not get emotional over what was happening to me. And the sound of my mum's voice, the pity, the sadness, and the sorrow that came out of her was just too much for me. I didn't feel strong enough to overcome that as well. I knew how much my mum would be worried about me, and that she wouldn't be able to sleep. Mum had taken care of me my whole life. When I was four and got salmonella, the hospital quarantined me in a glass room because they didn't know what I had, and my mum stayed with me the entire time. She took me to the ER both times I fractured my ankle, and when I had the flu, she would be the one who sat next to the bed with a damp cloth. But now I was an adult. I lived halfway around the world, and there was nothing Mum could do to help me. Our situation had changed a lot, and our dynamic had to change, too, as it wasn't serving me anymore. Eventually, it got to the point where I was anxious about talking to my mum, because I knew that as soon as we got on the phone, I would start getting knots in my stomach (the one place you don't want them when you have gut issues). I was trying very hard to stay strong, but her tone made me feel weak, even knowing full well that wasn't her intention at all.

At first, I just tried to shut her down and power right through to the next topic of conversation. That worked about as well as you might expect (remember how I said Greeks are stubborn?). So then, I thought maybe she just didn't understand where I was coming from, and it was my job to explain it better. So we had a full conversation about it, and I gently attempted to explain my point of view. "Mum," I said, "I'm trying very hard to think positively about my health, but when you approach it like that, I can't help but be reminded of the problems I'm trying to forget. I know you mean well, but when you bring it up, it's actually hurting me instead of helping me." "Okay, Lisa, okay. I think that was pretty well handled," I thought to myself. "I wasn't emotional. I articulated the problem and what I needed. Good job me, if I do say so myself." Mum assured me that she understood. Double score! Man, this shit wooooorks! The next time we got on the phone, the VERY FIRST words out of her mouth were, "So, how are you? Are you okaaaaay?" Like, literally! The verrrrrry first words out of her mouth. This is the part where I regrettably admit that I was no Cool Hand Lisa. I couldn't help but get upset, and when you've got health issues, stress is the last thing you frikin' need. It's like someone saying "We need to talk about our relationship" while you're trying to parallel park—not helpful. We started to get into a little tiff about it, and I asked her if she remembered our last conversation. She said yes. Then I asked her if she remembered what I had asked her to do, and she said yes to that as well. So I repeated what she had just said to me, and asked her what the disconnect was, because I wanted to give her a chance to explain.

"I want to know how you're feeling," she said.

"I know, Mum," I said, "but if I'm not feeling well and I need your help, I'll tell you, okay?"

"I know," she said, "but I want to be able to ask my daughter how she is." We went back and forth about this for a while, and then like the parting of the Red Sea, a miracle happened. I finnnnally got what she was trying to communicate.

"Wait," I said, "are you worried that if you don't ask, it will seem like you don't care and you won't feel like a good mum?" She was silent for a second.

"Yes," she said solemnly, "that's exactly it." So there we were. I needed my mum to stop asking about my health because it made me feel bad, but if she didn't ask me, then she felt bad that she wasn't doing her job as my mum. I was so busy looking at my own feelings and boundaries that it never occurred to me that I was crossing *her* unspoken emotional boundaries. So we decided to create boundaries together. Her boundary was that she needed to be able to ask, and my boundary was that she not ask right away in our conversation, and that she didn't do it in a pitying tone.

It took us a bit of negotiating to get there, but by being clear and honest about what each of us needed, we were able to get to a place where we could still have happy conversations—because you get a boundary. And you get a boundary. And you get a boundary. Er . . . well, you get it: Everybody wins.

Boundaries are also imperative if you're a people pleaser, because you probably have a bad habit of bending over so far backward for other people that you end up on the floor. And having clear boundaries is the first step in not getting stepped on. Having proper boundaries can help keep you from getting hurt, and keep you from hurting other people when you have to push back and break their heels—because once someone has overstepped your boundaries, you're going to have to push really frikin' hard to get them to move.

When it comes to setting them for yourself, the first thing you need to do is recognize what type of boundary you need to set. Now it's time to break it down. And, no, I don't mean MC Hammer style. I mean the boundary types. There are three main ones:

Material boundaries. Rules you make around your possessions. For instance, asking your sister not to borrow your clothes (though in the case of my sister and me, she was the one setting the boundaries). One boundary I've had to set with Tom is about my laptop charger. It drives me frikin' nuts when he takes it and doesn't put it back before I need it again. Tom and I are married, obviously, and a big part of being married is sharing your stuff. But this boundary was a big deal to me because my time is so frikin' valuable that any amount wasted—even a couple of minutes spent looking for a charger—is too much. (Babe, if you're reading this, and you should be reading this, because it's your wife's book: Get your own charger!)

Physical boundaries. Rules concerning the space around you. For example, I'm a hugger, even with strangers. This is my way of connecting with people—it breaks barriers immediately, which makes me more comfortable and, I hope, makes them more comfortable, too. But if someone isn't comfortable getting hugs (oh, the sacrilege), it can get us off to an awkward, standoffish start, because they will already feel like I've invaded their space. So, what I usually do when I meet someone new is tell them that I'm a hugger and give them space to set their own boundaries with their response. Maybe they come in for a hug and delightfully say, "Oh my God! Me too," maybe they offer their hand for a shake, or maybe they just wave from a distance (totally understandable in a Covid world).

As much as Tom and I talk about, work on, and renegotiate our boundaries, we also have some nonnegotiable ones. For me, from day one, I made sure that Tom knew that if he ever cheated on me or hit me, I was out the door. Adios. Arrivederci. Au revoir. Gooooooodbye! Immediately.

No discussion. No matter how much I loved him, or how long we had been together, if he even put a toe over either of those two lines, I was gone. And so in order to set us and our relationship up for success, I made those boundaries UBER clear without any chance of misinterpretation from the get-go.

Mental and emotional boundaries. Okay, so now we're getting down to business. These types of boundaries are the mama jamas. The big ones that are really hard to frikin' set. These are the rules around all the stuff that goes on in your head. They concern your thoughts, your beliefs, your opinions, your values, and your feelings, and no one—I repeat, no one—is ever going to agree with you on all of these, so you're going to have to hold on tight even when other people are trying to shut you down.

On our first date, when Tom asked me if I believed in God, it felt like he was crossing a huge boundary. I came from a world where NO ONE ever asked such a question—if I had ever said anything of the sort to my *yiayia*, it would have been the same as me taking a knife, stabbing her in the heart, and then giving it a big ol' twist. But Tom wasn't asking with an agenda or trying to upset me; he just genuinely wanted to know. And because I felt like he was asking from a genuinely curious place, I gave myself a chance to consider my answer with the same curiosity—even though in many other situations, with a different person and a different intention, I probably would have declared the topic a no-go zone. These boundaries are some of the most difficult to set because—hello!—they're emotional.

Now, I'd actually like to add an important disclaimer here. This advice should not apply to anyone who needs to set a boundary for their mental or physical safety. This is only relevant if it's a relationship you're looking to improve and work on, like the instance with my mum. When we're setting boundaries with people we love and trust, we need to understand that, like with my mum, our boundaries might directly conflict with theirs. This is why it's incredibly important to set these boundaries with respect, understanding, and a thick skin. Your boundaries are about your needs, just like someone else's boundaries are about their needs. When someone sets boundaries with you, it might sting a little bit, but just like that Monica song—don't take it personal.

So now that you know what kind of boundary you might need to set, you need to get uber frikin' specific—UFS—with it. Know the who, what, when, and why about the boundary you're setting. For example . . . The who: my mum. The what: asking me about my health. The when: when I speak to her on the phone. The why: It reminded me of how weak I was.

Get your UFSs down, and then you need to prepare. You probably already know by now that having conversations about boundaries isn't easy—it takes courage and bravery to do this. And that's where radical confidence comes in. Choose your words carefully, and practice what you're going to say. When Bruce Lee was asked about his badass ninja moves, he said, "I don't think 'kick.' I just kick." Meaning he had practiced sooooo much that he didn't even have to think about it. Repetition creates habit, repetition creates habit, repetition creates habit, and if you practice enough, you won't freeze up on the spot. Be prepared for pushback. Now in a dream world, everyone would answer and respond in the way you want them to. You set your boundaries, everyone is very agreeable, and then you hold hands around the campfire while singing "Kumbaya." Yeah, as if.

We're living in a world that is often not the world we wish it were, and people probably aren't going to respond this way. So what I do is practice different scenarios in my head, as if I'm going off a screenplay, so that if the other person says this, I have my next line ready to go.

Each boundary will be completely different for every person and every situation, but here are a few things you can do when setting them to make it easier:

Pay attention to how each boundary makes you feel. You, and you alone, have to deal with your emotions and, especially if you're new to setting boundaries, your emotions may not always be positive ones. You may feel guilty for setting them. You may feel like you're being selfish, you may second-guess yourself, and you have to approach this with no judgment. Don't beat yourself up for what you're feeling, and remind yourself that the more you practice setting boundaries, the more comfortable you will become when you do it.

You have to learn to say no. No is a two-letter word, but sometimes it feels harder to say than reciting the alphabet backward three times while simultaneously hopping on one leg while patting your head and rubbing your tummy. Another way to put it: not bloody easy at all. We all know to just say no, but damn it, sometimes that just feels very rude and disrespectful, which isn't our intention. So my strategy has evolved. I don't just say no; I say no and then explain why, though I'm also very careful not to justify it or position it as something that's up for debate. Don't apologize for setting boundaries, because an apology implies that you think you've done something wrong—and you frikin' haven't. If you find yourself in the middle of justifying your boundary or apologizing, just stop right there and move the eff on.

Read yourself your boundary rights. You have the right to say no without feeling bad. You have the right not to meet someone else's unreasonable expectations. You have the right to make your needs just as important as those of others. You have the right to set your own priorities, and you have the right to act on those priorities. You have the right to renegotiate your boundaries at any time. (You also have the right to an attorney, but, homie, I realllllly hope it doesn't come to that.)

Be aware of the impact boundaries can have on a relationship. You might want to buckle up and brace for that impact. While your boundaries are about what you need, they're also going to affect other people. If it's someone you care about, it's CRUCIAL that you go into these conversations with the utmost respect for them and where they're coming from. Again, this does not apply to abusers or people who are harmful to you; those people don't require respect or explanations. But with people you love whom you want to keep in your life, the ideal outcome isn't to beat the other person into submission but for you both to win, and if you don't offer them respect and a chance to be heard, then why would they do that for you?

Step into their boundary shoes. While it may never be your intention, you will run into people who will find your boundaries offensive. What you say, and what they hear, when you state your boundary might be totally different. It might be like Bill Murray and ScarJo, just lost in translation. You say, "I'd love it if you didn't text me before nine a.m." And they may hear, "Hey, stop bloody texting me. Ever!" Put yourself in their shoes, and imagine that you were on the other end of this. Imagine, for example, that you have a big event coming up; you've got nothing to wear and can't afford to buy a new dress, so you ask your bestie if you can borrow something. And she says no. The last time you borrowed something from her, she explains, she had to ask three times to get it back, and when you did return it, it had a stain that didn't come out even when she got it dry-cleaned. Well, shit, you think. You remember that: Work was crazy that month, and you kept meaning to get the dress cleaned because that drunk idiot spilled his drink on you, but it just kept slipping your mind. You can totally see where she's coming from, but it also stings a little bit because, let's face it, the subtext of this is that she thinks you're not responsible enough to take good care of her stuff. Ouch. That one's gonna leave a mark. But the worst part of it is that, from your past actions, she's got a point.

Having someone set boundaries with you can be a little tough to swallow. So when you're on the setting and not on the receiving end, consider how to phrase your comment in a way that reduces the possibility of putting the other person on the defensive. Instead of leading with what they've done wrong, talk about yourself and how you feel. Say, "I need your help, because I'm struggling with . . . " When you can explain your struggle, it shows them what you're going through and that you're vulnerable. You're not coming AT them—"Listen, dipshit, you keep crossing a line and . . . "—you're coming TO them: "Here's a problem I would like us to solve together."

Be ready for a do-over. Got everything so far? Okay, good. Now, deep breath, because here's the kicker. The next thing you do after you've finished setting your boundaries . . . is to set them again. Boundaries are a work in progress. You have to approach them the same way Marie Kondo approaches a closet: Take care of the ones that are important to you, and say goodbye to the ones that no longer spark joy.

It took me a long time to feel good enough about myself to hold my boundaries because I felt like I had used up every bit of courage I had just to set those frikin' boundaries in the first place. I was terrified of someone pushing back or saying no because I thought I would crumble if that happened, so I came in like Tony Soprano—"This is my fucking boundary. You break my boundary, I break your face, capeesh?" And I bet you can guess how well that went over—it frikin' didn't. I had to learn how to approach boundaries as teamwork with someone I loved and cared about, and once my boundaries became something we were setting and respecting together, it became a lot easier. And I didn't have to bust any heads in the process.

Over time, you'll get better and better at this. Setting and reevaluating boundaries will get easier and more automatic, for you and for the people in your life. Boundaries are enforced by habits, and habits are formed by repetition. They might not come out right the first time. Heck, when it comes to the reinforcing, you might not even get it right the second time. Or the fifth, or the sixteenth! If you set a boundary and someone crosses it, does that mean you immediately have to cut them out of your life? No!

It comes down to intention: If someone didn't intend to cross one of your boundaries, that's a mistake. We're all human, and we all make frikin' mistakes, and mistakes are forgivable. If someone is genuinely trying to respect your boundaries, give them the grace to keep trying to get it right, and encourage them along the way. You need to be able to say, "I really appreciate you making such an effort, and while you aren't there yet, it's really meaningful to me that you're trying," just as readily as you can acknowledge that you're going to accidentally cross boundaries, too. It's just as important to be able to tell someone else, "I realize I'm not there yet, and I really appreciate your understanding while I get into the habit."

However, if there's someone you love and want to keep in your life but they keep disrespecting your boundaries no matter how clear you've been, it's likely that there's a deeper issue that needs to be addressed. Did they misunderstand the boundary you wanted to set, or are they not respecting it? It's important not to assume that they're going out of their way to be malicious, but it's equally important that you have the conversation. If you get to the point where there's no improvement or they make zero effort, then it's up to you whether you allow them to still be in your life, knowing that they will forever be like that. If you decide you do want them in your life, then at least you know they'll never change and can stop hoping that they will.

Some situations will require that you take a step back, examine your relationships, and break down why a boundary is important to you in the first place. Is it for your own safety and sanity? Then that's probably one you don't want to renegotiate. But, sometimes, when you look closely, you might see that your boundaries are actually standing in the way. Maybe you put up the boundary a while ago because it was helping to protect you from something, but now it's actually getting in your way and keeping you from growing. If that's the case, then maybe it no longer serves you. For example, let's say your partner is a fitness junkie, but it's a sensitive subject for you and you aren't ready to focus on your health. So you set a boundary with your partner where they're not allowed to suggest that you skip dessert. You already have an unhealthy relationship with food, so this boundary is necessary so that you don't feel worse about eating that Adam's Peanut Butter Cup Fudge Ripple Cheesecake. But now let's say you're in a place where you really want to put your health front and center in your life. Well then, that once "healthy" boundary is now actually holding you back. And it will serve you and your new goal to smash that boundary into oblivion and let them advise away because now you're not only open to listening but you also just got an accountability partner . . . in your partner. A two fa' one!

Some boundaries need to be set in concrete, and some need to be on wheels, and radical confidence will help you identify which is which.

I Can Stop Saying "I'm Sorry."

Here are two rules I live by. Rule number one: Always apologize. Rule number two: Stop apologizing. Now before you chuck this book across the room in a fit of rage over the contradiction, let me explain. Stop apologizing does not—I repeat, *does not*—mean never having to say you're sorry.

You should say you're sorry, and you should mean it, in a ton of different situations. You forgot your best friend's birthday? You'd better say sorry! You crossed a boundary after someone explained why it was important to them? YOU ARE SO SORRY! You said or did something insensitive and hurt someone you care about? Girl, frikin' beg for forgiveness! If it's important that someone apologize to you when you feel like they've hurt you, then give them the same gift. Love includes being willing to say you're sorry; knowing when and how to apologize is a huge part of having successful relationships with other humans—and, in fact, with other creatures in general. If you've ever found yourself frantically apologizing to your pet because you've accidentally kicked them, then you know EXACTLY what I mean. If I step on Wookiee, you'd better believe that I'm apologizing to her in my squeaky mummy voice (and giving her a treat and tummy pets) because I don't want her to be scared of me or think I meant to hurt her.

But you have to stop apologizing for things that aren't your responsibility. A lot of us say sorry when other peeeeeople have done something wrong because it's so ingrained in us to not be a bother. A silly example that hammers the point home: Someone bumps into you, and YOU turn around and say sorry. WTF? Many times, we just apologize because we want people to like us. We want to be seen as sweet, kind, nonthreatening, and selfless. We've spent our whole frikin' lives being influenced to believe (whether deliberately or not) that this is how women should act. So we apologize to maintain that image.

Constantly apologizing leaves you justifying and second-guessing your actions. And if you're always second-guessing the choices you make, then you're constantly beating yourself up with no break, and that much negativity can start to turn into shame.

Here's a situation we've probably all been in: A friend invites you to a party, but you've had a rough week and are too damn shattered to go. You can barely peel yourself up off the couch to feed the dog, much less put on your glam and heels and go mix and mingle. You'd much rather zone out and smoke a joint while plucking your eyebrows and watching an episode of *Friends* for the zillionth time because that's all your fried brain can handle at the end of this week (not that I've ever done that, of course).

So you close the Postmates app (yay, your order is being prepared) and open up your texts to let your homie know you aren't going to make it, and the next thing you know, you're typing out, "I'm soooooo sorrrrrrry that . . . " By doing this, you're framing your decision as something that you've done wrong ("I should be going to the party") as opposed to prioritizing your own needs. By being overly apologetic, you're, in essence, shaming yourself and demeaning the reasons you're not going. You're basically giving someone else permission to judge your decisions and be upset with you about them.

So instead of apologizing, either explain that you're taking a self-care day and hope she has a blast (and if you're anything like me, this is followed by at least five emojis), or just politely thank her for the invite but say that you're unable to make it. Followed by pressing the send button. (This last part is really important.)

Now, I hear you asking "But, Lisa, what if it's both? What if it isn't that clear-cut and I find myself in one of those messy-as-hell conflicting situations where I know I need to set a boundary that's important to me, but I do truly feel sorry about how that impacts someone I care about?" I'm not gonna lie, that one's a tad trickier, but with radical confidence, it's definitely navigable! Recently, I was nearing total burnout. I had started writing this book, as well as working on a project for Webtoons, all on top of my normal workload of running the company, having my own show, and executive producing new content. My deadlines had deadlines, and that meant staying up waaaay past my 9:00 p.m. curfew. I was burning the candle on both ends and was starting to get warning signs that my gut issues were about to flare up. As all of this was going on, one of my best friends in the whole world, someone I love with all my heart, texted me in a panic, worried about her dog. He had stomach issues and was getting blood work done.

Now, trust me, one of my furbabies is seventeen years old, so I know what it's like to be worried about your baby. And in the moment that she texted me, "I need to talk to you," my heart was crushed. I was already near breaking with my workload and health load, and to take a couple of hours out of that would mean more stress, and less sleep because I'd have to make up the hours somewhere, and I wasn't sure my health issues could handle that. It crushed me that I couldn't be there for her, but I needed to be there for myself. It took every ounce of my being not to break under pressure, and I had to accept that I wasn't strong enough to carry both loads. And while it broke my heart and still actually hurts my heart to say it, I couldn't be there for her. But how did I tell her that? What did I say? I thought it through, and the truth really was that I was sorry I was unable to be there for her, but I wasn't sorry for putting myself first. And THAT is the golden nuance, and something I distinguished within myself before I apologized. Because even though it was the right decision, it didn't mean that I wasn't sorry for not being able to be there for her when she needed me.

The important part in all of this is that I didn't let the guilt dictate my actions. I knew where I was with my health and my emotional strength, and I knew that I was already walking a tightrope (and it was frikin' shaky up there). So I offered a genuine, heartfelt apology, stayed firm on my boundary, and explained to my friend why this was important to me. "I hope, in all the time we've known each other," I wrote, "that I've earned a reputation for always being there for you, so I hope you can understand that right now I'm on the verge of breaking and don't even know if I can be there for myself. I love you very much, and once I'm out of this, I will absolutely be there for you, because I know that what you're going through right now is really tough, and please, please let me know if anything with his situation changes." This last part was very important to me, because if her dog's situation did become life-threatening, then I would have dropped everything and she would have become my priority.

And what did she write back? "I understand." Her brief answer stung a little bit, but I knew that the whole reason I had been so honest was precisely because this relationship was so important to me. If I could also put myself in her shoes and thought about what it would feel like to get that text message from me, well, it wouldn't have been a weekend buffet fest in Vegas, that's for sure. But it was up to her to decide how she took my boundary, and I had to respect her reaction as much as I was asking her to respect my need for space. As soon as my deadlines had passed, and I was feeling better, I reached out to follow up.

"Do you want to talk?" I asked. "Or do you need space?"

"Look," she said, "it did bother me at first, but once I read it for the second and third time, it really hit me. You're always there for me when you can be, and this was just a time when you couldn't." My entire life, I've dropped everything for the people I love, and to now know that I could say no to that without having my loyalty questioned was frikin' huge. And the best part of it all is that this ultimately strengthened our relationship and brought us closer together by bringing even more honesty and respect into our relationship.

Instead of that . . . Say this.

"I'm so sorry I can't come."

"I'm not available,
but thanks for the invite.
I know it's gonna be a blast!"

*"I'm so sorry, could
you do me a favor?"*

"I'd really appreciate
your help with this."

"I'm so sorry I've upset you."

"I understand why
you're upset."

"I'm sorry I bothered you."

"Thanks for listening."

*"I'm so sorry,
I don't understand."*

"Could you explain that
last part again?"

*"I'm so sorry, but this
isn't what I ordered."*

"Excuse me, I ordered
the steak, and this is
a bowl of lettuce."

I Can Command Respect.

When we first started Quest, anyone could call me anytime, day or night. I always had my phone on. Didn't matter if I was in my pajamas and heading to bed, or even if Tom and I were on one of our very rare vacations. I foolishly took pride in the sheer number of hours I was on my grind, like for every hour I worked, I got a validation point and I could trade in my points at the prize counter for some much-needed self-worth. I felt like part of my validation came from being the person that people could turn to whenever they needed anything, but this also meant that other people ran my life. My phone number might as well have been 1-800-HELP-ME-LISA, and this hotline was staffed 24/7. "Yawn . . . hello, Lisa speaking.

How may I help you?" I remember being on our big Christmas trip to New York and sitting in a cab outside a restaurant on a call about a budget for a shoot that was taking place in LA the next day. Instead of being inside the restaurant doing vodka shots with the hubby, I was sitting in a car talking camera shots with the team. My lack of boundaries almost made us miss our reservation because I stayed on the call instead of just telling them to handle it.

As you can probably imagine, that kind of availability took its toll—on my health, and on the respect I received from the other people in the company. You teach people how to treat you, and I was teaching them that I didn't mind working nonstop (Tom worked even more than I did, but he was way better at shutting off when he wanted downtime). And contrary to what I might have thought, that wasn't doing me, my employees, or the company any favors. Boundaries are the opposite of selfish. Boundaries are self-care. Boundaries help you take care of yourself so that you can show up for other people. We've all heard this before, but it IS like putting on your own oxygen mask before you try to help those around you. As cliché as it is, it's cliché for a reason. And that reason is, because it's bloody true. If you don't, you're just going to end up passed out in the aisle, and then you're just deadweight and they're going to have to wheel you out on the drink cart.

I worked on this for yeeaarrrrs, and now I'm finally at a point where anyone can call me at any time they want—because . . . it's going to go to voice mail. My phone is off on the weekends, because I've learned (from my health issues) that I'm trying to show up as the best possible version of myself, and that version crawls into a hole like Punxsutawney Phil to shrivel up and die when she's been working nonstop.

Another boundary I had to set in the early days of Quest was that I had to stop being everybody's frikin' mum! First, there was a part of me that found the mum role very natural—I like taking care of people, and I genuinely want them to be comfortable and have everything they need. And, second, I'm Greek—my people like to give you two whole chickens to eat for dinner and get offended when you don't finish it. (Yes, true story! My *yiayia* made Tom TWO whole chickens when she first met him—and got offended when he left some.) So when I'm hosting someone—whether it's for a business meeting, a gathering of friends, or anybody else—I'd always ask if anyone wanted anything to drink. "Can I get anyone a tea or coffee?" I'd say when we had big influencers or other guests visiting the offices.

I truly didn't mind, and I didn't want anyone to be thirsty, but it wasn't long before people started *expecting* me to get them drinks. Finally, Tom, seeing my frustration, pointed something out to me: As long as I positioned myself as the caretaker, people were going to treat me as such. "Babe," he said, "you're so loving and caring, and that's great, but when you come into a meeting and the first thing out of your mouth is 'Can I get anyone something to drink?'—if you're trying to exude power in a meeting, this might not be the best strategy, even if you really don't mind."

Homie, this hit me hard. I care about what people think of me, I want them to like me, and I genuinely care about ensuring that people are taken care of and comfortable. But that caring seemed to be conflicting with the results I was looking to achieve, which was to be taken seriously as a businesswoman. So just like I had to ask myself all those years ago if I wanted to pass my art class or be right, I now had to ask myself (whether I liked the choices or not), what did I want to be known for: being the best at my job or making the best cuppa?

At the end of the day, you cannot get respect by simply demanding respect. Breaking frikin' news! Simply demanding respect is about as effective as telling a lame joke and then saying, "Please laugh." Homie, that's just not gonna work. But you can *command* respect through your actions, the way you treat others, and how you consistently show up for yourself and for them. When you set boundaries about how you expect to be treated, you command respect. When you show that it's not a one-way street, and you respect other people's boundaries, you command respect. When you're consistent on both . . . you command respect.

I still often offer to get everyone drinks, because it's a part of who I am and I like doing it. But if I find myself in a situation where I think showing up as the caretaker might move me away from my goals, then I'll hold off on boiling the kettle. At the end of the day, I like being a buttercup. I also know that being a delicate flower in some areas of my life doesn't mean that I can't be tough AF in others. Having radical confidence means you can break out of that invisible box to embrace dualities and all the conflicting parts of yourself. Now if you're thinking, "Lisa, I'm not confident enough to do that," then, oh girl, read on . . . coz I gotchooou!

RADICAL CONFIDENCE RECAP

- **Give a frikin' eff!** If you care what other people think about you, embrace that. It's part of what makes you special. Knowing when to listen to others' opinions can be part of your superpower arsenal. And stop trying to convince yourself that you shouldn't, because then you're trying to be someone you're not.

- **Whose life are you living?** If you're a people pleaser, it's important to ask yourself this question and answer it honestly. Are you living your life for your parents? For your partner? For your children? For strangers in the comments section? At the end of the day, no one will be as invested in your life as you are, so make sure you're choosing what will ultimately make you happy.

- **Cut it up one time!** Reframe your boundaries. You've been surrounded by boundaries your whole life, but it's just that you're so used to them that they've become as automatic as brushing your teeth (making sure you don't leave toothpaste all over the sink? That's a boundary). Realizing this makes the idea of setting new boundaries that you actually want a heck of a lot easier.

- **Cut it up one time—again.** Boundaries aren't one-and-dones. They're a constant negotiation, and it's going to be trial and error. That means you're going to eff up, and other people will eff up, too. The dictionary definition of "human" should actually read: "Creatures that make a whole hell of a lot of mistakes." So as long as someone is genuinely trying, appreciate their efforts and give them space to improve.

• **Beware the bad buttercups.** Abusers and people who are bad for your mental and physical health will try to sledgehammer through your boundaries. They don't deserve your respect or explanations but instead require a hard, nonnegotiable boundary. You should be open to negotiating boundaries only with people you want to maintain a relationship with.

• **If you don't like being a doormat, get off the floor.** Demanding respect is useless. You have to command it, and this might take time, especially if it's a new thing for you. Be consistent in showing others how you want to be treated, and don't beat yourself up about not getting it right the first time, or all the time. It took me years to embody the confidence of a leader and an entrepreneur, and to do this, I sometimes had to put the big picture ahead of my personal feelings. To build the trust of my community, I had to trust myself to keep showing up. You can't change your past, but you can change how you show up from here on out, Buttercup.

9

GET OFF THE COUCH AND PUT ON...
YOUR BAD-BITCH BOOTS

Bad-bitch boots (n):   1.   Your secret weapon that you only
                                 bring out when you need to feel like a
                                 frikin' beast.
                          2.   Commonly referred to as boots but
                                 actually can be anything you damn
                                 well please.

I get asked about confidence a lot, and the two most common questions I hear are "How do I feel more confident?" and "How do I get my confidence back? I used to feel confident, but now I don't."

First, let me pause a sec here. Because it frikin' blows my mind that anyone would ever ask me about confidence. Meeeeeeeeeee? Are you kidding? That always makes my jaw drop like in one of those cartoons when it becomes completely dislodged from your face. That kinda jaw drop. Because I still have days where I don't feel confident AT ALL, and there are so many things that still scare me shitless. Public speaking? Eeeeeeeeekkkk!

Writing a book? What the hell do I know about writing a book? I mean, will my editor even let me put a word like *Eeeeeeeekkkk* in here?

But here's my secret: I just don't let that bloody stop me.

Confidence isn't as important as you think it is, and people get this wrong all the time. Because confidence isn't a frikin' goal. It's not the endgame. We don't want confidence just for the sake of feeling confident. We want to be confident so that we can go out and kick ass and do all the things we want to do. You want to feel confident SO you can start your YouTube channel. You want to feel confident SO you can start dating. You want to feel confident SO you can take that dance class or ask for that promotion.

But here's the mic drop: You don't need confidence to do new things. Doing new things creates confidence. People want confidence to feel competent enough to begin, but it's actually the other way around. This isn't a chicken/egg situation, because here there is a clear answer: Competence hatches confidence. Cheep, cheep!

When you want to try something new, you want to be good at it already. Nobody likes the feeling of sucking. I get it, trust me, I really do. But the more you try to do new things, things that scare you, things that are risky AF, the more competent you will become. And the more competent you become, the more confident you will feel.

Right now, you're probably thinking, "That's great, Lisa. I hear you, and I understand you. But what about when I don't have confidence or competence? What about all those times when I'm so frikin' nervous that I think I might throw up in my purse? What the heck do I do then?"

Homie, it's okay to be shit-scared . . . but radical confidence means that cannot and should not stop you from going ahead and doing it anyway.

Confidence is a tool, like a hammer. And just like with tools, it's all about the results. Is the nail in the wall, yes or no? Yes! Then who the hell cares that you used a shoe to pound it in there? Your IKEA Eiffel Tower print is hanging on the wall now, isn't it?

I Can Be Shit-Scared and Do It Anyway.

In late 2018, I was still mainly behind the scenes at *Impact Theory*. While our company was growing like wildfire and Tom's interviews were going viral, I wasn't well-known in the personal-development world, and I felt way more like a student than a teacher. So when Tom and I got an email from the mind-blowing entrepreneur Gary Vaynerchuk (aka Gary Vee), asking us to attend a party he was throwing at CES, a major tech event in Las Vegas, I was stoked when it popped up in my inbox.

Subject: **VaynerX @ CES | Invites attached !! See you there**

Hey Tom + Lisa

Wild to think CES 2019 is less than a month away already.

If you're attending the conference this year, VaynerX will be hosting a few events throughout the week. We'd love for you to join us!

We'll be kicking off the week with a small friends and family dinner at TAO restaurant on Monday, January 7th, at 8 p.m.

On Tuesday, we'll be hosting a cocktail party at Catch @ 5 p.m.

Please let us know if you can make our events by RSVPing with the links below!

If these times don't work for you, we'd love to meet up with you at CES. Hope to see you there!

—*Gary*

"This looks frikin' awesome!" I was thinking to myself as I read all about it. "I definitely want to go." I was on my mission to help people, and going to an event like this would definitely help me do that: 1) I'd learn a lot. 2) I'd probably meet some really interesting, smart, inspiring people. So going to this event would be major for me. I mean, it's Gary frikin' Veeeeee! Plus, your girl (that's me) loooooves Las Vegas.

Then, before I could even pick up my phone to text Tom about how I couldn't wait to go, Tom responded from another room of the house:

> Hey Gary,
>
> Thanks so much for the invite! My CES plans are up in the air as I have a speaking gig that overlaps. I might be able to make it out for a day or two, though.
>
> Best, Tom

Well, shit. I didn't have any conflicts. The day of the event, my schedule was wide open. The invite had clearly been meant for Tom. But . . . Gary had said "you and Lisa," which meant that I was invited, right? But did that mean I couldn't go on my own? Was he just being polite by adding me? Was there a secret asterisk I couldn't see?

Before I could let that negative voice talk me out of it, I got up from my computer, walked down the hall, and stuck my head in Tom's office. "Hey, babe," I said, "that Gary Vee event looks really cool. What do you think about me asking Gary if I could go by myself?" I wasn't asking for permission, but I was totally unsure of myself, so I was using Tom (as I often do) as my sanity thermometer—my sanitimometer.

"Oh yeah, you should ask," Tom said. "Of course you should go." Part of me kinda hoped he'd say, "No, babe, I don't think you should ask," because then it was a get-out-of-jail-free card—I wouldn't have to handle a huge opportunity by myself without a safety net. Now I just had to ask Gary. What's the worst that could happen?

He could frikin' say no, that's what. And I ain't gonna lie . . . Ouch! that would sting. But if he said no, it would still just be over email—aka me hiding behind my computer—and so I wouldn't be getting rejected to my face. And I could deal with that.

If I didn't ask, then I knew for a fact I wouldn't go. It would be safe, and there was no risk of rejection, but I've also seen this one before, and it's just as predictable as one of those Hallmark Christmas movies where the big-city lawyer goes back to her hometown for the holidays and runs into her high school boyfriend, who owns the Christmas tree lot, and guess what? He's single! (Okay, wait, I would totally watch this movie . . .) Everyone knows how this movie is going to end, and that's why we watch it: Predictability is damn comforting sometimes. But to move forward, you have to do things you haven't done before. That's what makes this type of confidence radical—it's about having the courage and the momentum to do something even if you're not totally sure how it will turn out.

The worst part of not asking would be that it would mean I had seen an opportunity to grow, learn, further my mission, and work toward my goal, but had chosen to not even try to take it because I was scared of a little two-letter word: no. So I had to decide: Am I more afraid of rejection than I am committed to my goal? No way. Do I care more about having my ego bruised than I care about the progress I could make if I got a yes? No way: the sequel.

I Can Stop Feeling Like an Impostor.

You probably know what impostor syndrome is, but just in case you don't, Professor Google tells us that it's the persistent inability to believe that one's success is deserved. I personally am not a fan of the phrase "impostor syndrome." I mean it even sounds like a disease ("I'm sorry, I can't go out tonight. Yeah, yeah . . . I've got a bad case of impostor syndrome"), and it gets used a lot to describe any situation where we doubt our accomplishments, feel like we haven't earned our seat at the table, or don't know as much as others think we know. But in reality, we all experience moments like this, when we're doing something new or something that scares us, or even just something that's outside the norm. But impostor syndrome doesn't have to be paralyzing.

Maybe it's your first time leading a meeting at your new job, and you have no idea how you're going to get the room to respect or trust you. Maybe someone comes to you for advice because they admire your accomplishments, but you don't know how to tell them that you think you just got lucky. What about when you get invited to a conference where everyone is super successful, and you feel like you've only barely scraped by. When we were building Quest, I had these kinds of feelings on the daily—I'd been a housewife for eight years, whereas everyone else who was on my level within the company had years of business experience. But when feelings of impostor syndrome strike, don't panic! There's no need to pull the rip cord, and definitely do not throw yourself out of the plane. You can prevent it, and even if you do happen to feel it coming on, you can push through and fake it. Actually, let's not even think of it as fake. The reputation of the word "fake" has yet to make a comeback since its Pamela Anderson heyday. So instead of faking it, we're just going to pretend a tiny, eentsy little bit.

First, you have to believe that you can do something. Yes, really, truly believe. I'm not talking about believing that you will get it right the first time or believing that you will be perfect. What I mean is that you need to believe that you can TRY to DO YOUR BEST. That, in a nutshell, is radical confidence—believing that doing your best, learning from what happens, and getting out there to do your best again will get you where you want to go. If you believe you can't, you won't. If you believe you can, you will be able to figure it out. It's just that frikin' simple.

Here is the biggest, hugest, most valuable thing to remember about this utterly frikin' scary two-letter word: "No" is not a reflection of your self-worth. This is so true, and so important, that I want us to take a minute, right here, and say it together: "No is not a reflection of my worth. No is not a reflection of my worth. No is not a reflection of my worth."

The only thing it might have meant was that Gary Vee wasn't the right person to help me achieve the goals that I had. And if that doesn't get you to act, then let me tell you a story about a woman called Jamie Kern Lima, a very close homie of mine who was told "no" like a thousand times when she was getting her makeup business off the ground, often followed by the words "No one would buy makeup from a woman who looks like you." Years later, L'Oréal disagreed and bought said makeup company for $1.2 billion. Yes, billion, with a *B*. And here's my point: You would never know her name if she had taken "no" as a reflection of her worth. And by the way—if Jamie hadn't gotten so many nos along the way and someone had said yes to her earlier in her journey, she wouldn't have built a company worth $1.2 billion in the first place. Let THAT one sink in for a second. One of my favorite things I ever heard my girl Oprah say is that luck is when opportunity meets preparation.

A couple of years ago, I was on a mission to get Maria Menounos on my show. I've loved her since I first came to LA and saw her on E! I still remember scrubbing dishes while watching her on TV, living vicariously through her just to get through the silent tragedy that was my day. I mean a fellow Greek doing interviews on the red carpet with celebs wearing elegant gloves? That was a dream! The closest this Greek was coming to that was telling my puppies off for peeing on the carpet as I wore rubber gloves. Definitely not the dream. So when I heard that she was doing podcast interviews, we immediately reached out, and yep, you guessed it . . . we got a no. Now, while we've established that "no" is not a reflection of our worth, it sure as hell was a reflection of where I was in my hosting career. Because let me frikin' tell you, if Oprah had called, you'd better believe Maria would have found the time. While once upon a time, I would have let this crush me into smithereens, my radical confidence tools kicked into action. My growth mindset immediately went to one of my all-time favorite quotes from the great, wise Steve Martin (yes, the comedian): "Be so good they can't ignore you!" I was clearly being ignored, which meant I wasn't good enough . . . yet. I needed to be so good that she couldn't ignore me. This gave me something to focus on: Work harder, do better, keep learning, keep pushing, and eventually, with dedication to the consistency of these things, I would make her radar. Fast-forward a year: Our talent manager, aka Dr. Finesse, finesses his way into getting me and Tom on Maria's new podcast. That was the first time we ever met. I totally gushed, told her I was Greek, and how much she kept me sane during my mundane years. We got along so well that I immediately reached out afterward and asked her to come on my show—and . . . she said yes! Since then we've become really close homies, and during one of our girly nights, I finally told her this very story. Her response? She had no idea what I was talking about. We figured out the timing and realized that when I had first reached out, she was taking care of her mum, who had stage-four brain cancer, while at the SAME time finding out she had her own brain tumor. Her team were told to say no to any and all interviews she hadn't committed to. So it turned out she didn't even know I'd reached out in the first place.

When you hear the word no, use it as motivation. I know now that no really means one of two things: "not yet" or "not me." Sometimes that no means that you've got more work to do before you graduate to three-letter words and get a yes. Sometimes that no can mean that that person simply isn't the right person to be asking. If that's the case, keep asking until you find someone who is. But never does a no negate the courage and effort it took to ask in the first place.

As I sat in front of my computer trying to draft my email to Gary Vee, I kept in mind these three things:

1. Even if Gary did say no, it wasn't a reflection of my worth.
2. No matter the answer, I could be proud of myself. Even if I wasn't going to Vegas, I had still placed my bet. I had pushed myself out of my comfort zone in the name of practicing my skills and reaching my goals. I had shown up for myself.
3. A no today is just a to-do list for tomorrow.

"Lisa, just bloody email him."

Like I was signing my life rights away and this was the final contract, I read, reread, and read again my response before getting the radical confidence to hit the dreaded send button.

> Hey Gary,
>
> I would love to still come even if Tom isn't
> available...if the offer still stands.

Girl, there were four days between my asking and his responding. Oh, the agony! I'm sure he gets thousands of emails, so as each day went by, I assumed more and more that he wasn't going to respond. And as it was the holidays, I would follow up in the new year (that latter part was a decision I came to, of course, after having an entire debate in my head over whether it was appropriate to actually follow up or not). But then, as if Christmas was coming early, he got back to me on Christmas Eve, which of course I saw because I worked 24/7. His response? Not two letters but two words:

> Of course.

I Can Feel Good Enough.

Homie, I was so excited. But then, the meaning of "yes" really hit me.
Yes meant I actually had to go.
Alone.
Oh.
Crap.
I wasn't going to know a soul there, and it started to feel like I was about to roll solo to a wedding where the only person I knew was the bride. I knew Gary, but it wasn't like he and I were best mates or anything, and he had to host so many guests that it may have been a bit awkward if I cornered him to talk about the weather.

The event was taking place at a time when my gut was still super unpredictable, and that was a huge part of my main worries. I was so used to having Tom as my wingman; what if I had a major flare-up while I was there . . . alone? I had to recognize that it was my negative voice telling me that I wouldn't be able to handle a gut emergency during cocktail hour without backup. But I realized that what the voice was really drawing my attention to was the need for a backup plan. I just needed to do some extra prep work (like take my own food to mitigate the possibility of it happening in the first place) and have an action plan in case a health flare-up did happen (like suss out all of the emergency exit doors as soon as I arrive).

I started to realize that, as much as I would be going to Gary Vee's event by myself, I wouldn't really be alone. I'd bought a ticket for two because my negative voice was my constant traveling companion, and she wasn't *just* going to fight me on who got the window seat. She was going to fight me on my entire right to be there. I might not have been able to make myself confident, but I could at least lay out a game plan so that I could be completely focused and not let her distract me with her incessant internal negative chatter.

Before the evening cocktail event, I picked out what I was going to wear. As it got closer, I got my hair and nails done. Then, before I went to the event, I spent a little bit of extra time on doing my makeup. I knew I wanted to walk into that event feeling like a frikin' badass. Hair? Check! Nails? Check! Makeup? Checkity check check!

Now, while clothes and makeup may have helped me get to the event, I had to be honest with myself: Unless someone came up and complimented me on my hair (which I wasn't entirely ruling out), once I actually got there, the braids weren't going to do a damn thing. I needed a strategy for how to make the event worth all the trouble, which meant actually putting myself out there, talking to people, and being able to absorb as much of the brainpower and energy in that room of amazing people as I could. So I turned to another expert, Vanessa Van Edwards, a self-proclaimed recovering awkward person, a behavioral investigator and body-language expert, and author of the incredibly tactical behavioral book *Captivate*.

Now, Vanessa Van Edwards (I always three-name her, even in my contacts on my phone) is a frikin' genius, and in her book, she has literally mapped out the different zones in a party: the Start Zone, the Side Zone, and the Social Zone. As the name suggests, people in the Start Zone are just getting started. They literally just walked in the door—maybe they're looking for the bathroom, seeing who they know, wondering where to put their coat. Vanessa Van Edwards says that this isn't where people are looking for conversation. Okay, Lisa, if she says don't stand at the frikin' Start Zone, then don't stand at the frikin' Start Zone. Got it.

Then there's the Side Zone. If action's what you want, stay out of the Side Zone. It's where people go when they want to tap out for a while. If you need to check your messages, make your way to the Side Zone, but if you want to connect with other people looking for connections, steer clear. Okay, Vanessa Van Edwards says steer clear of the Side Zone. Understood.

The third zone is where she says you want to be if you want to create the opportunity to talk to new people, whether that be your next hot date, potential business contacts, or new bestie. This is the Social Zone, where people are comfortable, having fun, and open to chatting to strangers. Plus, VERY IMPORTANT: The Social Zone is where the bar and the snacks are. And if there are two things that put people in a good, relaxed mood, it's drinks and food.

So I tackled going to a party in Las Vegas by myself just like I'd tackled everything before. I broke it down, step-by-step. Here was my radically confident game plan, thanks to excellent coaching from my girl Vanessa Van Edwards:

- **Step one: Walk in the door, but don't stay there.** Okay, okay, got it. But then where the heck do I go?
- **Step two: Identify the next destination.** The bar. Cool, I'm on it.
- **Step three: Put one foot in front of the other, and walk there.** Yep, I can do that.
- **Step four:** Order a frikin' drink.

Now, Vanessa Van Edwards had another pro tip that has always served me well. She introduced me to a study from the University of Colorado at

Boulder that showed that people who have not just a drink in their hands but a HOT drink are perceived to be warm and approachable. So I beelined to the bar—in Las Vegas, of all places—and ordered myself a nice hot cuppa tea. To be honest, I ordered tea and then used my own tea bag, which I'd brought in my purse, because us Brits are damn picky about our tea.

So there I am, at Gary Vee's event in Las Vegas, and guess what prompts a conversation with a stranger? My frikin' tea bag. Because the guy next to me, ordering a drink at the bar, saw me take it out of my purse and asked about it. At one point in time, this would have mortified me with embarrassment, but now I just showed him the package and asked him if he wanted one. "But you have to get your own mug."

Before I knew it, I was so caught up in conversation that I forgot I had even been nervous, and I hadn't even noticed that my negative voice had called herself an Uber and gone back to the hotel room. This experience is 1,000 percent the thing I come back to when I'm feeling scared about doing something new. Now I don't think twice about attending a business event by myself. Now when something like this comes up, I'm not worried, I'm not tense, and I would never let the fact that I had to go by myself be a potential reason to not do it at all. In fact, I find it thrilling! I thrive off new challenges that let me put my growth mindset and my radical confidence to use. And falling? I don't worry about falling, because I know my plan is there to catch me.

So let's talk about the practical tools you can call upon to get you into your radical confidence headspace. Body language is super frikin' important, and how you hold yourself physically can have a direct impact on how you feel emotionally and mentally (as well as how other people see you). If you're slouching and trying to make yourself look small, then you will feel small. So, stand up right now.

- **Stick your chest out.** (Okay, you're probably starting to feel good . . .)
- **Bring your shoulders back.** (Feeling a little bit better . . .)
- **Put your hand on your hip.** (Yeah, baby, now you ARE a bad bitch!)

- **Practice it in the mirror.** In fact, do it five times in a
  row, and notice how your confidence intensifies with
  every step. I do this all the time, and just seeing myself
  standing like this, LOOKING more confident, makes
  me feeeeeeel more confident.

Even with all this prep, you still sometimes need a little extra oom-mmmppphhh. And that's what I like to call "You got this roulette." Open up your phone and type in "YOU GOT THIS!" (or whatever motivating phrase hits you) followed by an emoji, or emojis, of your choice. Whatever floats your boat. Now close your eyes and scroll through the alarm, and set it to go off at a few random times. Sure, this might just happen to go off while you're peeing, or while you're on a hot date, but that's the whole point. If you remind yourself "You got this" at enough random moments throughout your day, then soon enough, you'll start to believe it.

I Can Boost My Confidence.

When I was growing up, makeup was somewhat of a soothing balm for my lack of self-confidence. While it definitely was a great way for me to self-soothe my anxieties about my appearance, I can see now that it was a trap. I had painted myself into a corner—with eyeshadow and foundation—where I only liked myself when I was wearing makeup. I even remember once my mum and I got into a tiff because she was going to the grocery store and wanted me to go with her. I refused to go because I didn't have my makeup on, and she just thought I was being silly.

Now, my growth mindset and radical confidence have allowed me to evolve to the point where I don't base my confidence on my makeup and clothes, but I do use them as a tool to boost it. However, I want to always be wary of becoming dependent on them (because I know myself). And to do that, I have to polish up my crystal ball, gaze into it, and identify the traps that are coming my way.

Women are so often taught that our value depends on our youth and beauty. Unless you have a painting aging in your attic like Dorian Gray, these things don't hang around forever, and I always want to remind myself of this. I don't ever want to get trapped in a place where I'm trying to hold on to a temporary thing because that's where my self-worth comes from. When my good friend Lilian Garcia came on *Women of Impact*, she stopped me dead in my tracks when she told a story about how someone had once called her out for lying about her age. "You have two choices," they told her. "You either get older, or you die. Which do you want?" Obviously, I would rather get older than frikin' die. So bring on the sunspots. Bring on the wrinkles. Bring on the saggy boobs. Heck, I'll happily swing those bad boys over my shoulders so I don't trip over them and break a hip. Because all that stuff means that I'm still here and kicking.

I know how easy it is for me to get mired in the quicksand of external validation, so now I deliberately post stories on my Instagram with no makeup, no braids, and wearing my tattered, faded sweatpants. I may not look like Beyoncé, but I'm also not a corpse either.

When I was younger, I used clothes and makeup in an attempt to influence how other people felt about me (mostly boys, if I'm being honest). Now I use them to influence how I feel about myself. When I need to feel confident, when I need to feel like I can go out and do whatever the hell I want to do, I get radical confidence and dress for battle. If you've ever given a little kid a cape, you know what I mean: Within minutes, their fist is in the air, and they're flying off the couch, on their way to rescue someone and save the day. As kids, we're instinctively influenced by things like this, but as we get older, we only accept it, as a society, if it's Halloween (or Disneyland). Like giving a starved person a Cold Stone cake, some people go haaaaaam on their costumes just for that one day where they won't be looked at side-eyed. But what we wear doesn't just have to be determined by the earth's 365-day rotation around the sun. Clothes have the power to bring out our power every day of the year. And that's why when I have a clear vision for how I want my day to go, I prepare for it mentally, physically, and, yes, fashionally.

I don't have a cape or cuffs (at least, not yet), but I do have power items that may as well be. They act as such by helping me get into the right mindset: my jewelry, my hair, my figure-hugging tank top or corset (if, like shooting this book cover, the occasion calls for it), my tight-ass Spanx leggings (shout-out to the inspiring badass entrepreneur Sara Blakely); and, of course, no outfit is complete without . . . my bad-bitch boots.

I love my bad-bitch boots. My B3s. They're black leather (obvi), and they come up to my knees (double obvi). They're tight around my calves, which I like (because, just like Arnold, I've got skinny legs), and while they have high heels, they're not stilettos. The heel is a little chunky, so they have some weight to them. So when I walk, oooohhhh, man, can you hear me coming! Clonk, clonk, clonkety clonk!

Now, let me tell you how they make me feel: like a bad bitch. I put those boots on, I zip them up, I start walking, and oh yeah, now I remember who the hell I am.

There is so much judgment around how women look and what they wear, and let's get real, homie—we throw a lot of that shade at each other, especially when we're not feeling great about ourselves. I'm so guilty of this, because I used to looove the "who wore it best" pages in tabloids, and the pages where celebrities' outfits were ripped apart. "Eww—I would never wear that," we might think or say, when what we really mean is, "I wish I had the guts to wear that." When I was younger, I always got teased for how I looked (I had a caterpillar as a unibrow and buck teeth that would have made Bugs Bunny's feel understated), so the last thing on earth I wanted to do was give anyone anything they could use as ammunition to make fun of me. All I wanted was to blend in. I wanted to look and dress just like everyone else, and hell-to-the-no did I want to stand out. I always wore my hair long and parted down the center, and I remember once having a royal teenage freak-out because I wanted to tie my hair back in a ponytail—girl, a frikin' ponytail—but I was too scared to do it because it was different and I thought people would make fun of me. How would you even make fun of someone for wearing a ponytail? It would be hard. Like, "Oooohh, look, Lisa thinks she's going for a jog now?" Get the eff out of here!

When it comes to finding your own bad-bitch uniform, you don't know how you're going to feel until you try it. There's a bit of experimentation, and that's scary (if you ever have come home from the salon with hair that you HATE, you know exactly what I mean), but what makes you feel most like yourself might just be something you haven't even tried yet.

Including shaving the Wonder Woman logo on the back of your head. True story: I now rock that a lot and actually had it when I shot the front cover to this book. Having had long hair my entire life, shaving the lower part of the back of my head was a huuuuuuge deal, and once I did it, I couldn't stop stroking the stubble—just feeling it reminded me of how brave I was, because I'd wanted to do it for so long but always worried about getting criticism.

You have to play around and try different things. Maybe your bad bitch boots are jewel-covered flip-flops or your lucky top that you found on sale at Target (oh man, how I love Target). When I did my TEDx talk, I wore my bad-bitch boots, but I also knew that I needed a little extra something—so I got myself some Supergirl knickers that gave me a little extra support and a hit of confidence. No one else knew they were there, of course, but I got an extra boost of motivation when I peed for the forty-seventh time due to nerves before getting onstage. It doesn't matter what it is, because once you identify your own personal superhero cape—watch out, world, 'cause you're about to ffllllllly!

My jewelry is also a key part of my toolbox. I have my Wonder Woman necklace, just a little cheapie thing that I bought on Amazon but am obsessed with, and I pair it with my door-knocker Chanel pendant, which I could probably use as a nunchuck if the occasion ever warranted it. Both are symbols that communicate something to me when I put them on and when I see them in the mirror.

The ritual of putting on my jewelry is like foreplay for my confidence. My Wonder Woman necklace says, "Now I'm going into battle. Now I need to be brave. Now I need to remember just how frikin' strong I can be." The Chanel is a reminder of just how far I've come; when we started Quest, I never allowed myself anything extravagant. Feeling the weight of it around my neck makes me feel more confident and reminds me that I'm a badass who can bring it anywhere I want, anytime I want.

Every morning, as soon as I'm done working out, I start to think about what my day will entail and how to dress for it. A lot of people dress for the situation they're going to be in, and there are social expectations about the clothes we wear. If you saw someone show up at the gym in a suit and immediately jump on the treadmill, you might think it was a little weird but would just be glad, at the same time, that your work desk wasn't next to theirs. But I don't do that. One of our producers once suggested to me that I shouldn't wear yoga pants to conduct a serious interview, but I totally disagreed. I had specifically chosen that outfit because I wanted to feel sporty and energetic, as this guest was known for being in the fitness space, and it worked. I dress not for what I'm doing but for how I want to feel, and with radical confidence, I'll deal with any backlash accordingly.

As much as I can dress up to affect my mood, I can also do it in reverse, and dress down. Recently, I had one of those days where I had to be tough. I was in serious get-shit-done mode from the time I woke up, and it was go, go, go! As each hour passed, another stress bolt got tightened by some other problem ratcheting up. And so by dinnertime, I was a big ball of angst. And from all the years I had endured gut issues, I knew that stress was a recipe my stomach couldn't digest. What I needed was a mood change—and a hug from my hubby is always my go-to remedy. But the truth was, at that moment, I wasn't sure I even felt like being hugged.

For the same reason that I knew suiting up that day with my hair, clothes, shoes, and jewelry of armor helped me attack my day, I realized the same would be true in reverse. So I went upstairs, released the pressure along with my hair, wiped away the frustration along with my makeup, and changed my emotions along with my pants (and into my fluffy Wonder Woman pajama bottoms). Ahhh. Exhale. I was now ready to embrace my softer, feminine side. I went back downstairs, got that very needed big giant bear hug from the hubs, smelled his neck (which is extremely comforting to me), and as a result cut my stress, staved off the impending rebellion from my gut, and ate dinner without an extra side of anxious nerves.

I Can Be Motivated.

It's not all about the boots. Fashion is just one tool to have in your toolbox (or . . . shoebox), because motivation comes and goes. Sometimes you have it, and you're ready to bust the door down and carpe that effing diem. Other times, it feels like just making coffee is enough accomplishment for the day—because, let's face it, sometimes making coffee is damn hard (how are we out of filters again?). It's easy to look at confident people who are always hard at work on their dreams and think they've gotten so far because they were born with an extra motivated bone in their bodies. We think of motivation as something you either have or don't have, and that other people must certainly intrinsically have *more* of it. That's why we haven't gotten around to signing up for that open-mic comedy night, launching that cupcake cart, or going after that job prospect—we'll be able to do it when we're feeling more motivated, tomorrow.

But when that thought pops into your head, it's time to slam on the brakes and shift your mindset. What if every time you said or felt "I'm not capable" you were actually saying "I'm not motivated"? No one is intrinsically motivated 24/7—some people are just better at lighting a fire under their own ass. Other people shine once that fire is lit, because they know how to fan the flames. They're Tom Hanks in *Cast Away*, rubbing those sticks together like his life depends on it—because it does! Building a fire takes patience, practice, and persistence, and once it's going, you can't stop there. Now you're not Tom Hanks anymore; you're Sandra Bullock and Betty White in *The Proposal*, chanting "Sweat Drop Down My Balls" around that fire to keep it going. Am I mixing movies here? Yes, I am. Do I care? No, I do not. Because I'm trying to get you mooooottttiivvattted.

There is no one-stop shop, one-size-fits-all hack for motivation. Maybe you hate *Cast Away*. Maybe you hate *The Proposal* (no judgment, but really?). Maybe you hate both. The key is—and if you've been paying attention, you can probably guess what I'm going to say here—you have to find what works for you. If you listen to any podcast about personal development or success, if you hear any entrepreneur speak, there is a good chance that, at some point, they will mention how helpful they find meditation. Tom had been bugging me for years to try it because it had had such an impact on helping him manage his anxiety. I didn't really think I had anxiety, so I didn't try it. But as more and more guests came in and out of the house, I saw that I didn't really have anything to lose—especially if it might help my gut issues. I had heard meditation was good to help with stress, and at this point, I was willing to try anything. I gave it a shot. I gave it lots of shots.

I tried and tried and tried to meditate. My mum's partner, An, even tried to encourage me by buying me one of those little meditation cushions after I complained to her that my legs would fall asleep. I would sit down on that little cushion, close my eyes, and try to clear my mind. I thought about all the wonderful benefits I was going to gain from my newfound meditation practice—the clarity, the peace, ahhh the stress relief. All the benefits that Tom always went on about. Breathe in. Breathe out. And—nothing. Well, not nothing. Just a ton of uninterrupted time to think about everything on my to-do list. I found it extremely difficult and actually unpleasant. Despite all of the benefits of meditation that I'm sure work for other people, it just wasn't going to be my thing. In fact, I just found it to be anoooooother thing on my to-do list that I was desperately trying to check off. It was safe to say that I didn't like it. And that was okay.

So what does bring me clarity and peace of mind? And what helps me reduce my stress and feel more relaxed? Going to the gym and lifting heavy-ass weights. I lift weights first thing in the morning during the week, and this is when I have all my best ideas and get clarity on things like maybe a new business strategy, an employee review, or a puzzle we're trying to solve on the YouTube algorithm.

On the weekends, I reach for a different stress-reducing tool. I actually spend my Saturday and Sunday mornings drawing badass female superheroes. I want to clear my mind of all work and be totally present in just doing something for myself. I don't draw for anyone else. I draw with zero pressure. Zero external noise. I switch my cell phone off for the entiiiiiiire weekend. I eliminate the habit of going on Instagram, accidentally reading that work email with a problem that could have waited till Monday, or seeing the text I now feel obligated to respond to. But, Lisa, what if there is an emergency? Then ping Tom. But what if they don't have Tom's number? Said with love: We aren't close enough to warrant disturbing my self-care time. I totally get that many can't do this, for so many reasons, but the point is to give yourself time and space where you cannot be interrupted by other people's demands of you. And when I draw, it's just me and the pencil. I'm so focused on what I'm doing that I'm not thinking about the business or problems, just if the eye I'm drawing looks realistic. And that meditation pillow I had? I now use it as my footstool when I draw. So whether I'm picking up a pencil on the weekends or the squat bar during the week, I know that when I'm done, I'll feel more relaxed, happier, and better about myself.

The last, key piece in my radical confidence toolbox is Destiny's Child. And no, I don't have Beyoncé, Kelly, and Michelle hanging in my kitchen. I wish! I've just got "Survivor"—on repeat, and LOUD. Those lyrics are so frikin' powerful, and the song is my number-one go-to for a quick confidence boost. Now maybe Destiny's Child doesn't do it for you. No problem. Find a song that does, get it ready to go, and then use it as your hype song.

How hard it is to get off the couch will dictate what you use to get off the couch. Some days, all you may need is to read this chapter. But some days, when it feels like getting off the couch involves breaking the laws of gravity in a way that would make Sir Isaac Newton roll over in his grave, that's when it's time you play that hype song, buckle your "cuffs," put on those boots . . . and show Isaac who's frikin' boss.

RADICAL CONFIDENCE RECAP

- **Confidence is not the 26.2-mile mark.** It's not an end goal. You do the things you want to do and build the confidence along the way. I will repeat this until it's tattooed on your brain: competence breeds confidence.

- **Go Tom Brady on your game plan.** Map it out like you're trying to win the Super Bowl for the fourteen-millionth time. What are you going to wear? What are you going to do? What are you going to talk about ? Who are you going to throw the ball to? Oh, wait . . .

- **Play "YOU GOT THIS!" roulette.** Confidence comes and goes, and so you're gonna need reminders, even at the moments when you'd least expect it.

191

- **Dress for frikin' success.** Identify what that means for you, and then make sure it's easily available and ready to go. I know exactly where my bad-bitch boots are. Don't waste precious time tearing the house apart to look for your lucky pants; set out your power outfit the night before so that you have a smooth transition into go-time.

- **Shine your bat symbol into the sky.** What symbol makes you feel powerful? Find something that will help you remember, when you see it, what's possible. Is it a picture of Reese? A logo? A pair of socks? Make sure it's something that's visible all the time or that you'll see a lot. Like, put Reese in your wallet, right next to your debit card.

- **Pick your own personal theme song, then play it. LOUD.** Pretend you're on WrestleMania. You're coming out of that tunnel . . . You hear the crowd roar . . . Your leotard looks frikin' fire! What song is going to make you absolutely PUMPED to climb into the ring?

GET UNPISSED...
GAIN EMOTIONAL SOBRIETY

Emotional sobriety (n):
1. The ability to take a breather from an emotional high so that you can see what's really going on; recognizing an emotional response to a particular situation is not the same as the practical needs that serve you in that situation.
2. Resisting the temptation to have one too many shots of anger, get drunk on your emotions, and say something you might regret.
3. A term my genius hubby coined.

Have you ever had a feeeeew too many cocktails, gotten a little tipsy, and done something that let's just say you wouldn't normally do? Ever woken up the morning after a craaaazy night and thought, "Oh man, I'm so glad I chicken-danced on that table/yelled at that crowd of grandmas/tried to switch shirts with the bartender! I was really being my best self."

Yeah, me neither.

Emotions can be a frikin' mind-altering substance. When you get carried away by your emotions, you're just as likely to do or say something you'll regret as you would be if you'd gotten a little too familiar with the waiter. Never, not once in my entire existence, have I done something at the height of my emotionalness and found that it made the situation better. Instead, I hurt feelings, burned bridges, put my foot in my mouth, and just generally made whatever I was pissed off about a hell of a lot worse.

A saw is great when you need to cut something in two, but not all that great when you need to pound in a nail, right? (We learned earlier that you need at least a shoe for that.) And it's the same thing with emotions: Emotions are a frikin' fantastic tool to use to draw your attention to pain points and areas of your life that need work. However, emotions are usually total shit at helping you actually solve a problem. That's where emotional sobriety comes in.

Emotional sobriety is NOT about denying or repressing your emotions. It's about having them, feeling them, and knowing when to put them aside in order to accurately evaluate a situation based on the way it really is. That means pressing pause on the insecurity, the fear, the anger, the frustration, the negativity. I know that can sound harsh, but stay with me. I'm not saying your emotions aren't valid—they're actually utterly imperative to finding out who you really are and what makes you come alive as a person. Without our emotions, we'd be as full of life as one of the statues at Madame Tussauds. Our emotions are what make us laugh at jokes, cry at movies, fall in frikin' love, and all those things that make life worth living. But having zero filter and saying exactly how you feel when you feel it and letting those feelings run wild and damn the consequences just isn't going to fly when it comes to your goals. You will never achieve your dreams or have strong, long-lasting relationships if you can't learn emotional sobriety. Period. Why? Because going after the things you want means you're going to get pummeled in the process and experience frustration, sadness, fear, and all the other shitty emotions that might make you want to stop right before the going gets good—but that would be like driving from LA to NY on the trip of a lifetime but giving up in Philly because you're sick of being in the car.

You're going to be fearful. You're going to wonder, who am I to go after this? You're going to fail and feel like shit about it. You're going to encounter other personalities that make you frikin' mad, angry, frustrated, and annoyed. Emotional sobriety allows you to stop that game of insecurity hopscotch. Instead of just jumping to conclusions, you can actually take in the facts of a given situation (and of your choices) with radical honesty.

The more you start to pay attention and the more you know yourself, the more you can develop an emotional breathalyzer that helps you tell the difference between feeling your emotions, which is healthy, and emotional drunkenness, which is not. When it comes to alcohol, I'm a happy drunk. Through trial and many errors, I know my limits, and I know that after three drinks, I will be shaking my booty on the dance floor for six hours straight and hugging the doorman on the way out. Just like it's important to know your limits when it comes to alcohol or any intoxicating substance, it's important to know your limits when it comes to emotions as well. There's the angry emotional drunk who yells. There's the emotional drunk who turns inward and shuts down to the point where they can't even have a conversation. There's the hypersensitive emotional drunk who corners you in the bathroom and drowns her sorrows in "woe is me." Different situations bring out different types of drunkenness in all of us, but the important thing is to recognize when it's about to happen. What are your warning signs?

I know I'm emotionally drunk when I can feel a disconnect between how I'm acting and the person I want to be. I want to be Cool Hand Lisa, but when the shit hits the fan, sometimes Hothead Lisa comes out instead. When she takes over, I can't think straight. I start to stutter, because there's so much noise in my head that I can't choose my words. All the noise clogs my filter, and with my filter out of commission, something that I shouldn't say is likely to slip through and come right out of my mouth.

Sometimes you don't recognize emotional drunkenness until you've sobered up. Did you say something you regret? Did you act out of character? Do you feel shame or embarrassment about something you said or did? Then you were probably emotionally drunk.

I Can Get Angry Without Losing My Shit.

Anger is a tool that, in certain moments and situations, can really serve us. It can spur us into action, demand attention, and help keep us safe. Anger is a totally natural, normal thing; while I don't believe blinding anger can ever serve you, sometimes straight-up being pissed off can. If someone deliberately and maliciously crosses one of your boundaries, you, in my opinion, have every right to get angry. If you witness abuse or mistreatment of someone you love (or, to be honest, even a stranger on the street), you have every right to get angry. Anger can lift you up and out of feeling powerless and inspire you to fight. We're human beings, and there's no frikin' way we can go through life being totally happy all the time. Things are going to piss us off, and that's not the end of the world. But if you let your emotions control you, by definition you're then going to feel out of control. You may lash out at people, and instead of wanting to communicate with you, they'll naturally get defensive and shut down. And that's the frikin' opposite of what your goal is. When you find yourself getting mad, pissed, or frustrated, don't judge or beat yourself up for it. Just don't stay there.

Acknowledge that you're frustrated. Trying to pretend that you're not—or waiting for someone to ask you about it—only stifles the emotion. Too often, we wait for someone else to make the first move before we allow ourselves to address our emotions, and in that time those feelings just fester. For example, you're on a romantic dinner date with your partner, but after a heated argument, you end up at home hangry. You keep waiting for them to apologize. You wait some more. And by the time you microwave your frozen chicken breast in silence, you find yourself huffing and puffing and taking very loud bites so they know exactly how mad you are. And when they finally ask what's wrong, you reply, "I'm fine." Let me tell you, just in case you were wondering, they know YOU'RE NOT FINE. And when you stifle your anger, you're more likely to hold on to it and stay frikin' mad. Sometimes, you may not even know you're mad, because anger can show up in a lot of different ways when you aren't staying emotionally sober. You may feel sad, anxious, depressed, or resentful, but then when you start to dig down into it, you realize, yep, I've arrived at Pissed City (the opposite of Party City—there are no balloons or streamers in Pissed City). Watch for your warning signs. Is your jaw tight? Is your foot bouncing? Are you pacing? Are you scrubbing the kitchen sink extra hard so you can obliterate every last speck of dirt? This last one is me, so much so that I'll be cleaning the dishes and Tom will walk in, take one look at me with my rubber gloves on, and ask, "What's wrong?"

Emotions have to come out, and it's up to you to create a safe space for yourself to let those babies loose. Personally, I give myself a timeline so I can feel all the feels and then snap out of it. I tell myself that my layover in Pissed City (or Sad Suburb) will last thirty minutes, and then I have to get the eff out. I will literally set the timer and start licking my wounds or doing whatever else I need to do to fully explore the emotion I'm having. And we've all been there—sometimes a layover takes an hour, sometimes it's overnight, and that's okay. Give yourself as long as you need—just remember that the point of this time is to make sure that you don't let your layover turn into a permanent relocation. The goal here is to recognize your emotion, give it plenty of space to show you aaaaaall of its triggers and truths and to look at it nakedly to figure out what has really set it off. The goal is to slooooooow dooooown. Slow down enough to help that emotion take its foot off the accelerator. Slow down enough to be able to shift into neutral before you actually crash and burn into a big ball of flames.

Once you recognize that you're upset, you need to disrupt yourself and snap out of your own emotional spin. One disruptor that I use is super simple: I just walk away. Yep, I turn around, put one foot in front of the other, and don't stop until there's some distance between me and whatever emotional cocktail has currently got me seeing double.

If I don't walk away, I know that anything I say or do in that moment is NOT going to help the situation. By staying right there with it, you're leaving yourself open to saying or doing something that you're going to later regret, and it ain't gonna be pretty. Trying to solve problems while you're angry is like trying to light a candle with a blowtorch—it's just going to lead to a meltdown. Whatever you say, chances are it isn't really going to reflect how you feel or what you want to express. Take some time and space so that you can come back to the situation with a clear head.

If you're someplace or in a situation where you can't physically use your feet to move across the floor—like in a meeting with your boss, or dealing with your kid throwing a fit on a plane—then you still need to find ways to calm the eff down, and fast. Start with just simply breathing. If you're angry, you're probably breathing fast and shallow, so shift to deep, slow belly breaths that will start to calm your body down. In through the nose. Out through the mouth. In through the nose. Out through the mouth. See . . . you have radical confidence. And that means . . . you got this!

But none of this is enough on its own. You have to have an action plan for what you're going to do affffffter you've taken those steps. Otherwise, you're going to still be stewing—just in a different pot, I mean spot. You have to remove the immediate heated triggers so that you simmer down and get to the root of the problem.

Set your timer and do what you need to do to be alone for a while. Lock yourself in the bathroom if you have to, but if you can, go outside. A 2019 Harvard study showed that being surrounded by nature for just twenty minutes was enough to lower your stress hormones. Another reason being outside is good for you: the sun (aha, I knew choosing to lie by the pool instead of going hiking wasn't just because I don't like bugs). Studies have shown that soaking up the rays, so long as you aren't burning yourself to a Pringles crisp, increases the brain's release of serotonin (the hormone that stabilizes our mood, feelings of well-being, and happiness). And my last suggestion for what to do when you're pissed off is one that comes from personal experience: Take a bath! I don't have any big studies to back this up (though that's one study I would participate in!), but who doesn't frikin' like a bath? (Except for my old-man furbaby Banzai.)

I Can Sober Up.

Once your emotional timer has gone off, it's time to shift out of Big Feelings mode and into Problem Solving mode. Yes, I want you to feel your emotions, to acknowledge them, but don't let them take center stage and soak up the spotlight like when Madonna kissed Britney. Putting on the

Sam Smith to bawl your eyes out? Resist! Looking up pictures of your ex to remind you of what an a-hole he or she was? Don't! Repeating your last interaction like it's a boomerang you just can't stop watching? Stop right there! Focusing on and making a list of everything that's going wrong in your life? Just don't do it! Instead, do the opposite. Make a deliberate choice to do whatever silly, distracting, funny, happy thing you need to do to forcibly shift your mindset. Watch some funny TikToks. Sing Dua Lipa into your hairbrush. Shadowbox with your ficus. Because that is the choice that's going to allow you to emotionally sober up and put yourself back in control.

The key here is to disrupt, disrupt, disrupt! This is when our good ol' friend the squirrel can actually come in very handy. Do something that will help move you out of and away from your anger, and then do something that makes your heart sing. This is something that's entirely self-ish, and totally for you. But doing something that makes your heart sing doesn't have to be complicated or time-consuming—it can be as simple as popping to Starbucks for a venti. And treat yourself when you do. Get the Frappuccino with double whipped cream, if you want. Or heck, watch a cat vs. dog video. That shit is so funny I dare anyone to watch just one and not chuckle even on the inside. The most important thing here is that you spend a few minutes doing something that's just for yooooooou.

I don't know about you guys, but I need to be alone to calm down, and I need to resist calling THAT PERSON. You know THAT PERSON—your best friend, your sister, your cousin, your roommate, the person who always has your back, who will support you no matter what you do. THAT PERSON is your frikin' go-to when you need someone to push you to be brave, bold, and honest, but because they have your back unconditionally, talking to them in heated moments will get you even more worked up ("Yeah, girl, yeah! You don't need to take shit from him!" Or "Tell them to shove that job. You're too good for them anyway." Immediately followed by "Call me when you're done!"). This person may not be trying to rile you up—they're likely trying to support you, and when you're in the moment with whatever big emotion you're experiencing, you want that emotion validated. That's exactly why you call them—because they're the equiv-alent of pounding a shot of emotional Fireball. But while it's important to feel validated, it's equally important to recognize that what you really need is a cup of strong black coffee.

The final step in emotional sobriety is to plan ahead. Give yourself an action plan. Come up with a couple of things you can say the next time you encounter a situation that makes you angry. The more you can preempt what to say, the less likely you are to say something you might later regret. And this goes both for when you know your anger won't serve you and for when you know when it will. It might turn out that this is a situation where you need to channel some of it to turn a situation around.

I'll never forget a situation when an older, married neighbor crossed my line with some heavy flirtation. While it was physically harmless, it was utterly inappropriate and insulting, and after a while I could feel Hothead Lisa just below the surface whenever I even thought about it. Tom, being the protector that he is, asked me if I wanted him to step in, but I told him I had it handled. Because the inappropriateness was all in tone and suggestion, I knew I couldn't leave anything I said to him up to misinterpretation. So I wrote a script in my head of what I would say and practiced it in advance so that I could deliver it calmly, respectfully, yet firmly if it ever happened again. And so, as expected, the day came when he crossed my path—and my boundary—again. Cue radical confidence and my rehearsed lines . . . and action! "I don't think that's appropriate, and I would appreciate it if you never said that again." Clear. Concise. I wasn't making assumptions about his intentions, but I was letting him know that, no matter what those intentions were, the words that came out of his mouth would not be tolerated. This phrasing also let him know what I expected of him in the future. And I deliberately threw in the word "appreciate" so that I would appear calm and not disrespectful. Using anger or frustration to serve you is often about the escalation, and if you start at the highest point—basically, yelling at my neighbor to "Eff off already"— you're inviting people to meet you where you are, and you aren't leaving anywhere else for the situation to go except kaboom! This way, I calmly laid out my boundaries and gave my neighbor the opportunity to respect them. And if he didn't, then I could always move on to yelling and giving him the middle finger. Which I didn't have to resort to, because from that day forward he was never inappropriate again.

These kinds of confrontations still may not go according to plan, but my rule is that the more I can plan for what I say and do, the better the chances that I can leave with my head held high, even if things didn't end up the way I wanted. I can still be proud of myself for how I handled the whole damn thing.

I Can Choose How I React.

Controlling our emotions isn't always about anger—sometimes it's about shame, fear, guilt, or embarrassment. I'll never forget a night when I felt more shame than Cersei Lannister. Homie, this is something that LITER-ALLY the only two people that I've ever told are Tom and my sister. That's how embarrassing and shameful this story is gonna get. So, where are you right now, as you're reading this book? If you're out and about, wait till you're curled up somewhere private. Are we alone? Are you sure no one is listening? Okay, ready? Whhhhheewwwwww. Whhhheeewwwwww. Deep breaths, let me calm myself down. Okay, Lisa. Here we go.

It was our anniversary. I wasn't just excited. I was ecstatic! I was in the midst of my health issues at this time, and we were also full-on with *Impact Theory*.

Tom and I didn't get a lot of alone time, and on this particular night, there were still a ton of employees in our house as we were running out the door. I made them pinky-swear to leave within the hour, because, you know, we didn't want them there when we got home (to, uhum, you know, uhum, get in our pj's and, uhum, go to bed).

During this time, I was still trying to figure out what I could and couldn't eat, and my gut was unpredictable. I could be totally fine one minute, then bent over in agony the next, and I never knew how many times I was going to need the restroom. The hard truth of this was that I hardly EVER went out and was often nervous when I did.

This particular night was the anniversary of our first date. Every year on October 3, we visit, in order, all the places we went on that first date and take a photo in front of them. We start at that Chinese restaurant with a B rating (which is now a Thai restaurant with a B rating), then head to the Directors Guild of America. Our final selfie opportunity is outside Tom's old apartment building, where we stayed up talking until 4:00 a.m. After that, we go out to dinner.

Now, Tom might be the least pretentious person on the planet, so even once people started to know who he was, he never used his name or his connections to get special treatment. But this was OCTOBER 3, and we wanted to do a date night worthy of Richard Gere and Julia Roberts, so he called in a few favors to get us a booth at Cut at the Beverly Wilshire Hotel (which was more rare than the Hope Diamond). He got us the best table, and what's more, my loving hubby talked to the chef and broke down all the problematic ingredients so that they were fully aware of all my dietary restrictions in advance and we could really dig into our dinner without having to worry.

For the first three stops, as we snapped our selfies, I could feel my tummy rumbling, but I hadn't eaten anything yet, so I hoped it would quickly pass. By the time we were heading to the restaurant, though, it had started to calm down, and I could relax.

We got to the restaurant, the hostess greeted us by name, and showed us to our booth. I was so excited to have a night out, to have uninterrupted time with the man I love, and to eat some steak. We order drinks, and then, before I've even really had a chance to look at the menu, my stomach starts to go. We were officially at Defcon 1. "Babe," I say, pushing myself back from the table as quickly as I can, "I'll be right back."

I start walking a little faster than I normally would, but I don't run. It's a nice joint, after all, and I don't want to make a scene. So I'm walking, and I'm walking, and . . . oh my god . . . where the hell is the bathroom? "Excuse me," I asked, flagging down the nearest waiter, "where is your restroom?" He tells me that they don't actually have one. Yep, that's right: Because it's part of a hotel, customers are supposed to use the one in the hotel lobby. The lobby. The lobby, which is aaaaaaall the way at the front of the building.

Oh crap. My panic is building, but I thank him and start to walk a little faster, and a little faster. I start to rush to the restroom, and I'm going as fast as I can.

By now, I'm practically running, and I'm doing everything I can to clench every muscle in my body. I crash through the bathroom door and sprint into a stall. I get the door closed and start trying to take off my shorts. Except I'm wearing a belt. Of course I'm wearing a FRIKIN' BELT! . . . Oh crap oh crap oh crap . . . My shorts and my damn tight-ass G-string aren't even off yet and oh . . . crap. And right there in one of the fanciest hotels in LA, this grown woman, who helped build a billion-dollar company, who was on a romantic anniversary dinner with her husband, had just . . . shit herself. I was shaking. I was humiliated. I was so embarrassed, and I didn't even know what to do. I'm in fucking shorts. Shorts! In the Beverly fucking Wilshire Hotel. Shooorts! Shorts and a sexy tight tank top. I don't even have a jacket or sweater I can take off to wrap around my waist long enough to walk out of the restaurant. And I'd gotten up from my seat so quickly that I didn't even have my phone to call Tom and tell him. I'm totally crestfallen, and also—what the hell do I do now?

It was clear I had two choices. Option one: I could just have my mail forwarded and stay in this bathroom stall forever (Lisa Bilyeu, The Beverly Wilshire Hotel, Lobby Bathroom, Stall Two).

Or option two: I could get radical frikin' confidence and figure out how the hell I was going to get back to Tom, my home base. This was clearly the better option. So I trashed my G-string, cleaned myself up as best I could, put some tissue paper in place, then put my shorts back on and returned to our table commando.

By now, Tom is used to my stomach issues, but as I'm walking back to the table, he can tell by the look on my face that something is very, very wrong. "We need to go," I manage to get out. "Right now. And . . . give me your jacket." As this is incredibly out of character, Tom, like Dr. Dre, doesn't miss a beat and immediately, without asking questions, hands me his jacket, jumps up, leaves the waiter a generous apologetic tip, and hands our ticket to the valet.

The first moment he got, as we were standing there waiting for our car, Tom asked me what on earth happened. I just shook my head, so upset that I couldn't talk. Tom was so sweet and understanding, while I stood there beyond embarrassed and heartbroken. I had been working so hard to solve my gut issues, and I'd started to think that my worst days were behind me. I thought wrong, and now something awful and humiliating had just happened on a super-special night. I'd walked out the door of our house that night feeling like a sexy badass, but I was returning feeling whatever the total oppooooooosite of sexy was, as well as utterly ashamed. I also felt guilty, because I knew that Tom had been looking forward to this night just as much as I had, and now it was ruined. Totally frikin' ruined.

Or was it?

I had to remind myself that I had radical confidence. And radical confidence in this situation didn't mean not feeling completely and utterly red-hot-cheeks embarrassed. It meant being able to come back from it. And, right then, that meant emotionally sobering the eff up. On our way home, through my sniffles, I started to pull myself together. What had happened wasn't in my control. What I did have control over, though, was my reaction to it, especially if I remembered what was truly important. It wasn't the steak dinner—I could have a steak dinner anytime. But it was still our anniversary, and I was still getting to spend it with my favorite human on the planet, and that was irreplaceable. There was still time. And so I had to sober up quickly and make a choice to take control over what happened next. I could choose to stay where I was emotionally and allow what had happened to ruin the rest of the evening, or I could not let it dictate the hours I had left with the man I love on our anniversary. I went back to my emotional toolbox and thought about what I could do to help me get through this situation, because, as you probably already know, sometimes when you're thaaaaat upset, wanting to not be barely scrapes the surface.

I would often say that my health struggles were the best thing that had ever happened to me because they gave me so many opportunities for growth, as well as to help other people who were also struggling. Now it was time for me to prove it. How can this horrifically embarrassing thing, which was happening to me right now, be another chance to grow and get stronger and better? What can I do to empower myself in this moment, in real time, when I feel like all I really want to do is crumble into pieces?

And so here I was, writing my own story. I realized this moment was a future memory, and I could choose how I wanted to remember it. I could see it as something really shameful. Or it could be a story about how I'd used radical confidence to come through some difficult shit (um, literally) and lived to tell about it. I could pick myself up off the floor, or rather, out of the bathroom stall, and show myself what I was frikin' made of.

And, on that ride home, I made a promise to myself. And that promise was that one day, one day I would use this horrifically embarrassing story for good. And that thought, in that moment, was hella frikin' motivating. So here it is, homies: me telling the story and keeping my promise to myself.

"Okay, babe," I told Tom, "this is what we're going to do. I'm going to go straight into the shower, and then we're both going to put on our pajamas, and we're going to get in bed and put on the most wonderful, romantic movie that we can think of. I'm going to sip my bone broth [because that was all I could eat], you're going to eat whatever snacks you want, and we're going to snuggle and just enjoy our evening."

Sex went out the window. Ice cream went out the window. But neither of those were the whole point of our anniversary date night anyway. The point was for me to feel connected to my husband, and I could still do that, just in different ways. Yes, the plan had changed, but that didn't mean I had to settle for utter disaster. This story could have ended with me crying myself to sleep that night and allowing this to haunt my nightmares like a creepy-ass clown on Halloween. But it didn't. I proved to myself that I could be strong even at my weakest times. Tom proved once again that he's got my back. Tom and I don't just have a good relationship on our best days, we have a frikin' great relationship even when it's hard. And guess what? Out of twenty anniversaries we've had together, THAT'S the one I remember the most—the one when we cuddled all night, watching my favorite romantic movie of all time, The Notebook.

I Can Control My Emotions.

Building emotional sobriety doesn't just happen if the only time you take it into account is in the worst moments, the ones that are heated and emotional. You also need to take steps in your daily life, on those blessed stretches of time when nothing upsetting happens, to manage your stress so that you're less likely to lose it once things start piling on. The straw that broke the camel's back and all. Not that I'm calling you a camel, but you get the point. If you're stressed, you're more likely to be reactive, get emotionally triggered, and then fly off the handle. But if you take care of your mind, give it time to just be free of the stressors of life, you're less likely to react.

If you always live at max capacity, then it's more likely that you will overload. I use lifting as a way to keep my mind mentally healthy, clear, and strong. This is also a daily outlet that helps set me up for not getting mad in the first place. I also love drawing for these same reasons. That has been something I've come back to over and over, ever since I was young, because it allows me to shut out the rest of the world and focus on something that's pure creativity.

As you start to know yourself better and better, you will start to recognize your triggers—those things that make you feel like you're about to explode or break because you're just so upset. And you will also start to recognize the things that make you unpissed—like drinking a White Mocha Frappuccino while watching a tabby take on a chihuahua—and build your toolbox so that the next time you start to get pissed, you know exactly what to do. With a little bit of attention and retooling, you can swap your short fuses for long ones, and voilà! Now no one has to call the fire department because you just erupted and sent the whole house up in flames.

While I was running the media department at Quest, I was executive producing a huuuuge video with an absolutely dream budget. We were gearing up to launch a new bar flavor, one our customers had literally been begging us to make for, like, forever. So the stakes were just as high as the budget, and we all were working around the clock, knowing full well that the weight of the success of the launch was resting on our shoulders. It's day two and the final day of the shoot, and we have a bunch of big-name influencers in for it. Then halfway through the day, word spread that one of the main influencers, who was key to this video, decided that he needed to leave. Even though he'd signed a contract for two days of work, he wanted to take off because he had something else that was more important. The director and talent manager, try as they might, couldn't convince him to stay, and the more we delayed him, the more pissed he got. It soon became totally clear that he didn't give a shit about the contract. He thought he had other places he needed to be, and we were the big "corporation" that was holding him back. Which, of course, just infuriated him even more.

I had a reputation among my team for being a hothead, but when this situation popped up, and I saw just how panicked the team was that he would leave and our entire video would fall apart—I knew I had to have emotional sobriety and take a beat. This guy was already pissed off, and I knew that if I tried to meet him where he was, he was going to be even more mad. So I had to metaphorically step into his shoes and think of how I would be feeling right now if I were him. Whether I agreed with him about whether he should stay wasn't actually the issue. Because clearly HE believed to his core that whatever he had to go and do *was* more important to him than this shoot, even though he was contractually obligated to complete it. And there was no way I was going to convince him otherwise. So, if I were him, what could someone say to me right now that would make me want to stay? Immediately it struck me that I actually COULD relate to his situation. Here I was, wanting to do something that was incredibly important to me (this video) and someone else was standing in the way of that (him). What if I connected with him on this level? No BS, just two humans connecting about the difficulty of the situation they're both in?

I walked into his dressing room and asked everyone to leave so that I could speak to him one-on-one. He already knew me as the executive producer of the shoot, so I think he fully expected me to be a bull in a china shop and beat him over the head with the contract. But as soon as everyone else left, I took a seat and told him that I was in no position to tell him what was most important to him and that I could empathize with the situation he was in. I then proceeded to tell him my story. That I was not only the executive producer but actually a cofounder of the company. And this wasn't just another video to me but a symbol of everything I had overcome, and I was seriously honored to have him be a part of that. I then asked him if he wouldn't mind telling me why he needed to leave because, again, I wanted to respect where he was coming from.

And he opened up to me. What was said will forever remain private, but just as I confided in him, he graciously did the same with me. And after some back-and-forth, we came to a compromise. He agreed he would stay for a few more hours, and I agreed we would wrap a few hours early. We both stuck to our word, crushed the shoot, and bear-hugged at the end. The video got millions of views, and a few weeks later, he called . . . to thank me.

This—this right here is something I come back to time and time again. This was a situation where taking a beat and staying emotionally sober let me be the person I wanted to be. It was the first time I can remember where I was able to go from the Hulk to Bruce Banner. The first time I was able to achieve my personal and professional goals all in one emotionally sober shot.

And now we've come to the part of this chapter where I share my number-one tip for emotional sobriety.

1. Get yourself a Post-it.
2. Get yourself a Sharpie.
3. Use said Sharpie to write these four life-changing words on said Post-it. You ready? You got that pen? Did you take the cap off? Okay, good. Now go: "This too shall pass." Congrats! What you have in your hands is now a piece of game-changing technology that cures emotional drunkenness in one shot.
4. Stick that game-changing anger-management tool, which we will now call the Sober Up Shot, someplace where you will see it. A lot.

I used to have this Sober Up Shot (aka Post-it) stuck on my mirror because it reminds me that whatever I'm feeling right now won't stay. Seeing it so often helped me build the habit of remembering it when I needed it. I'd see it in the morning, so I could start my day with its message top of mind.

When you're really pissed off, or sad, or so steeped in any other emotion that the room is starting to spin, it's really hard to imagine how you could ever feel any other way. Sometimes, in the moment, you truly believe you will always feel like this. But that's not true. Maybe in thirty minutes, maybe tomorrow, maybe next month—these emotions will one day be a distant memory, and chances are it will pass completely, if you let it. It will be no more a part of your memory than the name of your friend's cousin's roommate who came to that party one time and knew your fifth-grade teacher.

And it's soooooo frikin' important to remember and to remind yourself that emotions are TEMPORARY. Emotions aren't diamonds—they don't last forever. They aren't like fine wine. They don't age well, and these are both good things. What you're feeling right now Will. Pass. And that's exactly what you want it to do.

And now I'm going to tell you something that you might not like to hear but that can be so damn powerful, if you let it. "This too shall pass" doesn't just apply to the bad emotions and bad moments. It applies to the good ones, too (I told you you might not like it). Life is full of highs and lows, but when we're on a high, it feels so good that we adjust our baseline and start to believe that we should always feel this frikin' good. And when we don't feel as good as we felt when we just got a new job, fell in love, or went on that magical vacation to the Bahamas, we feel like something is wrong. We're unhappy, and we then see this as a failure.

When I'm feeling really stoked on life, I remember: This too shall pass. This isn't to bring me down or to instill fear but rather to remind me, in the amazing moments, to exhale, take it all in, be in the moment, and be poised to take on whatever comes next.

Emotional sobriety is a skill you have to build, but once you have it, you don't just get to stop there. Building a skill takes practice. And how do you practice? You do something over and over and over and over and over and over again. You wax on, and then you wax off, and then you frikin' wax on again. It might be hard, it might be tiresome, but you know what? It works! And the next time you find yourself at the height of your pissed-off-ness, you will also find that you know just what to do about it.

I Can Be Too Sensitive.

Emotional sobriety also helps you process criticism and fear. And why do we need to know how to take criticism and handle fear? Because it moves us closer to our goals and helps us frikin' grow, and if there's one thing that I'm all about, it's growth. You grow, girl!

One time, at Quest, I was still struggling to own my seat at the table as one of only a few women in a management position, with no business experience, among experienced entrepreneurs. After a big meeting one day, at the height of my health issues, I found myself feeling insecure and frustrated. My hormones were all over the place, and my emotions were totally erratic, which was a new experience for me. As soon as the meeting was over, I bolted to the bathroom and broke into ugly tears (my first time crying at work). Tom, thinking I might have stomach pain, came in to check on me and was totally shocked to see me in tears and spouting how he was "mean to me." He very gently flagged that I was acting out of character. The fact that I even used those words meant that something was off because I'd, for the first time, taken a work situation and made it personal.

"Babe," he said, "is it possible that, because of your health, you aren't seeing things the way they really are? Can we agree that in all the years I've known you, you've never once broken down in tears in the bathroom over something I've said in a meeting? And if that's true, could it be pooooooossible that you're being too sensitive?"

Once upon a time, those words and that criticism may as well have been an invitation to a duel. But at this point, I had really been working on being open-minded to my blind spots. And there was no one I trusted more to be my guide dog than my hubby. Because I trusted him and knew he had my best interests at heart, I listened to what he was saying.

Now, "You're too sensitive" is a classic cop-out that a lot of people will use to make themselves feel better about having upset you, and in this case, you will have to use your emotional sobriety to be cool and collected while you make it clear that this isn't the case. But I knew that Tom wasn't one of those people. I genuinely trusted him. We had been together for over fifteen years, and he had proven sooooo many times just how much I meant to him, and it wasn't just words; he always acted in accordance with that. So if he said I was being too sensitive, then maybe—just maybe—I had to be open to the fact that . . . he had a point.

And as I sat there on the office bathroom floor and really examined the situation, I could see what he was talking about. When Tom and I disagreed about work, it was usually a back-and-forth debate, but because of how I was feeling on this particular day, I felt our normal debate as an all-out ATTACK. It's like the age-old adage of when your partner says you look nice on a day you feel great, you say, "Thanks, babe!" But if he says it on a day when you're moody, your response may be, "So, what, I didn't look nice yesterday?" The same comment can be taken as either good or bad, depending on your mood, and this was a classic example of that. I realized I was drunk on emotion; I wasn't seeing straight, and as a result, I was swerving all over the place. Getting negative feedback always stings, but there are times when you might want to listen to it. Because sometimes the reason it stings is because . . . it's frikin' true. Especially if it comes from someone who knows you well, like a friend, a partner, or a parent. So I thanked the man for sticking to his word and always being honest with me, got myself a grande Pike Place, and started to emotionally sober the eff up.

You will never be able to control everything that happens to you, but with emotional sobriety, you can control how you react to it. You can acknowledge your emotions, get unpissed, look at a situation clearly, evaluate it honestly, and then respond to it in a way that puts you back in the driver's seat of your life—exactly where you belong.

RADICAL CONFIDENCE RECAP

- **Get to know your triggers.** Think of a recent time when you had a big, fat emotional reaction to something important. Maybe your big idea was panned at work. Or you had an argument with your partner. Be kind and rewind the entire event in your head. Identify the moment you started to feel emotional about what was going on. What triggered your emotional response? Was it a specific comment? Continue the replay. How did you feel? At what point did you start to feel your heart race? Did your face feel flushed? Were there other triggers at play? Were there major red flags in the conversation, places where you could have changed how it went? Once you understand what your triggers and flags are, you can develop the best tactics to swap out in tough situations.

- **Practice, practice, and then practice some frikin' more.** Acknowledge your anger. Walk away. Snag some alone time. Do NOT call *that person* (yeah, you know the one). Do something that makes your heart sing. Rinse and repeat.

- **Stick that Post-it someplace you'll see it every day!** Whether it's good or bad, this too shall pass. Nothing lasts forever, especially not emotions.

- **Maybe you *are* too sensitive.** When someone YOU TRUST offers you this kind of feedback, look at the context of the situation. Are you tired? Are you stressed? Are you upset about something else? Did you eat? All of these things can affect your emotions, so set yourself up for success by being honest about where you're coming from, adjust, and then . . . frikin' up your game.

WHEN THE SHIT HITS THE FAN...
WEAR GOGGLES

The shit (n): Mistakes, failures, and other crappy situations that are totally necessary for giving yourself a kick in the ass, and which are setting you up for future success!

When the shit hits the fan, your first reaction may be to duck and cover. That's only natural, because no one wants to get hit with . . . the shit. And we've all been there and felt that awful feeling when it starts to dawn on you that you've messed up, and big-time. That feeling when the wave of *fucks* washes over you as you go from telling yourself, "There must be a mistake" to "Oh. Fuck. Fuck. Fuck. Fuuuuuck!" Your mouth goes dry, your heart starts to pound, and you start to think of ways you can just cover it up. You go full-on Frank Abagnale from *Catch Me If You Can.* "Okay, so if I go home and pack now, I can be on a plane to

Guatemala tonight, and by the time everyone realizes what happened, I will have changed my name to Isabella . . ."

But, homie, resist! It's all part of the process.

Even on your most badass of days, you will still make mistakes. Congratulations, you're officially knighted as a human. You're going to eff up, say the wrong thing, and probably take the wrong approach. And you're veeeeerry likely going to feel like shit about it. You know I'm not here to sugarcoat anything. Just to be super clear, here it is: You're going to fail.

It's inevitable that something in your life won't work out, no matter how bad you want it to. You can do your absolute frikin' best, try your goddamn hardest, and still have your face meet the floor. It's inevitable. All of the greats failed. Think about the case of Thomas Edison, who failed ten thousand times before creating the light bulb. Now, this is the part where if Edison were alive, he'd come and sue me for misrepresentation. Because he famously said, "I haven't failed ten thousand times. I've successfully found ten thousand ways that will not work." Get yourself some shit goggles as good as that, people! As you think about your next move, the question should not be "How do I avoid the shit hitting the fan?" The question is "How do I deal with it WHEN the shit hits the fan?"

A 2017 study from the Kellogg School of Management at Northwestern University found that failing at something early on, like in your career, will actually make you mooooore successful in the long run. Back in the early days of Quest—so early we only had about four people working the line—when we were working at max capacity and couldn't stand to lose a dime (like, if a dime rolled under the machines, we would have gotten a broomstick and some tape and then spent an hour trying to get it out), one of our employees came running in and said, "Oh my God, Tom, I'm so sorry, but we've messed up the batch." Props to this guy and his team for owning it, but still, this was a big frikin' mistake. We estimated that a batch of bars cost around five thousand dollars to make, and that was five thousand dollars that we certainly couldn't afford to lose.

I immediately went into panic mode, but Tom was coolio. "Well," he said, getting up from his desk, "what happened?" The employee shifted back and forth on his feet as he started to explain.

"We had a schedule where we were going to make one batch of the Peanut Butter Supreme bar, followed by a batch of the Mixed Berry bar," he said. "And all the ingredients were lined up, so when I went to put them into the machine, I put in everything—peanut butter, peanut flour, and . . . the berry flavoring." It was clear that this guy thought he was about to get fired.

"Let's just go in there and see what we're dealing with," Tom said, and we all walked into the production facility, and there they were: tubs filled with berry-flavored peanut butter bars. Reluctantly, we all took a chunk—when duty calls and all—and as we all took a fearful nibble in silence, something dawned on us.

"You know, this kind of tastes like a PB&J."

Now, I grew up in sunny old England, so this wasn't a flavor combination I was used to, so let me quickly educate my British peeps out there. They (being the Americans) put peanut butter on one side of a slice of bread, and jelly (what we call jam) on the other slice. Put them together, and ta-da! Like this bar, it's delicious. And that was the light-bulb moment. "Let's just turn it into a prototype for a new PB&J bar."

We immediately got to work wrapping the bars in plain silver wrappers, boxed them in our nondescript Quest-branded boxes, and then printed inserts from my Staples printer with the nutrition information of the new PB&J bar prototype. You see, you can't legally sell a food product without the nutrition value on the label, but because the bars were just the peanut-butter recipe with the addition of the berry flavor, the nutritional content hadn't changed at all, and we were able to use the peanut-butter nutrition info. Score!

We had a hard-core fan base of a few thousand people, so we posted on Facebook that we were giving them the opportunity to try our "brand-new," not-even-released-yet PB&J bar. Within a few hours, we'd frikin' sold out. Sold. Out! People were buying five boxes at a time! And it didn't stop there—once people got the bars, they were losing their frikin' minds. Our Facebook page was blowing up with comments: "You have to make this!" "This is my new favorite!" This only fueled the curiosity of the customers who didn't get to purchase a box, thus fanning the FOMO flames and pouring gasoline on the demand. The customers had spoken. Shortly thereafter, we officially introduced PB&J as a new flavor, and it immediately became our best seller. And all because once we had our goggles on, we could see the shit hitting the fan as an opportunity for success—just in a different wrapper. So keep your goggles in your purse. You never know when you will need them.

I Can Learn from My Mistakes.

Babies don't stop trying to walk when they fall the first time. They don't just throw their little puffy baby hands in the air and say, "Dddaaa dooonn," which means "I'm done" in Babyish (immediately followed by drool), but somehow life trains us out of the courage to keep trying. *Fail* is a big f-word. I mean, I won't be surprised if soon we have to write it like *fa*l*. There's such a stigma attached to failing that it holds people back from trying at all, but perfectionism Does. Not. Serve. You!

We need to stop being scared of making mistakes in front of everyone and of trying something new and failing. We have to normalize the experience of making a mistake, owning it, learning from it, and moving on. Having radical confidence means you can accept that you most likely won't nail things on the very first try. We have to own our failures and mistakes and wear them proudly like a badge of honor. Forget pins—sew that bad boy on and commit to it. If I make a mistake, and I act like, hey, it's part of the process, I'm only human, then it becomes an opportunity. Does that mean it won't suck? No, of course not. I'm not going to lie: No matter how many mistakes I make, it still frikin' sucks. But now I take comfort in the fact that each failure is going to teach me something, and that people around me will see someone who is unafraid and willing to try again. There's so much power in this—for ourselves and for other women.

So part of my preparation process—whether I'm getting ready for a meeting, or a presentation, a shoot, whatever—is to make a plan for failure. Imagine what could go wrong, and then imagine how you would get yourself out of that situation. This isn't about zapping yourself with a fear gun or driving yourself nuts over all those "what if" scenarios ping-ponging in your mind—it's about having a game plan. Just like how you probably already have a lot of boundaries in your life that you might not have noticed, you probably also have failure game plans in place already, too. If your house caught on fire, what would you do? Get everybody out, and then call the fire department—that's what you'd do. You need to implement that same type of strategy for the smaller situations you will encounter as you go after your goals.

There are two types of screwups: the kind where evvveryonnnne is watching, and the kind when no one is watching. And while we all might agree that the former is the most bloody terrifying, how you show up and handle both will equally dictate whether you're moving toward that dream or bye bye bye-ing it like NSYNC.

When I was preparing to go onstage for TEDx, I knew that I needed a plan to give me the radical confidence to go onstage in the first place, but that I also needed a plan for if—or when—I messed up. I worried that if/when my plan failed, I'd just freeze. So I reminded myself of the little kid who falls down and looks to his mum to see if they should be crying or moving on—other people will react to how yooooooou react. People will be nervous for me if I freeze. But if I laugh it off like no big deal, then no one will think twice. And it happened! Barely a few minutes into my talk, as I was telling a story about my family in Cyprus, I actually said, "My dad gave birth to my grandmother." Yep, those words came out of my mouth, and while I obviously meant the opposite, it was a very big misspeak. With all eyes on me, there was nowhere to hide. There was no way I could cover it up. So, what did I do? I laughed it off, and said, "Well, that would be weird," and I moved on. And so did the audience.

I Can Fail and Get Back Up.

While a public failure may sound worse to you than gouging out your eyes with a dull fork, I actually think it can be way more effective to your growth than a screwup when no one is watching. Because, let's face it, when no one is around, we immediately see the opportunity to protect our ego and sweep it under the rug. "Move along, people, there's nothing to see here." But pretending something didn't happen in no way, shape, or form changes that it DID happen. In the words of Keyser Söze, "The greatest trick the Devil ever pulled was convincing the world he didn't exist." In this case, the devil is your failure. And by pretending it doesn't exist, you miss out on the chance to grow and learn from the mistake. I will never forget one of the biggest times I messed up in the early stages of *Women of Impact.* My good friend Radhi Devlukia-Shetty had agreed to come on the show. Radhi is an amazing human, one of the sweetest people on the planet, and a conscious-cooking and conscious-living expert. We had an incredible conversation, the kind where the studio drops out, I forget the cameras are rolling, and we sit on the couch and talk like the homegirls that we are. We wrap up, and I give Radhi a big hug (I'm a hugger, remember?), and she leaves.

It's not long after that when one of our crew comes up to me, a pained look on his face. "Um, Lisa," he said, "something went wrong, and we lost the last fifteen minutes of the audio."

"Haha, that's a funny joke," I said, but his face said it wasn't comedy hour. "Yo—wait, what do you mean?"

"That interview was almost an hour," he explained, "and we've only got audio for forty minutes."

Crap.

At this point in time, I was still getting used to being on camera and was working hard to get my own show off the ground. A screwup this big could make us look like it was amateur hour and be a total waste of Radhi's time. So I'm not going to lie—my first instinct was . . . to lie. Well, not lie per se, but just cover it up a tad.

I knew content, and I knew there were ways we could have spun it and covered it up with a carefully placed fade-out, and no one watching would have known the difference. So there I am, on set, about to record a voice-over, saying, "Thanks for watching, to subscribe . . ." And then it hit me: What the hell was I doing? This wasn't what I stood for, and if I was going to inspire people to have radical confidence, I needed to show them that I did, too.

So, I told my team to switch on the camera, I stood on my mark, we racked focus, and with zero prep on what I was going to say (except for "to be honest"), I ignored my nerves, got radically confident, and we pressed record: "What's up, guys? You're probably wondering why the video just faded out and now I'm standing here talking to you. The truth is, we had a technical error, and we lost the last fifteen minutes of the episode. When the team told me, I tried to think of a million different ways that we could cover it up. Do we just fade to black? Do we fade to an end card with my voice-over on it? And just as I was about to film the voice-over, I realized, hang on—why am I covering it up? The whole point of this show, the whole point of bringing these incredible women on, is to show you guys that none of us are perfect. We all make mistakes. So if you're at home right now, fearing to try something because you're petrified that you're going to make a mistake and you want it to be perfect, I'm here to let you know that it's okay. I'm still here making errors. And the truth is, it's okay. As long as I look at what happened, how I fix it next time, and make sure it doesn't happen again, then I've just learned. I've become more powerful because of it."

And you know what? That video got more than 1.5 million views and comments like this:

Amazing! The ending was especially inspiring. I have always been afraid to make mistakes, and that has kept me from even starting. This was just the reminder I needed! <3

Dear Lisa, I love your message at the end! That was so funny and so inspiring, that you decided not to cover up that the video/audio stopped. Thanks for being such a light to the world 🤍🙏🌸🌿

I am so grateful I watched it to the end to hear your message about things going sideways and becoming more powerful because of it! Thank you 🙏

I can honestly say that this video was better, and moved me further toward my mission, BECAUSE we messed up. This was a humble reminder that mistakes happen, no matter how much experience you have, and there's always room for improvement.

No matter how often we hear the phrase "nobody's perfect" (apart from possibly being reminded of the Hannah Montana song), we still often think, "Oh, I'm the only one out here screwing up." And that's a lonely frikin' place to be. In 2016, a psychology and public affairs professor at Princeton University published a CV of his failures. He listed programs he didn't get into, jobs he didn't get, and places that rejected him. His "meta-failure," he noted, was that "this darn CV of Failures has received way more attention than my entire body of academic work." How crazy is that? More people are interested in a successful person's failures than alllllllll of their achievements COMBINED. Why? I'm certainly no expert, but I think it's pretty safe to say that there's tremendous comfort in not feeling like we're the only ones that mess up. There's tremendous comfort in a shared experience. So often, the shame and embarrassment that go along with failure and mistakes come from the fact that we think, "I'm the only one who has ever screwed up this bad." But—wrong! Everyone drops the ball—heck, many of us often miss it completely.

When you show up as flawed and vulnerable—aka human—people find it easier to connect with you than if you try to hide your vulnerabilities and screwups to appear more impressive. This was even demonstrated by psychologist Richard Wiseman, who conducted an experiment in which he hired two actresses to sell blenders at the mall. Actress One did her smoothie demonstration perfectly, to a T. Actress Two didn't tighten the lid and . . . whoops! But guess who sold more blenders? Yep, the klutz. The one who'd been smoothie-splashed. Why? Because people liked her more. Why? Because people felt like she was more relatable. Flawed, just like us. When you acknowledge your mistakes and failures, you feel less alone, and you make other people feel less alone in their own mistakes as well. There's strength in numbers, girl, and together we can turn our shitstorm goggles into this season's must-have accessory (eat your heart out, Louis Vuitton).

If you try to cover up a mistake, try to pretend it didn't happen, then all you're doing is burying that mistake deep inside you. It's going to stay in there and go all sauerkraut-like and ferment and fester, feeding your negative voice and feelings of unworthiness. And so, of course, the next time you take a risk or try something new, your negative voice is right there with her picket sign that says, "I TOLD YOU SO!" "Ummm, helloooo?" she shouts. "Need I remind you of the last time you tried something and fell on your face? Don't you remember the shame and embarrassment? Oh, the embarrassment!"

In order to keep that from happening, you've got to let yourself feel your failure. First, let the sting penetrate. This is the time to feel and process your emotions. Emotional reactions happen sometimes. It can't be all emotional sobriety all the time, and mistakes suck. Sometimes, they're NBD, other times they will be a BFD—the total opposite, a big frikin' deal. But either way, give yourself the time and space to feel the feels.

Just give them a curfew and kick them out before it's time to go to bed. Because when you get in bed, with no distractions other than trying to sleep, that's when the mistakes come creeping in, to replay over and over . . . and over . . . in your head. Your negative voice pulls up a rocking chair, grabs her knitting needles, and prepares to tell you the worst bedtime story ever—that one about the time you screwed up. No matter how hard you try—you throw socks at her, you cover your ears, you hum—you just can't get her to shut up. Lock her in the closet if you have to. Tune the bitch out, and give yourself some frikin' grace to relax. How do you put her on mute? When my mind is going at night and I can't stop replaying negative things in my head, I switch gears and focus on my body. I start with the top of my forehead and tell it to relax (unclench). I then work all the way down from my forehead, to my eyebrows, to my eyes, to my cheeks, to my jaw, moving, body part by body part, all the way to my toes, calling out each muscle and telling it to relaaaaaax. It's CRAZY how much I don't realize I'm tensing as I'm trying to sleep.

This strategy TOTALLY distracts you from whatever negative BS is skating around your mind like it's in a roller rink. No matter how bad you might want to, you cannot focus on relaxing specific parts of your body while simultaneously beating yourself up. It also gives you something to keep going back to if your mind starts trying to jump back into the rink. "Oh shit, yeah, I was at my jaw when my negative voice interrupted." The bonus is that when you do this, you actually start relaxing. You probably, just like me, haven't even noticed how tense you actually are, but when you start to unclench, you feeeeel more relaxed, and then it becomes easier to fall asleep—which is the whole reason you're lying there in bed in the dark in the first place.

And if that doesn't help you fall asleep, then rest assured, there isn't a human being on the planet who hasn't made a mistake. So let's all just put our hands in the middle and agree, right here, right now, that feeling worse about ourselves is never the goal. GO TEAM! And if we can agree on that, then we can also agree that judging ourselves isn't useful. You're probably thinking, "Okay, Lisa, I get it. You've told me all the things not to do, but I still don't know what to do." Never fear, Lisa's here! And, together, we got this.

Give yourself a big old pat on the back (or if you're anything like me and not flexible at all, the shoulder will do). Whatever mistake you just made might feel like shit, but chances are you were trying *something*. Don't you dare ignore that. Don't you dare do yourself that disservice, because trying is a million and one times better than not trying at all. You deserve some MAJOR frikin' props for just making it here at all.

Then, once you've felt all the feels, and reminded yourself that screwing up is universal, it's time to OWN THAT SHIT. Say, "I screwed up." Apologize, if you have to, and be prepared for the consequences. But you know what? The consequences for a mistake that you've admitted to, and that you're offering to fix, are going to be waaay less than the consequences for a mistake you tried to bury, only to have someone else dig it up later. When you bury your trash, it doesn't magically morph into treasure—it just starts to rot. When you try to hide your screwups by sweeping them under the rug, you deny yourself the opportunity to fix it, and that's probably just going to make the problem worse, because you won't ever learn from the mistake (plus, your rug will just get really lumpy). Whatever you do, do not try to pin the blame on someone else. Not even on the dog (unless of course it really was you that ate the shoe; in that case, yes, you blame the dog).

It's time to give yourself a kick in the ass. No dwelling. Mistakes don't happen because you're the only imperfect person on the planet—you're not. And mistakes certainly don't mean you're not good enough to achieve your goals. That line of thought is just impostor syndrome talking, and you know we don't let that bitch stand in our way. Having radical confidence allows you to reframe your mistake not as something shitty you did or didn't do but as an experience when you didn't fulfill what you wanted for yourself. Ask yourself, "How would the person I want to be react to this situation?" This helps me jolt my mind into action instead of smothering it with fear and killing the spark that made me want to try to do something new in the first place.

This is the most important question I ask myself when dealing with mistakes: What can I learn from this so that it doesn't happen again next time? After I messed up in my interview with Radhi, my entire team and I learned our lesson: We immediately switched to recording audio on three different devices, just in case one—or two—went out.

I Can Be Imperfect.

I like to always remind myself that even Oprah once sucked. I'm not out here trying to compare myself to Oprah—no, no, no! She's a God in my eyes. This is what I consider a useful comparison. I'm not comparing my unique journey to Oprah's. Instead, when I look at Oprah's success as a badass female entrepreneur, I think about how even *she* had to start somewhere and everything she has overcome since. Her hardships and the hurdles she had to get over are waaaaayyyyy harder than anything I've ever had to face. So if Oprah can frikin' make it, what's my excuse? When I fail, this inspires me to keep working at my goals, especially when I feel so far away from being great at them.

One of the biggest myths we have to bust is the idea that women are naturally competitive with each other. There's an African proverb that goes "If you want to go fast, go alone; if you want to go far, go together." I'm on a mission to empower fourteen-year-old girls, so in order to go the distance, I know I can't do it alone. Heck, I don't want to do it alone. It has zero to do with me and everything to do with my mission. It's about breaking glass ceilings, opening doors, and creating opportunities for women and girls everywhere. When I zoom out and remember what I'm truly working for, then you'd better believe I'm going to send out a rallying cry to any person who believes in this mission, too. When I focus on my mission, even if I fail, I'm even more motivated to seek out women who are way better than me. Unlike in my hairnet-and-sweatpants days in the shipping department, my growth mindset now allows me to see impressive women as people I can learn from, grow with, and be a teammate of, rather than the opposition.

I Can Be Inspired, Not Intimidated.

Once you start to see other people's success as proof that you can succeed, too, you can wipe some of the shit off your goggles and get a clearer picture. Whatever it was that you just failed at, there's a 99.99999 percent likelihood that there's someone out there who's waaaaay better at it than you—which, let's face it, can make you feel even crappier about yourself. But really Sherlock Holmes the circumstances and situations. Were you thinking that the launch of your first venture in entrepreneurship would impress someone who's thirty years into their career as an entrepreneur? Of course they're better than you. When you're thirty years into your career and some newbie thinks their first shot is going to knock your socks off, you can show them the light.

Who you are today is not—I repeat, is NOT—a reflection of the person you can become. Picking yourself back up after failure and deciding to face a situation again isn't about having blind confidence in yourself. It's about having the radical confidence to take it on the chin, and learning everything you possibly can. Experience can be your mouth guard. It doesn't stop you from getting bumped or bruised, but it protects your insecurities from breaking your teeth. When you're learning, you don't get knocked out; you can keep going. We spend too much time thinking our failures mean something about US. To be fair, they do—just not in the way we think. Our failures and mistakes say that we're trying, that we're growing, that fear isn't stopping us. Our mistakes say that we give a damn about our lives, and so we're trying to do big things because of it.

I Can Be the Learner.

You had your goggles handy, and you got them on in time. How do you make sure that this shit doesn't stick? Embody the identity of the learner.

When you're the learner, mistakes and failures are nothing more than teaching experiences that help you grow. Tom was the first person to give me this shift in perspective, which was key to building my self-esteem. I decided to own my impostor syndrome and ground my identity in always being the learner. If I identified with being the learner, no one could touch me; no one could say I was terrible at something or use the fact that I didn't know something against me (and to clarify, when I say "no one," I also mean the bitch in my head). Instead of having an emotional response to screwing up, or trying and *not* succeeding, I could look at the situation and say, "Thank you. I'm gonna go learn that." Woo-hoo! Learning! That means improvement! And then I run three laps around the room with my hands raised in victory with the *Chariots of Fire* theme song playing in surround sound.

When you're the learner, you can walk into a room where twenty people know way more than you do (something that, once upon a time, might have felt heart-attack-inducing to you), and now it doesn't have to knock your self-esteem. You've replaced the gut reaction of feeling bad or insecure about your abilities with a new identity that empowers you to keep going. And if the shit hits the fan, it's no big deal, because you already know you're there to learn, so even a failure is a win. When you can use your mistakes and failures to push yourself in new directions, you will be mind-blown at what you'll discover. But one thing you know for sure, homie: It's going to be radical.

RADICAL **CONFIDENCE RECAP**

- **Failure is not a dirty word.** You will fail and make mistakes, so you might as well embrace it. This isn't to bum you out or to get you to lower your expectations. This is just to remind you that failure is inevitable, for everyone. It will happen to you, and it won't define you. Embrace it and shout, "Bring it on!" (A cheerleader outfit is suggested but not required.)

- **Own the shit.** Take responsibility, and don't try to put the blame on someone else. Not only are you serving as an example for how other people can react when they make mistakes but owning it is the first step in fixing it.

- **Save what's worth saving.** Or at least try. If you can't fix it this time around, use it as a learning experience so that you can do better next time and prevent this from ever happening again.

- **Don't dwell.** Your negative voice might want to have a watch party where she can screen a compilation of your screwups over and over, but she doesn't get to just do whatever the hell she wants. It's okay to feel the feels, but know when it's time to move on.

- **Pats and hugs all around.** When you fail, or make a mistake, it's proof that you're pushing yourself and trying new things. Make sure to acknowledge this, and be proud of yourself for it.

- **Remind yourself that even Oprah sucked once.** Maybe Oprah doesn't do it for you, but pick a person you admire whose success you would love to embody. They had to start somewhere, didn't they? And if they could get from where they once were to where they are now, then so can you!

- **That's not gonna leave a mark.** Ground your identity in being the learner. Be a person who sees hardship as an opportunity to grow and change, and then all the shit you encounter will hit you like a pie to the face, not a punch. A little messy, sure, but doesn't hurt half as much.

BE THE HERO...

OF YOUR OWN LIFE

Hero (n): You.

I Can Do Whatever the Hell I Want!

Well, homie, we did it! I hope you read something that made you laugh so loudly that people around you started to stare. I hope you had moments that touched your heart so much because something you read made you realize you weren't alone. But most important, I hope you're feeling radically confident, fired up, and ready to go out and kick some serious ass in your life!

You now know that it's possible to create a life you absolutely love from scratch, no matter where you're starting. You know that it's okay not to have a clear sense of where you want to end up, as long as you know how to be honest with yourself about how you do (and don't!) want to feel. You can recognize when you're buying into your own bullshit, and know when you're making excuses that are holding you back. Most important, I hope that you no longer believe that "fine" is good enough—you will settle for nothing less than that audacious dream you have for your life. And the bigger the dream, the harder you put the pedal to the metal and chase after it.

Having a growth mindset means that you can learn to do any-frikin'-thing you want. YOU define your identity—rather than letting someone or something else define it for you—and you're an escape artist who knows how to Houdini it out of those velvet handcuffs of external validation that previously kept you trapped in something that didn't make your heart race. You can ask the hard questions in your life, and you can answer them honestly, without fear of the answer. When shit gets uncomfortable, you can strap in and ride it out for the greater good.

You've befriended the bitch in your head, and know that when she starts giving you lip, she's really just trying to help you identify pain points and areas in your life where you can do better. You've stopped seeing your insecurities as your weaknesses—instead, you've turned them into your superpowers and know that they only make you stronger.

You can set boundaries. You can motivate yourself. You're no longer steered by your emotions. You can laugh in the face of failure. You're the expert in your own life, and you save yourself instead of waiting (and waiting, and waiting . . .) for someone else to come along and do it for you.

I'll never forget the day when I was lying on my bathroom floor, clutching my stomach in absolute agony. It was in the early days of my gut issues, and the cramps were so severe that I'd dropped to my knees, my face on the cold tile from the pain. Just taking a breath was excruciating. I needed my husband, but he wasn't picking up his phone. How the hell was I going to get up off the floor if he didn't come save me? Then it hit me: I didn't need Tom to save me. I didn't need anyone to save me, because . . . I could save myself. That's the moment. The moment I got up off that bloody floor and finally took the first step toward becoming my own hero. And what I didn't realize at the time was that was also the moment that would change the course of my mindset for life. Pulling myself up off the bathroom floor showed me how strong I REALLY was. Whenever I start to doubt my own strength, I come back to that moment and remember what I once did for me, and me alone. I hope that this book allows you to recognize moments like this in your own life—those moments when you pick yourself up and realize just how fucking badass you truly are!

With radical confidence you can try new things despite the embarrassment, shame, fear, guilt, or any other emotion that may be paralyzing you. With radical confidence you can go balls to the wall and risk falling on your face. And you can do It knowing that even if you do break a cheekbone, you can Get. Back. Up. With radical confidence you don't have to fear failing, or fear whether you're the only woman, or the only one with no experience, or the only one who shit themselves in a bathroom stall at the Beverly Wilshire Hotel, because, homie, with radical confidence you can zip up your bad-bitch boots, remember who the fuck you are, and be the hero of your Own. Damn. Life!

*G*et me a megaphone, because my first shout-out deserves one! Without this man, this book wouldn't have been possible—and I don't mean that as just a nice thing to say. No, I actually mean I wouldn't be the woman I am today without this man beside me. And those are just facts. He pushed me when I doubted myself. He stood by me when it was easier not to. He believed in me when I didn't believe in myself. He never wavered. He never faltered. He was the best decision I ever made in my life. My hubby, Tom, aka the hubs/Me Baby/Bilyeu . . . sink or swim, baby, we go together!

Now to my fam! My mum, my beautiful butterfly, the very first Wonder Woman in my life! Thank you for always loving me unconditionally. And thank you of course for just being the coolest mum ever! I mean, you could make the car dance! To my pups, the very first Superman in my life! The man who loves his kids more than life itself! Your heart, wisdom, love, and guidance throughout my entire life have shaped me into the strong woman I am today. Παπά, σε αγαπώ για πάντα! To Beeve, not just for protecting me from strange boys as a teenager and letting me sleep in your room on Christmas Eve but for always being there. No. Matter. What. To my Lullenshki, not just for keeping me safe from spiders and standing in line for hours so Nicole and I could meet Mariah Carey but for alwaaaays accepting me completely. One soul forever, my Lul! And to both you and Beeve: ΛΣΛ. To Demetra, aka Tim, for being my second mother. To my bros Harry and Mario, who are making their big sis resort to having to ask in her book to please join the family Zoom calls more! Spurs can wait ;-). I miss you! To Flamin, my ride-or-die homie, my confidante. I frikin' love you, girl! Having you in my life has impacted me in ways you will never know (besides the fact that Sexxxi B wouldn't have existed without you). To my SissyLaw, for being the best SissyLaw alive (and for our Sunday *Destiny 2* escapades, of course). To my Mil, Mikey, Tom, and Jean, for being the best in-laws a woman could ask for and always accepting me just the way I am. And a big, huuuge shout-out to my OG homie, my first official partner in crime, Nicole! Even though we didn't like each other when we first met at the age of nine, we became inseparable, and all the crazy—um, I mean very sensible experiences we had are what kept me going. Nicasayli forever!

A huuuuge part of how I'm able to keep showing up every day is my very, very close homies who, on the regular, show up for me, who accept me, who give me advice, who inspire me, listen to me, and support me behind the scenes. My homies Brenda Gilbert, Jamie Kern Lima, Vanessa Van Edwards, Nicole LePera, Jenna Kutcher, Mel Robbins, Adhrucia Apana, Cassey Ho, Emily Morse, and the badasses Audrey Hussey, Martha Higareda, and Danielle Canty; ladies . . . I love you! To Brendon Burchard, who has been a huge cheerleader in my life; I will be forever grateful for your support, love, time, energy, and encouragement! To my fellow US-living Brits Jay and Radhi Shetty, who make me feel at home. And a big, huge shout-out to the Beachgang, a frikin' badass group of peeps who inspire me on the daily!

And now to the people who are the beating heart of everything I do—the entire Impact Theory team! You are some of the most loving and hardcore people I know, and so many of you helped with aspects of the book process that I never would have been able to do alone. Each and every one of you has my utter gratitude; it's an honor to be your teammate. Casey Elliott—who was brave enough to take the plunge with us and jump in with no life raft. To Michelle Strand, for being my partner in crime and starting a show called *Women of Impact* when we had zero women to impact. To Will, who took a huge chance interning for an unknown company with a bunch of YouTube videos and big dreams. And to Andru, who poured his heart into this book with me and never gave up!

MAD SHOUT-OUTS

To all the people who made this book actually happen, starting with the first person who believed in me as an author and offered me a ticket on the roller coaster ride that was writing this book! A woman I'm not only honored to have worked with but whom I'm truly thankful to now call a dear friend, my homie Celeste Fine of Park and Fine. She and her team—Sarah Passick and Charlotte Sunderland—are one of a kind. To the incredible Kate Williams, who was the other voice in my head: This book truly wouldn't be what it is without you! One of the best things about writing this book was bringing you into my life! And now to my Simon Element peeps: every single one of you contributed to this, so you deserve single shout-outs in my book (literally). Jessie McNiel, Allison Har-zvi, Laura Levatino, Ben Holmes, Jessica Preeg, Elizabeth Breeden, Michael Andersen, Richard Rohrer, Doris Cooper, Libby McGuire, Maria Espinosa, and, of course, the woman behind it all, the frikin' badass legend who took a chance on this unknown to write a frikin' book—my editor and bad-bitch-boots (but sometimes slippers) wearing homie Leah Miller! (Now picture a standing ovation.)

And finally, my last mad shout-out goes to you—you, homie, reading this! You deserve a frikin' parade in your honor! I'm talking a Macy's on Thanksgiving kinda parade. You did the first hard thing: you picked up this book, because there's a part of you that knows you want and deserve more. And that, homie, is my North Star. So, actually, I'm not only shouting you out for taking the first step but also saying a big, massssssive thank you for being *my* motivation to have the radical confidence to write this book in the first place! Thank you, because this book truly wouldn't exist without you.

Much love,

LISA

Lisa Bilyeu is an entrepreneur, bestselling author, public speaker, and YouTube host and producer with half a billion views to her name, but that's not where she started! For nearly a decade Lisa was stuck at home, helping her husband live his dream. But, ultimately, she learned to manage her fear, deal with failure, and build her inner badass. In the process she cofounded the billion-dollar brand Quest Nutrition, launched the modern media studio Impact Theory, built a massive global audience, and learned how to teach others to do the same.

Part comedic catalog of failures, part road map to success, *Radical Confidence* destroys the myths about what it takes to turn dreams into reality. This book is NOT a memoir but rather a side-splittingly funny guide for people with big dreams who want to know how they can go from utter insecurity to radical confidence.